Talking Sociology

# Talking Sociology

Gary Alan Fine
University of Minnesota

ALLYN AND BACON, INC.

Boston   London   Sydney   Toronto

Credits

Production Administrator: Jane Schulman
Editoral Production and Design: Kailyard, Inc.
Cover Coordinator: Christy Rosso

Library of Congress Cataloging in Publication Data

Fine, Gray Alan.
  Talking sociology.

  1. Sociology. 2. Social problems. I. Title.
HM51.F535 1985   301   84-24179
ISBN 0-205-08358-7
Printed in the United States of America
10 9 8 7 6 5 4 3 2 1   90 89 88 87 86 85

Acknowledgment for Quotations in Text:

Page 30: Irene Barth, "Bruising a Parent's Image to Protect a Battered Child," *Minneapolis Star and Tribune,* September 13, 1983, p. 13A. Reprinted with permission of the *Minneapolis Star and Tribune.*

Page 32: Jim Klobuchar, "Will Kindergarten Kids Caucus?" *Minneapolis Start,* April 11, 1979, p. 1B. Reprinted with permission of the *Minneapolis Star and Tribune.*

Page 34: "Family Discipline, Intimacy, an Children's Rights," *The Center Magazine* November-December 1981, pp. 36–39. Reprinted with permission from *The Centre Magazine* a publication of the Center for the Study of Democratic Institutions.

Page 57-7: William Loeb, Editorial, Manchester (N. H.) Union Leader, November 11, 1977. Reprinted with permission of the Manchester (N. H.) Union Leader.

Page 94–5: David Wagner, "America's Non-English Heritage," *Society,* November-December 1981, p. 37. Published by permission of Transaction Inc. from *Society,* vol. 19, no. 1. Copyright © 1981 by Transaction Inc.

Page 97, 102: Nathan Glazer, "Pluralism and the New Immigrants," *Society,* November-December 1981, pp. 34 and 36. Published by permission of Transaction Inc. from *Society,* vol. 19, no. 1. Copyright © 1981 by Transactions Inc.

Page 118–19: Kenneth V. Greene, "Inheritance Unjustified?" *Journal of Law and Economics* 16 (1973), pp. 417–19. Reprinted by permission of the University of Chicago Press © 1973 by the University of Chicago.

Page 163: Nathan Glazer: "Toward a Self-Service Society?" *Public Interest* 70 (1983 p. 67, 80–1. Reprinted with permission from the author and from *Public Interest* © 1983 by National Affairs Inc.

Page 174: Mary and Herbert Knapp, *One Potato, Two Potato . . . The Secret Education of American Children.* W. W. Norton and Company 1976

Page 263–4: Ira Reiss, "Some Observations on Ideology and Sexuality in America," *Journal of Marriage and the Family* 43 (1981) pp. 279–80. Copyrighted 1981 by the National Council on Family Relations, Fairview Community School Center, 1910 West County Road, Suite 147, St. Paul, Minneapolis 55113.

Page 268 and 273: David Carline, Jr., "The 'Squeal Rule' and 'Lolita Rights' ", Commonweal 10, September 9, 1983, pp. 465–6. Copyright © Commonweal Foundation, 1983.

To Dan Alexander

My first teaching role-model who always used to tell his students, "You are only limited by your desire." A belief I find I understand less and less and think about more and more.

Contents

Contents

Contents

Acknowledgments

I wish to extend thanks to a number of individuals who made this book possible. Ira Reiss, D. Stanley Eitzen, Ramona Asher, Albert Chabot, Dennis Teitge, Maurice Garnier, Michael Bassis, and T. S. Schwartz commented on parts of the manuscript. Judith Ann Williams, Randy Stoecker, and Sari Fried ably served me as research assistants, sniffing out clever quotations as if they were truffles—a metaphor which pays heed only to their powers of investigation and not to any similarity to our porcine colleagues. The manuscript was ably typed— again and again—by Gloria DeWolfe and Joanne Losinski; both suffered through the original version of my lame jokes. Allen Workman and Jane Schulman at Allyn & Bacon made useful suggestions for improving the manuscript without defenestrating it. Rebecca Davison of Kailyard weeded the manuscript, allowing my writing to reach its harvest. I appreciate her thyme. Finally, thanks to Al Levitt of Allyn & Bacon who convinced me, over several fine dinners, to write this book. If any portion of this book causes indigestion, remember its origin.

 **Introduction**

Murder and Martyrdom

What would you die for?
What would you kill for?

Before reading on, spend a few moments pondering your answers. Is there anything for which you would either give up your life or take the life of another?

WOULD YOU BE WILLING to die to prevent your child from dying? Would you kill to prevent your sister from being raped? Would you lay down your life to prevent a military invasion of the United States? Would you murder an oppressor to end brutality against your ethnic, racial, or religious group? Around the world, young people, in most respects identical to you, are choosing to die and to kill for their beliefs. Americans were willing to die and to kill to gain independence from the British, to defeat the Nazis, and to control the Viet Cong. We have died in the struggles for union rights and civil rights. We have executed murderers, lynched those accused of crimes, and knifed members of rival gangs.

Yet, if you compose a list of what you would die or kill for, I predict that it will be short. If you are like most students I have asked, the only answer you will give has to do with individuals for whom you have intense personal feelings. You might kill someone who attacks your family. You might choose to take a risk in giving birth to a child. Of course, not everyone would assent to these hypothetical emergencies, but many would. Some would agree that they would pick up arms and lay down their lives for the sake of national defense against a hostile enemy, if asked by our government.

Few of you will name a cause that you might kill or die for. Americans today do not care enough about causes, even those they deeply believe in, to take or give a life. Yet, when we read the newspapers we learn that a lot of people around the world are doing just that. Whatever you might think about the morality of terrorism, you must admit these terrorists have a passion for their causes. Many Protestants and Catholics believe it is literally a matter of life and death who controls those six counties of Northern Ireland. Most Americans think of Great Britain and Ireland as civilized democracies, both with good governments. Protestantism and Catholicism are both respectable religions; some of our best friends belong to each. Because they cannot understand the nationalistic or religious impulses, most Americans see this violence as silly, futile, and tragic. The terrorists on each side do not share our perspective, and the violence shows no signs of ending. We look, for example, at India, Sri Lanka,

Introduction

Indonesia, the Philippines, Nicaragua, El Salvador, Argentina, Cambodia, Lebanon, Quebec, Puerto Rico, Cyprus, Chad, Nigeria, South Africa, and Italy and see essentially the same thing. People do care enough to kill and be killed, even when, from the view of outsiders, their deadly crusades are pointless. Consider two important American political issues. The first stage of the fight over the passage of the Equal Rights Amendment is now history. That constitutional amendment, which meant so much to so many women, was defeated by enough state legislatures to prevent its passage. An interesting side-light to this struggle is that during the decade in which the Equal Rights Amendment was a political battleground no one was killed, no one took his or her own life. Although the passage of the Amendment was vital to many women, no woman felt it appropriate to assassinate state legislators who opposed them, no woman saw fit to become a gasoline-soaked martyr for the cause. This political moderation is in sharp contrast to the battles for suffrage in Great Britain and the United States, where acts of violence were part of the campaigns. Although it may be horrible for us to consider the tactical value of a well-placed bomb, apparently many terrorists constantly consider this a possible course of action.

The civility shown by those who hold strong beliefs applies not only to progressive causes. Many members of the pro-life (anti-abortion) movement believe that each year some 1.5 million babies are being *murdered* in the United States. Surely such genocide—as some have termed it—is ample reason for direct political action. Yet, the prolife movement, with few exceptions, has worked within the conventional political rules with few violent acts. Each day they let thousands of innocent babies go to their grave without raising a finger. Why?

In suggesting that Americans do not see murder and martyrdom as acceptable political alternatives, I do not mean to imply that we should. We are not politically deficient because we lack a tradition of organized political terrorism. Presumably this *relative* (but not total) lack of collective violence is one reason for our political stability. Americans are largely pragmatic and centrist in political outlook. We vote overwhelmingly for

3

two parties that often seem to not have "a dime's worth of difference" between them. This is particularly striking when we consider the much broader range of political beliefs accepted in Great Britain, France, or Canada. While we should not ignore the real differences between the Democratic and Republican parties, their basic values and policies are similar. Both claim to believe in a strong national defense, a social security system, aid to the needy, support for the arts, nuclear arms talks, and free enterprise. The two parties differ in the *level* of funding for these programs and in the way specific programs are administered; however, when we consider them against the full range of possible alternative political policies, our two major parties are huddled very much in the center. Each wishes to convince voters that it is the real centrist party, the party of moderation. When a Barry Goldwater or George McGovern is nominated, he is overwhelmingly defeated. Socialist, nativist, populist, and libertarian parties have had little success in selling their nostrums to the American people.

Because of the success that the two parties have had together in making America strong at home and abroad, most voters feel the general centrist positions that the major parties push are correct. Furthermore, Americans have accepted the idea that compromise and civil discussion are more effective than forcing one's opinions on others. Americans typically are pragmatic in their political orientations and often stay away from all-encompassing ideologies, despite their strong opinions on many issues. We seem more concerned with getting the job done than in how it gets done.

Of course, there are other good reasons for not wanting to kill—and be killed. Some accept the principle that nothing is as valuable as life and that there is no excuse for shortening it. Better to be Red than dead or, for that matter, better to be blue than dead. No political issue, these thinkers believe, can take priority over the destruction of human life—a point emphasized by the Indian revolutionary Mahatma Gandhi and his followers who believe non-violent civil disobedience can achieve the same end. In theory we all probably agree with this approach, but

4

whether we believe it will work depends on our view of human nature.

I used killing and being killed as an opening gambit to indicate how strongly some people feel about social issues and political ideology. (I have no desire for students to raise arms.) Yet I wonder whether our American lack of ideological concern is a good thing; how far can political pragmatism be pushed before it becomes a willingness to accept any policy so long as it is nicely packaged? I have written this book to expose students to the philosophical bases of social life. Sociology is the proper place to begin to understand the underlying questions of social order.

I believe that people are better off if they are consciously aware of their basic principles—that is, those beliefs and values that structure how they view the world. From these basic principles, their attitudes toward particular issues will emerge in logical and consistent ways, to the extent that human psychology allows. Most people do not have strong feelings about human nature or about the role of the government in individual affairs. I assume that most students have never considered these two issues in any detail, yet most students do have beliefs on particular social problems. Since I believe that these two issues, human nature and government intervention, are at the heart of all sociological understanding, they deserve to be considered in detail.

Over three centuries ago, the British moral philosopher Thomas Hobbes raised an intriguing and important question that continues to haunt sociologists: How is social order possible? In other words, why, in a world of individuals with their own needs and personalities, is society as orderly as it is? Just as the physical world rarely fools us, the social world (perhaps a little less consistently) rarely surprises us. As adults, we usually know what to expect from our fellow citizens. How, in a world of four billion people, do we so neatly fit our personal routines together? The answers that a person gives to this puzzle of social order depends on how he or she evaluates human nature, and from this answer, one can draw conclusions about how people should be governed.

We do not expect people to go through their daily routines constantly aware of these fundamental questions; people generally act on the basis of immediate circumstances and options. While this is fine for small decisions, such an approach presents difficulties when we confront momentous decisions. These decisions may be erratic or inconsistent since they derive from immediate concerns and not from basic principles. Thus, some critics have suggested American economic and foreign policies lurch from position to position to position, depending on what the public is most clamoring for and how close it is to an election. We try to control inflation just when inflation is subsiding, only to push the country into a recession; we deal with rising unemployment by establishing social welfare programs, which increase inflation; or we stimulate the economy by cutting taxes, which leads to increased deficits, which is solved by raising taxes. Conservatives support high deficits when to do so is in their political interest; liberals support massive arms buildups when this is what the public wishes to hear.

A dilemma inherent in a pragmatic approach is one of morality. The pragmatist sees problems in their immediate setting but often without concern for their long-term consequences. Some solutions may be morally right, even though they are less effective than others. For example, sterilizing "genetically deficient" individuals might decrease the incidence of mental retardation; yet, many who believe this is possible to institute would reject this policy on moral grounds. Such forced sterilization may be wrong, even though it works. Ethics may take precedence over technical efficiency.

Finally, by considering issues only pragmatically, we are prone to ignore the global sociological principles. Sociology strives for insights with general relevance. It is hoped that what sociology can tell us applies to more than narrow, local problems but rather can address a wider range of concerns. As we shall discuss later, the sociological principle of *functionalism* allows us to understand many social spheres. The same can be said of an alternative approach—*conflict theory*.

Do not make too sharp a distinction between decisions based on principles and those based on the needs of the moment. Many sociologists believe the world is too complex to be completely dominated by any single set of principles or ideologies. We should be sensitive to each of the sometimes contradictory principles that are widely held. Many claim no single set of beliefs can possibly hold all the answers. Whether or not this is true, political reality typically means that some principles must be compromised. Politics is, after all, the art of the possible, of learning to make adjustments to the wishes of others. Although you should be aware of your principles in making decisions, this does not mean you should always blindly and coldly act on these principles. Pragmatism is not a dirty word: in a democracy it is essential in reaching consensus.

The Social Order

There exist many possible prescriptions for how society should be ordered. Each society, each tribe, each nation has at least one, sometimes several, ways of seeing their world. In this book I will examine three of the most common views in American life: *social democracy, libertarianism,* and *conservatism.* I do not claim these are the only three perspectives that Americans hold, but they do have several things in common that make them good subjects. First, each presents a reasonably consistent and complete view of human nature. Second, each contains within it the principles by which a government could make policy. Third, each of these views is accepted by a significant number of Americans, and elements from each have penetrated the general, pragmatic political view. Finally, each perspective described here is consistent with democratic government. Certain important philosophies, that are not readily amenable to democracy are not considered: communism (Marxist-Leninism), fascism, or benevolent monarchy. In addition, I consider only "Western" political philosophies; those of the great empires of China, Japan, India, Persia, Mexico, Peru, and West Africa are ignored.

I don't pretend to discuss the details of the three approaches that I have selected. Each is a complicated point of view with many nuances of thought and objective. There is no single, correct interpretation of any of them. I only try to capture their basic ideas. Keep in mind while reading the following descriptions that few people are "true believers"; most individuals pick and choose the best ideas from each philosophy. Furthermore, it will be helpful for you to read these points of view sympathetically. In other words, try to see the world from each particular point of view. After you have finished reading, ask yourself which view you find most appealing and why. Why do the other two approaches seem wrong? Ask your study partners and classmates the same questions.

This book will not tell you that one approach is more correct than any other. If I can give you something to think about, something to argue about, and something to help you understand the buzzing, booming social order a little better, then I will have accomplished my purpose. Ultimately, I want to prod you into thinking about your basic assumptions about the world, and how your assumptions lead to positions on important contemporary issues. Although sociology is, in some measure, a science grounded in empirical investigation, it should not be forgotten that it is also a branch of social philosophy.

The Libertarian Point of View

Of all three approaches, the libertarian perspective is probably the easiest to describe, as libertarians pride themselves on their logical consistency and principled positions (which reaches absurdity in the eyes of some critics). Libertarians hold individual freedom as their highest value. They believe that each person should have the right to do what he or she wishes, if it does not directly coerce or interfere with the freedom of others. The libertarian strives to uphold individual rights in all ways.

Although many social democrats and conservatives hold public office, few strict libertarians do. One reason is that libertarians are often perceived as extremists who are unwilling to compromise. This stems from their reliance on pure logic, cold logic, some might call it, to make their case. The 1980 Libertarian Party platform endorsed the following programs, which most Americans would find difficult to accept: 1) eliminating all laws requiring gun registration, 2) ending government payment for psychiatric treatment, 3) eliminating all anti-pornography legislation, 4) ending all government operation and subsidy of schools, and 5) abolishing the Consumer Product Safety Commission, the Environmental Protection Agency, the Federal Aviation Administration, and the Food and Drug Administration. In conventional political terms, libertarians are very conservative on economic issues (ultimately opposing all government regulation of businesses) and very liberal on social issues (allowing any and all acts that do not directly harm another person). How, you might ask, have libertarians come to adopt such views?

These positions are derived from the libertarians' understanding of human nature, especially the belief that individuals are largely responsible for their own actions, and are part of what many call the "Protestant Ethic." If people are successful, it is because they have the skills that enable them to be successful: they have chosen to be successful. They are hard-working, sincere, honest, diligent, and educated. All of these traits are ones that are not inherited but are acquired through personal effort and moral strength. Of course, the libertarian would not deny that some things are hereditary, but those are seen as less important. Likewise, the libertarian does not deny that some individuals have social handicaps—race, parents' income, sex: however, the libertarian believes that in a fair society discrimination would not exist and, anyway, people should be able to overcome these obstacles without government help. This may strike some as naive, but it follows from a belief in free will. (We would do well to recall in all the philosophies we examine matters of degree, rather than absolutes.) The libertarian believes that people are rational decision-makers, relatively free to do what they wish; success or failure in this life is due to one's own efforts. The libertarian believes you are free to get an "A" or "D" in this course, and the fact that you attended a poor high school or just split up with your lover, or that your grandmother recently died, does not change your own responsibility for the grade you get.

From this belief follows the libertarian's view of government. The libertarian assumes, in Thoreau's words, "that government is best which governs least." Since people have the knowledge and ability to make themselves happy and successful (if they choose to), it follows that government can best serve its citizens by maximizing their freedom. This position derives from the writings of eighteenth and nineteenth century British liberals, such as Adam Smith, John Stuart Mill, and Jeremy Bentham, who mistrusted the power of the State. These thinkers, and others who followed them, raised the individual to a pinnacle of power in the social universe. They also believed reason would ultimately provide the means by which human beings could live happily with each other. If everyone would try to maximize his or her happiness, without infringing on the rights of others, the world would be a nice place to live in.

The greatest sin for the libertarian is coercion. Although libertarians recognize that some people can coerce other people (muggers or rapists, for instance), libertarians' primary concern is the power that is taken away from individuals by the government. Although at first this concentration of power might seem innocuous—someone has to provide for national defense and for a police force to prevent anarchy—such power can easily be misused. As the American revolutionary Thomas Paine wrote in *Common Sense* (1776): "Society in every state is a blessing, but government, even in its best state, is but a necessary evil; in its worst state, an intolerable one." Libertarian economist Murray Rothbard uses the metaphor of the state as "a criminal band" to explain the libertarian philosophy.[1]

As a result, the libertarian believes passionately that the government should not entangle itself in the private lives of its citizens. If a person wishes to have sexual relations with a sheep, so be it. If someone chooses to use heroin or commit suicide without involving others, that is no cause for concern. The government should not protect people from themselves. Thus, rape is not a crime against the social order but rather a crime that violently eliminates the right of a particular person to refuse intercourse. All crimes are crimes against individuals, not against society—an argument to which the conservative would object.

One problem in libertarian theory concerns the boundaries of coercion. When are a person's rights infringed? A libertarian believes people should be allowed to play music if they wish, but suppose they do this at three o'clock in the morning in your dormitory. Are they infringing on your rights? There are no easy answers to these conflicts of rights. The libertarian, however, more than the conservative or the social democrat, is likely to side with the actor, rather than with the person being inconvenienced by the act.

In the realm of economics, the libertarian's position is *laissez-faire* (translated from the French: "leave it alone"). This phrase, derived from the writings of the eighteenth century Scottish economist Adam Smith, refers to the theory that the government should not attempt to manipulate the economy. The economy is best stabilized through the laws of supply and demand. When more people want something, its price increases. Price increases will typically increase the supply (because of increased profit) and will decrease the demand, and this increased supply and decreased demand will decrease price. Furthermore, the economy operates by the rational decisions of free people, and it assumes a "free" market, not one artificially controlled by large monopolies or cartels. Social democrats are likely to object to *laissez-faire* economics and government nonintervention on this point because, they claim, the market is not really free.

Another problem with libertarian theory is its border with anarchy. Indeed, anarchy is closely related to libertarianism, with the primary difference being that the libertarians accept the fundamental right to property, whereas most (left-wing) anarchists do not. In emphasizing freedom, the libertarian deemphasizes equality and order. The libertarian would qualify this by saying that with rational human beings working together for their common end, order will emerge, and that equality means only the equality of opportunity, rather than the equality of outcome. Equality of opportunity is always present in libertarian theory because of the free will inherent in life. The great virtue of libertarians is their lust for freedom; their great failing is their cold-hearted lack of compassion for their neighbors who simply cannot keep up.

The Conservative Point of View

Ambrose Bierce, in his *Devil's Dictionary*, defined a conservative as "a statesman who is enamoured of existing evils, as distinguished from the Liberal, who wishes to replace them with others."[2] There is some truth in this sardonic comment. Conservatives do have a high regard for the tried and true, and fret about the new and untested.

The term Conservative is derived from French political thought during the Napoleonic era and refers to a guardian of principles of justice and the nation's civilized heritage. Conservatism largely originated from opposition to the radical changes brought about by the French Revolution. Sociologist Robert Nisbet, in tracing the history of sociological thought, makes a cogent case that sociology is derived from conservative political thought with its love for community, order, and authority, although relatively few sociologists today would define themselves as politically conservative.[3]

Russell Kirk, a leading conservative theorist, argues conservatism is not really a political system nor an ideology.[4] He makes this claim because conservatives are in favor of preserving what has come before, that is, whatever has worked for a society in the past. Thus, a Peruvian conservative would legitimately differ from a Swiss conservative, who would differ from a Kenyan conservative. Unlike the libertarian, who has the same principles wherever he or she might be, the conservative's policies are based on the society in which he or she lives. So, if an innovation (for example, Social Security or enforced racial equality) has proven successful, despite the original opposition of the conservative, the conservative will now support it. Conservatives do not suggest any single set of policies are necessarily superior.

Kirk, making particular reference to British and American conservative writing, points to a set of "first principles," that are shared by most conservatives.[5] I shall draw heavily on his analysis in my discussion.

Unlike the libertarian who sees human beings as fundamentally rational and basically decent, conservatives believe that humans are imperfect. Human nature is faulty and, as a result, no perfect social system can ever be devised. The conservative sadly concludes that all we can hope for is a *reasonably* happy, just, and fair society. Finding absolute goodness is no more likely than finding a unicorn. The human lot (perhaps due to "original sin") is to live in a world where some evil, misery, and unfairness exist. We can't eliminate pain; we can only hope to control it. The conservative perspective is most likely to present human beings in an unflattering, pessimistic fashion. They are apt to agree to some extent with the seventeenth century British moral philosopher, Thomas Hobbes, that human beings without government to control them are destined to live a life that is "solitary, poor, nasty, brutish, and short."[6] This belief in the weaknesses of human nature leads the conservative to accept the rightful place of a variety of social institutions to control these excesses.

Most conservatives include God in their social equation. That is, they accept the existence of a "transcendent moral order"—moral authority that cannot be challenged by other people.[7] Conservatives reject the libertarian idea that all individuals should do their own thing. They believe in a moral authority that is set by divine principle or "natural law."

Conservatives also accept the value of social continuity—preferring the devil they know to the one they are yet to meet. They believe most changes are for the worse, and so changes should be made gradually, cautiously, and often not at all. The church serves in some regard as the model for the state. Just as theology changes very slowly—after all, it is supposed to be God's law—so should secular law. The radicalness of revolution, particularly of the French and Russian revolutions, is profoundly frightening to conservatives. Implicit in conservative thought is a deep respect for the past. The wisdom of the past has been replaced by the foolish babble of the present. This romanticism for what has come before leads some to claim conservatives are reactionary. Yet, it is not so much that conservatives revere particular historical figures; rather, they revere the trial-and-error learning to which they are heir. In eighteenth century conservative philosopher Edmund Burke's words: "The individual is foolish, but the species is wise."[8]

Finally, conservatives share with libertarians the belief that everyone should not be treated equally. While social democrats wish to minimize the class system, conservatives believe that classes produce a healthy diversity in a society. Leveling of classes leads to a stagnant society. If all people are equal, there is no need for anyone to exert himself or herself to do better; motivation is lost. Furthermore, conservatives cherish the existence of other social institutions besides government. They see the church, the community, and the family as particularly important social forces that have authority equaling or surpassing that of the government. The state, on the other hand, is a secondary or artificial institution, not derived from the natural relations of human beings.

For the conservative, government is not the evil that it is for the libertarian; it is just secondary. When other social institutions have failed, then government must step in. As a result, conservatives often believe government involvement should staunch the tide of moral decay and, as long as the economic system is functioning, allow business to operate on its own without government regulation. The conservative is not afraid of the fact that some people are poor and some people fail; these unfortunate facts simply represent the natural diversity of a social system.

Unlike the social democrats, who admire a just and strong government, and the libertarians, who mistrust governments of all kinds, the conservatives are neutral toward government. It is simply not the most important thing in society. While government is needed to preserve order, it is weakened by the frailty of human nature and doesn't compare with natural, primary organizations. The conservative's greatest virtue is order and, according to Russell Kirk, their particular vice is selfishness—the desire to let things rest in a way favorable to them. Despite popular stereotypes, conservatives are no more anachronisms than social democrats are wild-haired firebrands.

The Social Democratic Point of View

Of the three philosophies, the least clear and most broad is what I have termed social democrat. Although you will find Americans who are proud to call themselves libertarians and conservatives, few Americans call themselves social democrats. In the United States, such people will typically refer to themselves as liberals or progressives and will be called by their opponents leftists, left-liberals or socialists. None of these terms really do justice to their social and political approach. Perhaps liberal comes closest, but the history of the word is so muddled up with libertarianism that it does us little good. (Some of the founders of libertarianism were known as liberals.) So, I have chosen to use a European term to refer to this group of Americans. In West Germany, the major left-liberal party is known as the Social Democratic party. In other European countries, the leading party on the nonCommunist left is a social democratic party—committed to democracy but also to a strong, involved government. Although this term does not precisely fit the American situation, it is the best available. I have combined an uneasy blend of contemporary liberalism, welfare-state economics, democratic socialism, and progressive democracy. More than the other two approaches, the social democratic perspective casts a wide net, possibly slightly too wide.

Unlike conservative theory, social democratic philosophy accepts the possibility of the betterment of human nature. It is not that people are naturally good, but they can be made to be good. Social policies can bring out the best in people. This perspective can be seen most clearly in the social democrat's fight for civil rights legislation. The social democrat starts with the assumption that all people have been created equal and that they should be treated equal. Of course, in the tough, cold, real world they are unfortunately not treated in this way. Thus, in the early 1960s social democrats vigorously and successfully fought to have the United States Congress pass a civil rights law that would outlaw discrimination in restaurants and other places of public accommodation. They believed that by preventing whites from segregating racial minorities, this would increase the toleration among the races. Social democrats believed that changing the laws would eventually produce a change in attitudes—that stateways precede folkways. In this case at least, the philosophy appears to work. For example, white southerners, forced by law to eat at the same coffee shops with black southerners, discovered the moral order of society did not come crashing down. Southern politicians such as George Wallace discovered when they were forced to desegregate they really did not mind blacks as much as they thought they would. Civil rights legislation provides a textbook case of how government involvement led to positive moral outcomes and a presumed improvement in human nature.

Perhaps most central to the social democrat's philosophy is the potentially positive role of government. President Andrew Jackson gave a wonderful metaphor that reflects the social democrats attitude, "There are no necessary evils in government. Its evils exist only in its abuses. If it would confine itself to equal protection and, as Heaven does its rains, shower its favors alike on the high and the low, the rich and the poor, it would be an unqualified blessing."[9]

State power need not necessarily be scary; it can increase human happiness. Likewise, change need not be the fearsome foe pictured by the conservative. Although some changes can be harmful (no one is in favor of every possible change), other changes, even radical ones, are sometimes for the best. The social democrat sees a multitude of crimes committed by a multitude of governments as not necessarily true of every strong government. The obligation of the government to promote equality and justice must take priority. In this desire for equality the social democrat parts company with the libertarian and the conservative who welcome the diversity brought by a class system, a social system in which some succeed and others fail.

Behind this belief in equality lies a different view of motivation. Social democrats believe that people will work hard because that is the right thing to do. Unlike the conservatives who are constantly complaining about the many people who will try to cheat on welfare and try to get by without working, the social democrat sees the number of such individuals as rather small. Most people have strong internal moral compasses, and while they are not perfect, they do have good hearts. The social democrat ultimately paints a rosier picture of human beings than does the conservative. The problems for the social democrat are those traditional social arrangements that prevent people from living happily and equally—racism, social inequality, sex discrimination, and prejudice against old people, people of a different nationality or religion.

Ultimately, the primary problem for the social democrat is poverty; poverty destroys human dignity. In the words of Democratic presidential candidate Adlai Stevenson: "A hungry man is not a free man."[10] This reflects the attitude of the social democrat who, in working against poverty, is concerned with insuring that government takes an active role in preventing these offenses to human dignity.

One of the problems with such a broad category as the social democratic perspective is that adherents have different attitudes about what is the appropriate governmental response to poverty. Some (the welfare-state liberal) wish to restrain the government's effect on the market to as little as is necessary to cure the symptoms of poverty. Such a person favors a collection of welfare programs to help those who are disadvantaged because of their position in society. He or she also believes government should play an active role in combatting the *excesses* of business. On the other side, some democratic socialists consider it appropriate for the government to manage large segments of the essential industrial and service economy of the nation. Thus, in Great Britain, the government controls the railroads, much heavy industry, medical practice, and other areas of concern to the people as a whole. Some areas are left to private industry, but often these are not the most central industries and services. Critics have noted inadequacies of government intervention in all its forms, and wonder whether an efficient government is ever possible.

In the area of morality, the social democrat often stands with the libertarian. Since private institutions of religion and the family have no special position in social democratic thought (as they do for the conservative), the government should allow a full flowering of lifestyles. Morality is a private matter, while economic insufficiency is a public matter. Morality is a matter of individual choice, whereas economic position is related to the social structure. Since morality has no special place in society, the social democrat thinks it unwarranted that some groups suffer discrimination by others because of differing beliefs and practices. For example, the social democrat finds it easy to support legislation prohibiting discrimination against homosexuals. Discrimination poses a structural barrier to the well-being of these citizens. A group's right to protection takes priority over an individual's freedom to discriminate.

The leading virtue for the social democrat is equality. All social democrats believe in the equality of opportunity, and many believe in the equality of outcome as well. There is a point below which a society should never let its members slip—a view not shared by the extreme libertarian or conservative. Just as equality is the social democrat's virtue, envy is their weakness. Some say that social democrats are envious failures, who wish to grab from the successful those rewards that they have not been able to win through personal efforts. Social democrats who are personally successful may be accused of being naively optimistic, painting too rosy a picture of those they wish to help. Redistribution of wealth is particularly appealing to those who have little, just as the status quo is appealing to those with much to lose.

The Structure of the Text

In the remaining chapters we will examine twelve controversial social issues from these three major standpoints. The issues were deliberately chosen to reflect major sociological concepts, those found in most textbooks for introductory sociology and social problems courses. Each chapter has a sociological concept for which the question asked is a reflection. So, for example, when discussing culture, I ask whether Hispanic children should be taught in bilingual education programs.

The chapter begins with a short discussion of how the relevant concept has been treated in sociological writing. This does not replace the discussion in the text or in class but rather provides a basis for the discussion that follows. I try to present the major concept in a straightforward and simple fashion. In order to provide continuity between the concepts, I will typically include in each chapter some discussion of the three major theoretical approaches to sociology: functionalism, conflict theory, and interactionism.

Functionalists see society as similar to a living creature. By this they mean that all of the systems (or "organs") of society are interrelated. The life of that society is a result or "function" of the interplay of these systems (for example, religion, the family, the economy, culture). The functionalist is likely to emphasize consensus and stability in a society. A smoothly functioning society is a stable society which is a happy society. While functionalists do not totally ignore change, they tend to deemphasize it and see it as a threat to the functioning of the society, something that disturbs the systems in society. The functionalist believes that each system has a role in preserving the society and that, when functioning properly, its form is best suited for its tasks. Furthermore, systems should mesh without conflict. For the functionalist, conflict should be avoided—it is perceived as dysfunctional because it undermines the existence of society. Thus, it is easy to see why functionalism is often seen as a conservative approach to society.

Of course, it is not always easy to see what the function of a social system is; as a result, functionalists distinguish between *manifest* and *latent* functions. The manifest functions are those that are easily observable. The family has a manifest function in providing for the systematic moral socialization of children. Latent functions are those which may be unintended and unseen. Some suggest the family has the latent function of preserving the sexual division of labor, of keeping women out of the work force. The problem with this approach is that one person's latent function may be another's oppression. Functionalism with its orientation toward the status quo may be charged with having an ideological bias in favor of the dominant classes.

Conflict theory contrasts with functionalism. Contemporary society for the conflict theorist leaves a somewhat sour taste. Just as consensus is basic to the functionalist, struggle and change are basic to the conflict theorist. This approach considers the existence of rival groups with contrary interests as inevitable and even healthy for preventing a stagnant society.

The conflict theorist is prone to ask: Who gains from current social arrangements? How are opposing groups trying to change systems or society? In practical terms these sociologists tend to side with those whom they see as oppressed, and so the conflict approach can easily be likened to the social democratic philosophy in its desire for change.

Interactionism, the third major theoretical approach in sociology, is less overtly political than the other two. Interactionism focuses on the relations among individuals and the meanings these relations have for the participants. It suggests that the society has no inherent meaning but that individuals give meaning to events. A gunshot, for example, means nothing by itself; whether it is part of a murder, a prank, a hunting expedition, or a suicide depends on the context. Likewise, a minister and a drill sergeant will define "curse" in very different terms; it would be the same word but with very different meanings, provoking very different reactions. The interactionist believes that meanings can change over time and in negotiation with others. In the recent past two men hugging in public would have been censured; today such behavior is tolerated. Even those who might still condemn this action if they assumed that the two men were gay, would quickly change their attitudes if assured that the two were long-lost brothers. Behavior is subject to change in interpretation at a moment's notice.

Crucial to interactionist theory is the belief that human beings have the power to define their own world. Unlike the functionalist and the conflict theorist, who both emphasize structure, the interactionist is likely to point to the power of individuals to create their own sets of meanings. It is because of this emphasis on the power of the individual that we can liken interactionism to libertarianism; although, in this case, because of the generally apolitical stance of interactionism, the connection is tenuous.

After examining each broad sociological concept, there is a general examination of the chapter question. I present some background material that will allow you to make sense of what all the fuss is about. Each question has a long controversy behind it and, while it cannot be dealt with in as much detail as the disputants might provide, a brief description of the basic issue is sketched out. That section is followed by a discussion of how proponents of the libertarian, conservative, and social democratic point of view address the question. I have chosen to present the approaches in no particular order, choosing as the first perspective that seems to be the most vehement about the issue under discussion. This is fair because the order that one makes an argument affects the way in which an audience will respond. By changing the order of discussion, I provide some semblance of balance.

I do not pretend to have provided an exhaustive treatment of any of these subjects; I hope only to give you enough material for debate and controversy and to make you consider the basis of your own beliefs. I do not encourage you to accept any particular perspective or, for that matter, any of the perspectives. I recognize that Marxism has not been adequately covered; neither have many non-American ideologies. Because of the breadth and diversity of each philosophy, some who hold that view may disagree with portions of my discussion. This may, in part, be due to my errors of understanding, and part may be attributed to the difficulty of describing a complex philosophy in simple terms. In presenting these issues, I have attempted to draw from a wide variety of sources, some of which rarely appear in reputable sociology textbooks. I have chosen quotations that are written in a lively fashion and that capture the essence of an argument in a memorable way. Some of the sources make truly strange bedfellows, but at least I try to change the sheets frequently.

I then turn to a research case study that relates to the question being discussed. My goal is to demonstrate how various styles and methodologies of research can be used to examine these theoretical questions. While the studies selected represent a variety of approaches to social problems, each is respectable. Even though the assumptions of each will be held up for scrutiny, they represent a collection of the best research studies that sociologists have to offer. (You could profitably read the original version of each of them.) The point I wish to make here is that the debates I present are not mere idle speculations but are empirical questions on which researchers can throw light. Although the research will *not* tell us how to solve the problem, it will help us to recognize more easily the dimensions of the problem.

The final section of each chapter connects the sociological concept with the particular question that I have addressed. Here I raise the basic questions that underlie the specific question. So, in the chapter that deals with race relations, I ask the possibly horrifying question: What is so wrong with discrimination? It is my belief that unless we understand the foundations for our beliefs, we cannot hold them strongly and steadfastly. While these broad questions are not destined to be answered satisfactorily, at least they have been raised, to fester or flower in your mind and in discussions. Do not forget that sociology ultimately is based on questions of human nature, and addresses questions of how the social order should be organized. With that in mind, "Let the wild rumpus start!"

For Further Study

Conservative

Buckley, William F. ed. *Did You Ever See a Dream Walking? American Conservative Thought in the Twentieth Century*. Indianapolis: Bobbs-Merrill, 1970.

Gilder, George F. *Wealth and Poverty*. New York: Basic Books, 1981.

Kirk, Russell, ed. *The Portable Conservative Reader*. New York: Penguin, 1982.

Libertarian
Friedman, Milton. *Capitalism and Freedom*. Chicago: University of Chicago Press, 1962.

Hospers, John. *Libertarianism: A Political Philosophy for Tomorrow*. Los Angeles: Nash, 1971.

Machan, Tibor R. ed. *The Libertarian Reader*. Totowa, New Jersey: Rowman and Littlefield, 1982.

Social Democratic
Galbraith, John Kenneth. *The New Industrial State* Boston: Houghton Mifflin, 1969.

Mansfield, Jr., Harvey C. *The Spirit of Liberalism*. Cambridge: Harvard University Press, 1978.

Spitz, David. *The Real World of Liberalism*. Chicago: University of Chicago Press, 1982.

General
Nisbet, Robert. *The Sociological Tradition*. New York: Basic Books, 1966.

Notes and References

1. Mark Paul, "Seducing the Left: The Third Party Wants *You*," *Mother Jones*, May 5, 1980, p. 47.
2. Ambrose Bierce, *The Devil's Dictionary* (New York: Dover, 1958), p. 24.
3. Robert Nisbet, *The Sociological Tradition* (New York: Basic Books, 1966). See also Everett C. Ladd, Jr. and Seymour Martin Lipset, *The Divided Academy*: Professors and Politics (New York: McGraw-Hill, 1975), pp. 107–115, 369.
4. Russell Kirk, ed. "Introduction," *The Portable Conservative Reader* (New York: Penguin, 1982), p. xiv.

5. *Ibid,* pp. xv-xviii.
6. Thomas Hobbes, *Leviathan* (New York: Collier, 1962; original ed., 1651), p. 100.
7. Kirk, *op. cit.,* p. xv.
8. Kirk, *op. cit.,* p. xvi.
9. President Andrew Jackson's message to Congress vetoing the Bank Bill, July 10, 1832. *Bartlett's Familiar Quotations,* 13 ed. (Boston: Little, Brown & Co., 1955), p. 399.
10. Adlai Stevenson, campaign speech, September 6, 1952, Kasson, Minnesota. *Bartlett's Familiar Quotations,* 13 ed. (Boston: Little, Brown & Co., 1955), p. 086.

 **One**

Socialization: Should Parents Be Allowed to Hit Their Children However They Wish?

THE BRITISH FOLKLORIST Douglas Newton once remarked "The worldwide fraternity of children is the greatest of savage tribes, and the only one which shows no signs of dying out."[1] Despite the affront to our vanity, Newton's point is crucial for our understanding of how sociologists view the social process by which human beings mature. When we enter this complex and confusing world, we are nothing but a bundle of cute and complicated biological mechanisms; we are not social beings. We must be trained to live in a world in which we have been placed without our consent.

We are "uncivilized." Our guardians, especially our parents, are given the formidable challenge to make us into responsible Americans, Britons, Poles, Haitians, Nigerians, or Vietnamese. Within these nationalities, we are taught to be Black Americans, Scots, Moslems, Hottentots, socialists, or upper-class. Finally, but not least important, we must learn to fit into the culture of our family. Socialization is the process by which an infant human child is shaped into a responsible, mature adult. Primary socialization is the learning that occurs through the primary institutions of society, most particularly the family, and occurs largely, although not entirely, during childhood. Secondary socialization typically refers to more specific, formal training—such as learning one's occupation or how to behave properly in some public association.

Socialization results from a combination of factors, both biological and social. Often children are simply unable to learn something until they are biologically ready. Most parents at some time or another become frustrated in raising their children because the child seems unwilling to master something that the parents are sure the child "should" be able to do. Ask a parent about toilet training, for example. Despite the parent's frustration, the child is probably not so much unwilling to learn as not ready to learn. Experts in child development look at this biological readiness in terms of a series of stages through which each child will pass. These stages do not only involve such obviously biological factors such as bladder control, but intellectual skills as well. The Swiss child psychologist Jean Piaget has argued that there is a series of intellectual or cognitive stages that a child will reach. For instance, until children reach approximately the age of seven, it is difficult to teach them that the larger of two objects need not be the heavier (a pound of feathers versus a pound of lead).[2] When they reach the appropriate stage (what Piaget terms the "concrete operational stage") such a connection is obvious to them.

At times children seem like information vacuum cleaners. Even a youngster who does not do well in school frequently picks up some other kind of knowledge and can become a street performance virtuoso or mechanical wizard. Learning is as natural as breathing, although what is learned is not always what parents want to be learned. For this reason parents strive to set up reward/cost structures so that it is in the child's

interest to do what the parents want. The fact that children consider the consequences of their actions, and eventually
internalize the rewards and punishments, supports a behavioris-
tic (or Skinnerian) understanding of socialization. Many people
believe reinforcement does change behavior. Parents are constantly orchestrating a dance of treats and punishments to
direct the behavior of their offspring, including using physical
force.

Through socialization children learn who they are. They become familiar with the core of personality: the self. The self is
what people believe makes them special, different from everyone else, uniquely themselves. Development of the self-concept
is too complicated to explain completely here, but some aspects
should be mentioned for purposes of this discussion. Perhaps
most important from a sociological viewpoint is the fact that the
development of the self is a social process. The American social
psychologist Charles Horton Cooley recognized that we come to
know ourselves after we know others. In other words, our self-
concept is a function of the "reflection" of others. We discover
how others view us and in time we see our self in the same or
similar ways. If others see us as great beauties or unendurable
prigs, we will use these attitudes to build our own self-concept.
Cooley refers to this as *the looking glass self*.[3] George Herbert
Mead,[4] a prominent American philosopher and social psychologist, extended this by emphasizing the importance of *role-
taking*. This is the process by which children come to internalize
the expectations that others have of them. By understanding
how others see them, children can shape their behavior to be
perceived in a favorable light. Later children expand their role-
taking to include the expectations of large groups or of the entire
society; Mead called this skill "taking the role of the generalized
other."[5] The acquisition of these skills helps people to be able to
"present" themselves in desirable ways—a technique that sociologist Erving Goffman has named "impression management."[6]
This skill is largely mastered by the time a child reaches adolescence, although it has roots much earlier, stretching back to
infancy.

Question:

Should Parents Be Allowed to Hit Their Children However They Wish?

All studies of American child rearing practices[7] indicate that corporal punishment has been and remains a common form of discipline. In these studies (particularly about younger children), approximately three-quarters or more of those who answer admit to punishing their child physically. The parent who claims never to have hit his child is either a saint or, more likely a liar. Hitting children is part of the American way of life, and, yet, consider one mother's account of what happens when this "normal" behavior gets out of control: "I started abusing my boy because he was an accident and a screamer. When he was four months old, I hit him so hard my engagement ring carved a deep bloody furrow across his soft face. His screams shattered my heart. I sank to the floor with self-loathing. Then I held him tightly in my arms, so tight he turned blue. I told him he had to do his share. Why didn't he stop screaming? Deep down, I knew he couldn't understand. But I also thought he was doing it on purpose."[8] This account could make you want to cry for and strangle this woman all at once. As anyone who reads the newspaper knows, there seems to be an epidemic of child abuse in America. Statistics on its extent vary so widely that we do not know how widespread the problem is nor do we know if it has increased in recent years. Figures for the number of abused children each year range from 650,000 to a million to six million. We simply do not have very good ways of measuring the problem, nor do we have an agreement on the definition of "child abuse". Some researchers include any form of corporal punishment as family violence, which would probably label all of us as abusers; others allow welts and bruises as part of normal, strict parental discipline. Of course if even one child dies at the hands of a parent (and the figure is close to 1,000 each year),[9] this is cause for alarm.

Many of the sociological studies that attempt to measure

child abuse or violence in the family use broad definitions that include any kind of physical action, including slapping and shoving. This broad definition, while alerting us to the possibility of serious abuse in families, also suggests to some that the figures on child abuse are so inflated as to be meaningless. Although much remains to be studied, there are some things that we do know about family violence. First, there is a cycle of violence; those who had violent and abused childhoods are likely to be violent and abusive as parents. Second, family violence is directly related to the amount of stress on a family and to the extent of its social isolation. Although strict discipline and child abuse are found in all economic classes, it is relatively more common among poor families.[10] Finally, there does seem to be some evidence that strict and humiliating corporal punishment is slowly moving out of favor[11] and is being replaced by a philosophy that emphasizes permissiveness.

Nevertheless, we face a cruel paradox. As civilized people, we probably all react with disgust when we hear of some atrocity, violent or sexual, that has been perpetrated on a child. And we can all probably agree with Sergeant Dick Ramon, head of the sex-crimes division of the Seattle police department, when he says, "child abuse is the ultimate crime, the ultimate betrayal."[12] Yet most Americans do hit their offspring and were hit themselves by their parents, and many people believe corporal punishment is valuable in teaching children right from wrong, even if there is no definitive scientific evidence to support this view. Somewhere there is a hazy wobbly line that separates guidance from villainy.

Most Americans would argue that there is some need for a law against child abuse. The question is how far should it go? Should it go as far as the Swedish law, passed in 1979, that says: "The child should not be subjected to corporal punishment or other humiliating treatment."[13] Or should it restrict as much as possible the intrusion of the state into what some feel is mostly a matter for family decision-making. Where shall we draw the line, and on what grounds shall the line be drawn?

The Social Democratic Point of View

The social democrat is particularly concerned with insuring that the rights of all groups are protected, particularly those groups, such as children, that cannot easily protect themselves. When a social democrat hears of a problem he or she is likely to suggest the government should step in and do something about it. Even if the action infringes on the "rights" of individuals and families, government intrusion may be necessary to protect a greater right—that of not allowing a child to be beaten. Irene Barth, an editor for *Newsday,* writes

> Recently, the public has been treated to accounts of a 5-year-old snuffed out by means of a plastic bag placed over her head, a 3-year-old boy beaten to a pulp with a bat and a 2-year-old shaken into the hereafter with bare hands. Another 3-year-old, a girl, according to police, was shredded with a belt because she showed too little interest in arithmetic flash cards. . . . Because of increased public awareness, the number of tips [to social service agencies] is up. Now comes a suit charging that social workers caused $6.5 million worth of "anguish and humiliation" to a family by looking into an unfounded allegation of child abuse. Richard and Dee-Ann Marrone complain that they were asked personal questions and that their children were undressed by a child-welfare worker looking for bruises. The family doctor, friends and school officials are said to have been told of the investigation. . . . Even if the plaintiffs are the tenderest of parents and the accusation against them was malicious, their suit has terrifying implications. . . . What is worse than the anguish visited upon innocent parents is the anguish visited upon the innocent children of guilty parents. . . . In an ideal world, all parents would receive thoughtful instruction in child-rearing and all homes housing young children would be visited at least once or twice by family experts. . . . Children's rights to protection from cruel and unusual punishment should outweigh adults' right to secure their houses against searches.[14]

Barth makes a strong and coherent argument in favor of the social democratic position. She believes the rights of a group of ✓ vulnerable individuals take priority over the property and privacy rights of parents. That individual parents might be hurt is more than offset by the fact that children are not abused. Of course there is no certain way of knowing how many parents will be hurt by this intervention and how many children will be spared pain.

Ms. Barth is explicit about her "ideal world." Parents would be thoughtfully trained in child rearing (presumably by the government), and every home would be visited by "family experts." This, however, is not everyone's idea of utopia. Conservatives would react with horror to this proposed army of bureaucratic intruders. Some might see thoughtful child-rearing instruction as ideological manipulation of youngsters by an all-intrusive state apparatus. While Barth is obviously sincere in her proposal, which is congruent with social democratic thought about the positive role of a helpful government, it would be a living hell for her critics.

Which position you adopt may relate to the faith you have in families and governments. If you see individual parents as ignorant, apathetic, or primitive, you are likely to be more willing to grant that there is a place for the thoughtful, altruistic government official. The cases rhetorically presented by the advocates of large-scale government intervention attempt to paint this picture: what kind of a world do we live in when a father could "shred" his three-year-old daughter with a belt for not caring about mathematics? On the other hand, there are an equal number of horror stories of bumbling, incompetent bureaucrats. Do-gooders may intrude on your family espousing their own narrow ideology or following government regulations to the letter. Each position has its own fantasies associated with it.

To understand where this government concern with the health and well-being of young children might lead, let us turn to Sweden. In 1979 this progressive Scandinavian nation passed a law that outlawed spanking, slapping, locking a child in a closet, or in general humiliating the child. This law was in addition to strong Swedish laws that provided stiff punishment for child abuse.

The law was not primarily designed to be punitive but rather educational. As a Swedish Ministry of Justice spokesman put it: "We hope to use the law to change attitudes. If we launched a big campaign on the subject, it probably would be forgotten in a year. But the law stays, and it enters the public consciousness."[15] Even if it is unlikely to send parents who swat their kids to jail, the proposal does have the force of law.

The Swedish politicians who passed this legislation believed that it is a legitimate role of the state to insure "proper" child rearing practices. The majority were convinced that children who are hit or threatened do not respond positively, and being convinced of this fact, they took action.

Of course this social democratic legislation has been subject to heated attacks and ridicule by those with a more conservative bent. Jim Klobuchar, a popular Minneapolis newspaper columnist, imagines satirically the length to which government interference might go:

> My cousin [from Sweden] said the family had torsk the other day, or whatever the Swedes call cod, and the kid refused. The wife tried all the gentle, loving approaches and when that didn't work, the guy ordered the kid to eat the torsk. The kid angrily refused. He said he was studying to be a vegetarian and the old man was intruding on his right of choice. When the predictable impasse developed, the old man said Ingemar couldn't go outside to play. The kid then went into his room and came out with a banner four feet high, which he put in the picture window, announcing: "This house practices grounding and other methods first used by the Spanish Inquisition." The guy might go to jail.[16]

As silly as this scenario might be, the social democrat does believe that the government has a place in the home. The family is not seen as a sacred institution, but government and its laws are. Government can right the wrongs caused by others. The social democrat believes that people can be made better and happier through legislation. When they see child abuse or any social wrong, they have no difficulty in correcting the problem by the most direct and universal solution—a law.

The Conservative Point of View

No conservative enjoys being beaten. Yet, it is more likely to find a conservative approving of and applying corporal punishment than a member of the other two groups. Conservatives believe that those tried and true methods of discipline are the best. They believe along with the Bible that: "He that spareth his rod hateth his son: but he that loveth him chasteneth him early" (Proverbs 13:24). They believe like Odin, the Norse God of War and Wisdom, that: "He who goes without corporal punishment will go lawless and die without honor." The conservative is far less likely to agree that reason is the guiding force of child development. A child must learn to accept and obey legitimate authority. Physical discipline is a forceful (if perhaps not totally effective) means of impressing the power differential between child and adult on the former in an emotional, rather than rational, way. A nineteenth century minister put it this way:

> [Corporal punishment] must be viewed not as simply the pain produced, but pain as the expression of disapprobation of a moral governor; and the dread of it, or the appeal made to fear, must be on account of the association it recalls of the displeasure of the beloved parent. To fear such displeasure, is a proof of affection; and the appeal made to such a feeling, even by means of external infliction, has no tendency to produce or cherish slavish submission . . . the family is a monarchy, though not a despotism; the father and mother, considered as one, are invested with patriarchal authority: and we carry out our idea still further; for we say that a holy family is in a sense a Theocracy.[17]

The authority of the family is central to conservatives, who would agree with philosopher Herbert Fingarette's claim:

> In terms of child abuse, [critics of corporal punishment] include the notion that it is wrong for the parent to use, or even to have authority to use, any kind of disciplinary action that involves what we call corporal punishment, which means laying a hand on the child. Now, if that is child abuse, then it is something which many people over the ages, and many people today . . . are well-convinced is a perfectly reasonable way to run a family. . . . [When] you deal with the family, you are dealing with an institution . . . that is the one fundamental opportunity for intimacy in a little community, a kind of peculiar, special intimacy, one which is rooted in aeons of traditions. We don't know what we are fiddling with when we fiddle with that. It is an enormously valuable thing that a family should have a certain kind of intimacy.[18]

Of course one should not caricature this position by pushing it too far. As conservative columnist William F. Buckley writes: "It is sometimes difficult to draw the line, but a line simply can and must be drawn between domestic discipline and domestic savagery."[19]

Fingarette is particularly concerned about the possibility of legislation damaging the integrity of the family. Rather than emphasizing the problem of child abuse, he sees a totally different problem: that of preserving and strengthening the family. The strength of the traditional family is considered one of the foundations of Western society, but now conservatives believe the family is being attacked from all quarters: delinquency, feminism, sex education, divorce, and premarital intercourse. Of course, when conservatives speak of the family, they refer to the traditional nuclear family (two parents and their offspring). This structure has never been as common as its staunchest defenders have implied. Throughout history numerous family forms have existed—extended, single-parent, communal, and the like. The conservative, then, is protecting an ideal, rather than a universal reality.

This point of view makes little sense to the extreme libertarian or social democrat. They view the family as little more than a contract between consenting individuals. Admittedly, children do not consent to this contract at birth and must be slowly given rights; still, they see nothing particularly sacred about the nuclear family structure. It may be efficient, but not *specially* moral, and so does not deserve to be specially protected by tradition or by law. It is the rights of individuals or protected classes that are more relevant. One critic of Professor Fingarette has reminded him that the same argument that he makes about families and children might be made of plantation owners and slaves.[20] A conservative would counter this by saying the family has a special privileged status that did not apply to ante-bellum cotton plantations.

Whereas the social democrat is concerned with the "epidemic" of child abuse, the conservative is equally concerned with the "epidemic" of permissiveness. Conservatives attribute the so-called moral decline of America to the permissive childrearing techniques of the past few decades and to the shunning of the basic and traditional values of society. The list of troubles is long and depressing: divorce, unwed mothers, public homosexuality, recreational drug use, and the decline in religiosity, to name but a few. Some Americans (particularly some libertarians) do not see these problems as problems but simply as the diverse flowering of a free and open society that should be allowed to flourish, rather than be repressed. (Of course, some conservative concerns such as an increase in violent crime worry everyone, regardless of their philosophy.)

Despite this concern with moral laxity, conservatives are not in favor of harsh discipline for its own sake. No one argues that a child be hit as an end in itself. Conservatives emphasize that pain and love should be mixed and that corporal punishment is only a last resort and a sign of parental concern. It is a sad commentary on the chasm between attitudes and behaviors that many parents who share these reasonable beliefs, find themselves engaging in unloving, brutal behavior.

The Libertarian Point of View

The debate over the issue of whether parents should be allowed to hit their children is primarily between social democrats and conservatives. For libertarians the debate pits two undesirable consequences against each other. Corporal punishment seems, in general, alien to the spirit of libertarian child rearing, which attempts to maximize the freedom and dignity of the child. Many child-rearing books of the post-war era are more or less congruent with the libertarian emphasis on the individual child as a person worthy of respect and responsibility. Bernice Weissbourd, president of a Chicago area agency that provides drop-in centers for parents of young children, made the following remark, which is consistent with the libertarian view. "A child learns many lessons from being spanked, but responsibility is not necessarily one of them. He learns that there are forces in his world to be feared. . . . He learns that the bigger and stronger you are, the more power you have. He learns that hitting is a way to express feelings and solve problems."[21] Libertarians consider such lessons harmful because they undermine the personal respect and rationality that is necessary in a free rather than controlled society. Likewise, corporal punishment is demeaning to the parent. From a libertarian's position, it really does "hurt me, more than it does you". Lillian Katz, a professor of early childhood education, warns of the dangers of spanking. "Overall, spanking can best be thought of as something we use against our better judgment. It is something we do in "hot" (as opposed to "cold") blood. To spank in the heat of the moment is not recommended; but, once in a while, it is inevitable and forgivable. But to spank in cold blood, as a matter of deliberate, premeditated policy, is sadistic."[22] Violence is outside the pale of libertarian thought because it denies the validity of a society based on maximal freedom.

Libertarians also fret about the intervention of government in child rearing. A tenet of their philosophy is the right of privacy. Consider the comments of John Maher, the founder of San Francisco's Delancy Street Foundation, a self-help foundation for drug addicts and criminals:

> Children's rights seems like something I would like to be in favor of. On the other hand . . . my fear of intervention in my family by the kind of clowns I find in our juvenile justice

system would increase the possibility of violence in our culture. I would be outraged. On the other hand, the concept of children's rights sounds like something I should support. But I can't get my teeth in it. Does this mean we simply add rights for children to the Constitution, or do we create intervention agencies that we must then deal with?[23]

Unlike the true conservative, the idea of children's rights is not offensive to the libertarian; the problem is rather the government's enforcement of these rights.

As is true for conservatives, most libertarians will grit their teeth and agree that the government has a right to be involved in cases of extreme child abuse—one legitimate role of any government is protecting its citizens from harm. This does not imply that the libertarian will be happy with the government's involvement in personal relations. Even though the family does not have the same sacredness for the libertarian as it does for the conservative, government intervention provokes the same concern.

Child Abuse and Social Research

There is little consensus on the social effects of physical punishment on children. While we can say with considerable conviction that child abuse is morally wrong and ineffective because it produces parents who will abuse their children, it is not entirely clear what constitutes the problem. Despite the fact that spanking is unfashionable among many child educators, it is widely practiced. Many Americans feel they are what they are because of child-rearing practices that included corporal punishment. Punishment can either be a horrible crime or a necessary evil, depending on its motive and its extent.

What can sociologists contribute to the understanding of child abuse? How can they, as social scientists, integrate their personal concerns as citizens with their desire to understand an objective reality? Sociologists are only beginning to explore in their research the extent and degree of punishment of children.

Richard J. Gelles, one of the most influential scholars in this area, was the first to conduct a national survey on parental violence toward children. In early 1976, Gelles interviewed 1,146 parents of children ages three to seventeen as part of a larger study of family violence. All of these parents (about half mothers and half fathers) were living in two-parent households. Parents were asked whether they had ever engaged in physical actions toward one of their children (the child used as the subject of the interview was randomly selected). The participants were given a series of possible actions: slapping or spanking; pushing, grabbing, or shoving; kicking, biting, or hitting with one's fist; "beating up"; threatening with a knife or gun; or using a knife or gun.

Before discussing Gelle's findings, note that he considers *all* of these behaviors as indicators of family violence. Gelles comments:

> For the purposes of this study, violence is nominally defined as "an act carried out with the intention, or perceived intention, of physically injuring another person." The injury can range from slight pain, as in a slap, to murder. . . . We chose a broad definition of violence (which includes spanking as violent behavior) because we want to draw attention to the issue of family members hitting each other; we have defined this behavior as "violent" in order to raise controversy and call the behavior into question. . . . Indeed, one thing that influenced our final choice of a concept was that acts parents carry out on their children in the name of corporal punishment or acceptable force could, if done to strangers or adults, be considered criminal assault.[24]

Gelles' concept of "violence toward children" provides a legitimation of government intervention and creation of a social policy. If the study was on "parental discipline," it would not have all the same implications, despite identical findings. The way in which a sociologist describes his or her study will direct the public's attention. While Gelles is not *wrong* to describe his study as he does, he has made a choice that is based on his own view of the world.

Gelles sees his findings as supporting his assumption that there is a great deal of violence within the American family. For example, 71 percent of the sample of parents admitted to having slapped or spanked their children, with 58 percent saying they had done so within the previous year; 46 percent of the parents had pushed or shoved their child with 32 percent saying they had done so within the previous year. As for using a gun or knife, only one father admitted he had done so recently, and only 2.9 percent said that this had occurred at least once in the child's 'fe.

Does this represent an extraordinary amount of violence or normal home life? It depends. If we choose to consider spanking, slapping, pushing, and shoving as acceptable parental behavior, the figures seem less daunting. Relatively few parents admit to going beyond this. Even with regard to the more troubling use of knives or guns, we don't really know what this statistic means:[25] horrible brutality or protection from a violent teenager, throwing a dinner knife or slashing a child with a switchblade, murdering a child in cold blood or frightening him with an unloaded pistol. Gelles admits that a weakness of the study is a lack of information on the consequences of these behaviors. Yet, public policy will be based on the *imagined* consequences of these actions.

The choice of conducting interviews with a random sample of the adult population also affects the conclusions that Gelles can draw. First, he can claim that the survey is representative of the American people because the results could approximately be duplicated if additional surveys were conducted. Second, Gelles can estimate the actual number of instances based on his sample. He found 2.9 percent of the sample of 1,146 parents used a gun or knife on their children. By extending this percentage to the total number of children in the United States, Gelles can estimate that from 900,000 to 1,800,000 have experienced such brutality.[26] (This technique is called *extrapolating* from data.) Finally, because this is self-reported data (that is, what

parents said they had done), Gelles can argue that the "real" figures of family violence are much higher since some parents
would probably choose to make themselves look good by
claiming to be less violent than they are actually.

This piece of research can be used by partisans in several
ways to emphasize or minimize the significance of the problem.
Gelles wants to emphasize the seriousness of family violence in
our society, and to suggest that action needs to be taken; by implication, he would fall closest to the social democratic point of
view. While it would distort his position to claim that he is a conflict theorist, he does criticize American family behavior and the
social norms, such as traditional sex roles, that stand behind
them.

Spanking and the Socialization Process

The type of discipline parents use is a major factor in how their
children develop. Parents are the primary role models for children. Children are likely to define their morals by what they see
their parents do. If a child is spanked by a loving parent, he or
she could feel that, in some circumstances, inflicting pain is
morally right. If parents insist that children obey them, this may
lead children to have respect for authority. If children receive
love from their parents or guardians they will probably be accepting of others and contented with the justice of the social
order.

Children see their reflection as adults in their parents. The
interactionists tell us parents are the primary "looking-glass
self" in our culture, serving to allow the child to "create" his or
her own identity through that of the parents. It is likely that the
faults children resent in their parents, their children will resent
in them. Those things children most admire about their parents,
their children will admire in them. Children, in other words,
are the products of the parents who socialize them. This is the
reason why family violence is so troubling. One of the strongest

predictors of child abuse is whether the adult was abused as a child. Child abuse is not only a social problem but a self-perpetuating one.

Yet, a completely undisciplined child poses problems as well. Children are, alas, not "naturally" obedient; so parents must, somehow, impress their will on their offspring. Perhaps the discipline used in the home will also reflect itself in the courts of law and in the prisons of society. The question this chapter has raised involves whether the decision of child-rearing disciplines are best left up to parents or are better left up to the community.

Social democrats believe that there is a moral imperative to protect the vulnerable members of society—the children—and the government in some sense serves as an advocate for the child. The libertarian, on the other hand, is more willing to let children fend for themselves in the rough and tumble of family life. The power of the government to decide for the child is as abhorrent as the tyranny of the family. For the conservative, there is no contest; the family is a "natural" institution whose autonomy must be protected. It is the family, rather than the government, that prevents society from breaking down. These views are reflected in the source of socialization of three philosophies; while the conservative looks to the family, the social democrat to the society, the libertarian stresses the autonomy of the children, mothers, and fathers.

Questions

1. Do you believe that under some circumstances parents should spank their children?

2. What lessons do children learn from being spanked?

3. What does the term child abuse mean?

4. What is the appropriate punishment for a parent convicted of child abuse?

5. Should doctors and teachers be forced to report all suspected cases of child abuse?

6. Should welfare agencies interview friends and neighbors of a family suspected of child abuse before it has been proven?

7. Is Sweden's law forbidding all corporal punishment a proper use of government power?

8. Should the government be involved in family discipline?

9. Since people who are abused as children are prone to become child abusers, should they be forbidden to have children?

10. Is it a good idea for every home to be visited by a government child care expert once a year?

11. Is America too permissive or too violent in its child rearing practices?

For Further Study

Cable, Mary. *The Little Darlings: A History of Child Rearing in America*. New York: Scribner's, 1975.

Erlanger, Howard. "Social Class and Corporal Punishment in Childrearing: A Reassessment." *American Sociological Review* 39 (1974):68–85.

Gelles, Richard. *Family Violence*. Beverly Hills: Sage, 1979.

———. "Violence in the Family: A Review of Research in the Seventies." *Journal of Marriage and the Family* 42 (1980):873–885.

Gil, David. *Violence Against Children*. Cambridge: Harvard University Press, 1970.

Kett, Joseph. *Rites of Passage: Adolescence in America 1790 to the Present*. New York: Basic Books, 1977.

Pfohl, Steven J. "The Discovery of Child Abuse." *Social Problems* 24 (1977):310–323.

"Violence Toward Youth in Families" (special issue), *Journal of Social Issues* 35 (1979):1–176.

Straus, Murray A.; Gelles, Richard J.; and Steinmetz, Suzanne K. *Behind Closed Doors: Violence in the American Family*. New York: Doubleday, 1980.

Notes and References

1. Iona Opie and Peter Opie, *The Lore and Language of Schoolchildren* (London: Oxford University Press, 1959), p. 2.
2. Jean Piaget, *The Origins of Intelligence in Children* (New York: International Universities Press, 1952).
3. Charles Horton Cooley, *Human Nature and Social Order* (New York: Schocken, 1964), p. 184.
4. George Herbert Mead, *Mind, Self & Society* (Chicago: University of Chicago Press, 1934), pp. 150–152.
5. *Ibid*, pp. 152–163.
6. Erving Goffman, *Presentation of Self in Everyday Life* (New York: Anchor, 1959), pp. 208–237.
7. See, for example, Claire Safran, "Mother Love, Guiding Words— and an Occasional Spanking," *Redbook*, April, 1981, pp. 27, 29; Howard Erlanger, "Social Class and Corporal Punishment in Childrearing: A Reassessment," *American Sociological Review* 39 (February, 1974):68–85.
8. Ed Magnuson, "Child Abuse: The Ultimate Betrayal," *Time*, September 5, 1983, p. 20.
9. U.S. Department of Health and Human Services, Children's Bureau, *National Study of the Incidence and Severity of Child Abuse and Neglect*, September, 1981, Washington D.C.: D.H.H.S. p. 18.
10. Erlanger, *op cit.*; Richard J. Gelles, "Violence in the Family: A Review of Research in the Seventies," *Journal of Marriage and the Family* 42 (November, 1980):878–9.

11. Herbert Costner, *The Changing Folkways of Parenthood: A Content Analysis* (New York: Arno Press, 1980).

12. Magnuson, *op. cit.*, p. 22.

13. Amelia Adamo, "New Rights for Children and Parents in Sweden," *Children Today*, November–December, 1981, p. 15.

14. Irene Barth, "Bruising a Parent's Image to Protect a Battered Child," *Minneapolis Star and Tribune*, September 13, 1983, p. 13A.

15. John Vinocur, "Swedes Shun Norse Adage, Ban Spanking," *New York Times*, April 4, 1979, p. A7.

16. Jim Klobuchar, "Will Kindergarten Kids Caucus?" *Minneapolis Star*, April 11, 1979, p. 1B.

17. D. Newell, "A Holy Family—Parental Government and Discipline," *Christian Family Magazine*, 1842, pp. 123–24.

18. "Family Discipline, Intimacy, and Children's Rights," *Center Magazine*, November–December, 1981, pp. 36–37.

19. William F. Buckley, "The Child Beaters and Their Critics," *National Review*, April 16, 1982, p. 449.

20. "Family Discipline, Intimacy, and Children's Rights," *op. cit.*, p. 39.

21. Bernice Weissbourd, "A Good Spanking: A Bad Idea," *Parents*, September, 1981, p. 100.

22. Lillian G. Katz, "Spank or Speak?" *Parents*, February, 1980, p. 84.

23. "Family Discipline, Intimacy, and Children's Rights," *op. cit.*, p. 39.

24. Richard Gelles, *Family Violence* (Beverly Hills: Sage, 1979), pp. 78–79.

25. *Ibid*, p. 89.

26. *Ibid*, p. 82.

 **Two**

Race and Ethnicity: Should Minorities Be Given Preferential Treatment in Hiring?

PEOPLE SAY YOU can't judge a book by its cover. This folk belief, of course, extends beyond books to human relationships, and, unfortunately, is as ignored in this case as it is in the case of books. The melancholy fact is that people act toward others on the basis of which racial, religious, national, or ethnic category they belong.

While many people diligently try to rid themselves of all discriminatory tendencies and sincerely believe that prejudice on the basis of another's race, color, and creed is morally objectionable, this attitude is rare in the history of humankind. Few societies have been without ethnic or racial prejudice. To be without any prejudice is to be convinced that your genetic or social group is without special merit ("the chosen people", "the best and brightest", "the center of the universe"). This totally nonegocentric attitude is rare. Indeed, the names of many tribal groups throughout the world label their group as special. For example, Hottentot means "the people." Killing in the name of race and ethnicity is still occurring frequently even today. The moral belief held by many Americans that no group is better than any other must seem unusual and incomprehensible to some.

Despite our belief in racial and ethnic equality, prejudice is still very much with us. Equality is easy to mouth but difficult to maintain. Most Americans recognize that prejudice and discrimination still exist against many racial and ethnic groups. The term *race* in this context refers to genetic differences between individuals and groups and is typically related to skin color but also to other anatomical features, such as shape of facial features and average height. We still know too little about other genetic features that are related to race, particularly cognition and intelligence, to make any definitive statements. For example, although black Americans on average regularly score lower on some standard intelligence (IQ) tests than white Americans, the reasons for this difference are hotly debated—with test biases and environmental factors being put forth as alternatives to a genetic explanation. Until there is definitive proof of genetic racial differences in cognition and behavior, it is best to assume that "racial" differences in test scores are due to environmental differences and, thus, are subject to change.

Ethnicity refers more directly to culture. An ethnic group is a group that shares a culture and perceives themselves as a cultural group. When members of such groups marry within their own group, they may have common genetic traits (such as some hereditary diseases), but typically the genetic component of ethnic groups is less salient than their cultural unity.

Unless you happen to be a white, male, Episcopalian, from Vermont, of English descent (on both sides of the family), you have probably experienced some form of prejudice or discrimination. Even if you are one of the very few who do fit this facetious description, your mother or sister may have been discriminated against. (See discussion on sex roles in chapter three.) Very few people have not experienced some kind of discrimination, but some groups have suffered more than others.

The blacks and American Indians, for instance, have been the victims of slavery and genocidal wars. American Jews have found their synogogues defaced with swastikas; Japanese-Americans were unfairly placed in internment camps during World War II; and Polish-Americans, until recently, have been regularly portrayed as ignorant boobs on television. The large *majority* of Americans are members of racial or ethnic groups that have been the targets of prejudice and discrimination.

Sociologists distinguish between the concepts of prejudice and discrimination. Prejudice refers to a negative attitude toward some group because of their perceived characteristics. Obviously those characteristics that typify a group do not apply to all or even most group members (e.g. blacks being musical, the French being culinary geniuses, or the English keeping a stiff upper lip). Whereas prejudice refers to attitudes, discrimination refers to behavior that is directed against a group or its members, in particular the refusal to provide opportunities or rewards to members of a group even though they are qualified. Although the extent of prejudice and discrimination has declined in the United States over the past few decades, both remain ingrained in certain segments of our society.

Difficulty in ethnic and race relations can occur on several levels. Prejudice and discrimination are individual-level concepts; that is, they are things individuals feel and do because of personality (for example, an authoritarian personality) or experience (such as never having had contact with a member of a minority group member). On another level racial or ethnic groups may be harmed without anyone deliberately or maliciously planning to do so. Sociologists term this *institutional racism,* or *institutional discrimination.* This refers to those established, customary ways of doing things, that keep a minority in a subordinate position. For example, many minorities are channelled into low-status, dead-end jobs because of poor education, in part, which means they are unable to move to better neighborhoods. No one person has forced them to take these jobs; ostensibly it is their own choice, but their social circumstances or environment makes it difficult to improve their lot.

It is relatively easy to see the effects of this treatment on minorities, but it is not necessarily clear what the consequences are for society. Sociologists differ on the effects that intergroup relations have on a society. Some functional theorists argue that racial and ethnic segmentation, unpleasant as we might find it, has a hidden or latent benefit for society as a whole, in that it provides for a division of labor. Someone must do the physically demanding, low-paying dirty jobs; by categorizing some people as second-class citizens, society has a supply of cheap labor. Conflict theory, while not disagreeing that there must be a division of labor, would emphasize that the whole society is not benefiting from this situation but only certain segments, mostly the powerful and wealthy members. Open conflict between groups may be necessary in order to increase the standing of the subjugated groups. While functional theorists imply that large-scale social movements indicate a functional imbalance in society, conflict theorists are more likely to welcome such movements as a sign that a society is still changing and growing. Such movements may represent a healthy redistribution of power and resources, for instance. Although neither approach welcomes racism and prejudice, they approach the problem from different angles.

Question:

Should Minorities Be Given Preferential Treatment in Hiring?

"Affirmative action" has become a prominent part of the political lexicon within the past decade. Americans have recognized that certain groups in this society are underrepresented in certain jobs and overrepresented in others. Blacks and Hispanics represent about one-fifth of the American population, but are 20 percent of the sociology professors black or Hispanic? Are 20 percent of the bankers or astronauts black or Hispanic? Are 20 percent of all cleaning women, farm laborers, and dishwashers black or Hispanic?

The list of statistics demonstrating that blacks and Hispanics are disadvantaged is almost endless. For example, the median black family income was 59 percent of that of whites in 1978, a figure that had changed little from the previous decade. Black levels of unemployment are approximately twice that of whites. A smaller percentage of blacks than whites attend college. Despite these inequalities, most overt discrimination has vanished. Employers no longer tell black applicants that they have been rejected *because* they are black. Nevertheless, it is certainly understandable why many black Americans, after listening to this list of statistics, feel that discrimination is in the minds of many white Americans, if not on their tongues.

Since we can assume that the reason there are fewer white Americans, proportionately, among farm laborers or menial workers is not because they are discriminated against, the real question is what can be done to increase the number of minority professionals and white-collar workers. To see this as a *problem* we must make two important assumptions: The first assumption is that minority members wish to hold these positions. That is, that they are in the relevant labor pool but are not being hired. The second assumption is that they have the qualifications to be hired and that enough minority applicants meet the *minimum* criteria necessary for employment. Although specific job classes may not meet these assumptions, we shall assume that for our discussion, these two assumptions have been met.

In order to correct the absence of minorities in employment, affirmative action programs have been instituted. The term *affirmative action* is tricky to define precisely. Its meaning has changed with time and with circumstances. The first formal government action on the subject of racial discrimination was Executive Order 8801, issued by President Franklin Roosevelt on June 25, 1941. The Order barred discrimination in defense industries and government because of race, creed, color, or national origin, and stated, "it is the duty of employees and labor organizations . . . to provide for the full and equitable participation of all workers in defense industries."[1] It was not until 1961 that the phrase "affirmative action" was used in a government order. President Kennedy, in requiring government contractors to recruit workers on a nondiscriminatory basis, wrote, "The

Contractor will take affirmative action to ensure that applicants are employed, without regard to their race, creed, color, or national origin."[2] No longer was it enough for employers to refrain from discrimination, now they had to actively *recruit* applicants who belonged to minority groups.

During the mid-1960s people went further and assumed that *hiring* be "without regard to race and ethnicity." By the late 1960s and through the 1970s this "race-blind" view took another turn. It was not enough for employers merely to recruit minority workers openly. Increasingly they were expected, or even required, to balance the number of minorities in their work force. By 1971, under the Nixon administration, federal orders called for the establishment of goals and timetables for increasing minority employment. For some, these phrases and the way they are implemented smack of quotas and "reverse discrimination" against "majorities." If the work force is not integrated according to the estimated racial composition of the pool of workers, the employer has the burden of proof to demonstrate that there is no discrimination.

The 1978 Supreme Court ruling on Allan Bakke's case (*Regents of the University of California v. Allan Bakke*) was a blow to affirmative action. The court found that the University of California, Davis Medical School, could not exclude nonminorities by reserving a precise number of places for minority applicants. Most Supreme Court decisions since then have supported programs that have targets and goals. This difference is, according to critics, one of semantics rather than substance. In a world with limited resources the fact that one person, or group, gets something means that other people, or groups, do not. The question then is should people who belong to a minority be given preference in hiring if they are equally or slightly less qualified—provided that they meet the minimum requirements necessary for doing the job. Should "preferential treatment" be a matter of government policy?

Throughout the last few pages I have been using the terms "majority" and "minority" quite deliberately, but it is not clear just who comprise these groups and who should be the beneficiary of preferential hiring programs. To the extent that women are a discriminated group, they can be considered a "minority" even though they are a numerical *majority* of the population. They are, in other words, a majority with the power of a minority. Also, other groups that are covered by affirmative action plans have changed somewhat over the years and for particular purposes. The 1977 Public Works Employment Act requires that 10 percent of all federal public works contracts be reserved for "minority-owned" construction firms. Minority in 1977, however, was defined as black, Spanish-speaking, American Indian, Eskimo, Aleut,[3] and Oriental. One might ask why a language group was included since speaking Spanish implies neither race or ethnicity. Furthermore, the inclusion of Orientals might strike one as unusual if the concern is to help the disadvantaged. Although Chinese-Americans and Japanese-Americans have both suffered discrimination, as have Jews and Finns, they have higher incomes than many ethnic groups not included, such as German, Irish, Italian, or Polish-Americans.[4] Clearly such a criterion is based primarily on skin-color and not entirely on being disadvantaged. Thus, it is not surprising that Jews, Italian-Americans, Polish-Americans, and other "non-minority" groups with histories of discrimination and current economic problems, should feel resentment toward a system that rewards others and ignores their troubles. The decision of which groups deserve special treatment is a complicated one grounded in politics as well as in economic circumstance.

The Social Democratic Point of View

Preferential hiring, even that which is government-mandated, poses little problem for the social democrat. Individuals have always been treated as members of groups, often to their detriment, now it is time to change that for the better. Government at its most moral should intervene to insure no group is being systematically denied justice and equal treatment. Even if it means a few people who belong to the majority group are denied jobs, society must help disadvantaged people to compete *fairly*.

51

Equal opportunity, alone, ignores the heavy weight of history and oppression. Lyndon Johnson expressed the same sentiment in his famous address at Howard University:

> Freedom is not enough. You do not wipe out scars of centuries by saying "now you're free to go where you want and do as you desire." You do not take a person who for years has been hobbled by chains and liberate him, bringing him up to the starting line of a race and then say "you're free to compete" and justly believe that you have been completely fair. All of our citizens must have the ability to walk through those gates; and this is the next and most profound stage of the battle for civil rights.[5]

The social democrat recognizes the effects that historical injustice has on groups. Regardless of whether this injustice is equally applicable to everyone within a group (for example, injustice may be less for the son of a black doctor than for the son of a recent Haitian immigrant), it is group justice that is central. This justice will have benefits for the society as a whole in that it produces a "truly open" society in which all groups can participate equally. The *Philadelphia Evening Bulletin* ran an editorial on the social value of preferential admission to medical schools in light of the Bakke case:

> Some people argue that to provide special consideration for black students is to discriminate against whites. The sad fact is that if the effects of years of discrimination against minorities are to be undone, for awhile some individuals in the majority are going to suffer deprivation. That isn't pretty, but it is a fact. . . . Until effective equal opportunity programs have made it possible for minorities to catch up with the rest of society—and that will take decades—minority people must receive some special consideration. That way the ideal of a truly open society will be brought closer to reality.[6]

Some people argue that without meaningful affirmative action programs, we are courting disaster. It is in the interest of society to protect itself by insuring justice for everyone. George McAlmon, Director of the Fund for the Republic, observed that millions of Americans, the chronically unemployed and the propertyless, could actually do better under communism. Why, then, should they be committed to free enterprise and private ownership? What morality prevents these citizens from engaging in violent and destructive behavior?[7]

Supporters of preferential hiring point out that hiring criteria may systematically discriminate against minorities because it uses a measuring stick that is particularly favorable to the majority. Scores on standardized tests, past work histories, attendance at prestigious schools are only some of the criteria that are used to predict success. Moreover, supporters of preferential hiring note that not all hiring and admission is based on criteria that predict success. For example, some schools give preference to in-state residents and athletes. Some unions make it impossible for anyone but relatives of members to join. Some organizations give special weight to veterans. Some employees prefer individuals who are married or who dress in a particular style. Thus, consideration on the basis of race is not unique, but is only one more means by which people are hired. The existence of seniority is another indication that "ability" is not the only criterion for employment. In many companies when employees have to be laid off, it is those who were last hired who will be first fired. This flies in the face of the belief in merit as the sole means of judging people. Why not lay off those workers who are least qualified? Such a process, however, would prove offensive to many unions; the seniority system assumes that there is a level of competency above which ability does not really matter. Once people have met the level of acceptability, termination should be on the basis of years with the company. Without seniority, companies might choose to hire only young, and cheap, workers, and replace them when they become older and more expensive.

Social democrats see the controversy over preferential hiring as an issue that involves the rights of groups, rather than that of individuals. The question for them is how can we insure equitable representation for disadvantaged groups, rather than how can individuals be treated fairly. Frequently the major concern is insuring "equal representation." Although some writers[8] have claimed that this need not derogate individual rights since there are other factors that go into job hiring, others have vigorously criticized this position,[9] suggesting that invidious discrimination is inevitably involved. Surely in some cases whites are being denied rewards that would otherwise be theirs if there were no program of preferential hiring. The social democrat's concern, then, is with equalizing the positions of groups, rather than insuring that people are treated equitably as individuals. Supreme Court Justice Thurgood Marshall stated this crisply in his dissent in the Bakke case: "In order to treat some persons equally, we must treat them differently."[10]

The Libertarian Point of View

The 1980 platform of the Libertarian party clearly and emphatically states the party's position on preferential hiring:

> Discrimination imposed by the government has brought disruption in normal relations of peoples, set neighbor against neighbor, created gross injustices, and diminished human potential. Anti-discrimination enforced by the government is the reverse side of the coin and will for the same reasons create the same problems. Consequently, we oppose any governmental attempts to regulate private discrimination, including discrimination in employment, housing, and privately owned so-called public accommodations. The right to trade includes the right not to trade—for any reasons whatsoever.[11]

For the libertarian the rights of the individual must remain paramount. This includes property rights and the right to trade. Thus, libertarians assent to what may seem to be a paradoxical position: individuals have the right to ignore the "equal rights" of others. This position, however, is only paradoxical until one considers the libertarian concept of freedom. People have freedom to do what they wish providing it does not coerce others; they do not have the freedom to make others act toward them in any particular way.[12] This is based on the view that each individual has the freedom to acquire as much power and wealth as he wishes—a philosophy perhaps more applicable in the ideal world in which all are created equal, than in the real world in which some are born with social handicaps.

The libertarian is particularly incensed by the government's attempt to intervene in human relations. Most libertarians do not personally support discrimination; yet, they don't see discrimination by its nature as being coercive. In this sense, the libertarian believes voluntary preferential treatment plans are acceptable, although perhaps not desirable. If white employers choose to hire all whites (or, for that matter, all blacks), this would not require any kind of government intervention because the employers are engaging in their own rights to use their resources as they see fit. To the extent that affirmative action is a voluntary decision by the employer, and not coerced by the government, the libertarian would not stop it.

A recent, controversial court case, *Kaiser Aluminum & Chemical Corporation v. Brian F. Weber et al.*, illustrates the conflict for libertarians posed by private decisions versus government interference. In 1974 Kaiser Aluminum & Chemical Corporation and the United Steelworkers of America agreed together to set up skilled-craft training programs at fifteen Kaiser plants around the country. Half of the positions in the programs were set aside for minorities and women. The whites who could enter the program were determined by seniority (who had worked at the plant longest), and the minorities and women were selected by a separate seniority list. Such a program was easily justified because of the very low representation of women and minorities in these mostly all-white male jobs. When Brian Weber, a white male laboratory analyst, applied for this training program, he was rejected because he did not have enough seniority. He then learned that several of the minority applicants on the other seniority list had less seniority than he had. He subsequently charged racial discrimination under the 1964 Civil Rights Act.

When the case finally wound its way to the Supreme Court, the court decided by a vote of 5-2 that the Kaiser plan was legal under the 1964 Civil Rights Act, even though the act appeared to outlaw discrimination on the basis of race or ethnicity. Weber contended that if he were black he would have been trained, a point which was not contested. The Supreme Court majority brushed aside the surface reading of the law and pointed to its intent—to reduce discrimination in employment. Pertinent to the libertarians' theory was that ostensibly this was a private decision that was not directly dictated by the government. The Kaiser company could, if they wished, train and hire whatever percentage of minorities they chose provided they did not discriminate against minorities, which all agreed was illegal under the Civil Rights Act. Although some noted that government intervention was not totally absent, in that Executive Order 8801 did call for federal contractors to take "affirmative action" to insure that minorities were represented in the workforce by telling companies they could lose their federal contracts, the coercion was indirect. Still, it is somewhat ironic that the supporters of civil rights were now taking a similar position to those, such as Senator Barry Goldwater who, speaking against the Civil Rights Act, said employers should have the *freedom* to take race or ethnicity into account in hiring.[13] A business should choose the best person for the job *regardless of race*, or it will suffer by having a less qualified workforce than its competitors.

There is a second part of the libertarian attitude toward preferential hiring that finds such practices abhorrent. The libertarian philosophy is based on the moral stature of the individual. Libertarians believe every person should succeed or fail by virtue of his or her own abilities. Preferential hiring goes against this by promoting some citizens simply because they are of a different race or ethnic group over others who are "objectively" more qualified. While libertarians would acknowledge that other nonability based criteria are used in judging hiring, these are equally as questionable as race or ethnicity as a means for making a hiring decision. Libertarians argue with Supreme Court Justice John M. Harlan who says "the Constitution is color-blind and neither knows nor tolerates classes among citizens."[14] Furthermore, preferential treatment is akin to punishing the children for the sins of the fathers. Brian Weber did not discriminate against minorities; American society did. Yet, it is Brian Weber who is forced to carry the burden. People are made to suffer for acts that have been carried out by other people. Many libertarians see this as unfair, even if they might be satisfied with the end result. In this case the ends truly do not justify the means.

The Conservative Point of View

It is ironic that some who at one time felt blacks were inferior and not deserving of any but the most menial jobs are now in the forefront of those who call for scrupulously equal treatment. Perhaps, though, they should be given the benefit of the doubt just as we give the benefit of the doubt to the social democrats who once spoke out in favor of the Civil Rights Act saying it would not mean special treatment for minorities.

Consider as an example of conservative thought, the blunt comments of the late William Loeb, the ultraconservative editor of the *Manchester (N.H.) Union Leader,* writing about preferential admission to graduate school:

> It makes no sense to try to make up for the wrong of discrimination against blacks in the past by now discriminating against whites. What we are trying to do in this country—at least what this newspaper thought we were trying to do in this country—is to find the ablest people in our society and give them the best possible education so that they can then best serve the nation. . . . If we are going to lower the standards and say to incompetent black students, "You may not have any brains, but we will let you in college anyway because years ago we discriminated against blacks," at the same time we would be saying to many white students, "You are more qualified, by the proven level of your intelligence and your entrance examinations, to become a lawyer or doctor or architect, etc., but we're sorry, old boy or old

girl, you will have to step aside and let this less qualified black take your place because we are discriminating now in favor of blacks."[15]

Although libertarians and conservatives share a distaste for programs of preferential hiring for minorities, they dislike them for somewhat different reasons. The libertarian focuses on the unfairness to the individual, while the conservative suggests that the new system is unfair to the majority group. Of course, many who argue against preferential hiring use both arguments and may not even distinguish between the two, but the bases of the two arguments are different. The conservative dislikes the radical change the concept of preferential hiring will bring in the relationship between employers and workers and the government-sponsored changes that will affect race and ethnic relations. The conservative believes citizens increasingly share the belief that race should not be a factor in hiring, and, so, they do not like the government attempting to alter public values, instituting in their place sanctioned discrimination against unprotected groups (whites). Black economist Thomas Sowell, a vocal conservative critic of preferential hiring, notes that by including women under the banner of affirmative action, "discrimination is legally authorized against one third of the U.S. population (Jewish, Italian, Irish [males])—and for government contractors and subcontractors, it is not merely authorized but required."[16] Leonard Walentynowicz, executive director of the Polish-American Congress emphasizes this point: "If America's job opportunities and money are to be parceled out to groups, we are a definable group, and we want our share."[17] If preferential treatment is extended to every group that is underrepresented in the upper-level of the workforce, what will this do to those groups that are overrepresented. Jewish leaders, for example, worry that a strong and large-scale program of preferential hiring would actually be anti-Semitism in disguise.

Conservatives also point out that despite the continuing steps that have been made toward affirmative action and preferential hiring, many political leaders and most Americans—white and black—oppose it. The policy changes during the growth of affirmative action demonstrate the clout of an unelected bureaucracy, which runs the day-to-day operation of government, not the clout of a majority of citizens. Thomas Sowell offers some concrete support for this argument:

> The insulation of administrative processes from political control is illustrated by the fact that (1) administrative agencies went beyond what was authorized by the two Democrats (Kennedy and Johnson) in the White House who first authorized "affirmative action" in a sense limited to decisions *without regard* to group identity, and (2) continue to do so despite the two Republican Presidents (Nixon and Ford) who followed, who were positively opposed to the trends in agencies formally under their control as parts of the Executive branch of government.[18]

Surveys, too, indicate that the American public is overwhelmingly (83 percent) opposed to preferential treatment in hiring,[19] and blacks reject preferential treatment 64 percent to 27 percent.[20] Thus, the conservative claims, government policy flies in the face of public opinion and social tradition. Regardless of whether white Americans discriminate against black Americans, people should hire the best person for the job. It is this belief that is being undercut by a government that conservatives are afraid will only succeed in promoting racial tension. The leading conservative journal, *The National Review*, suggests, perhaps sarcastically, that it would be simpler if Congress passed a "Black Reparations Act"—a point of view with which some social democrats might sincerely agree, in spirit, if not in name.

Black Unemployment and Social Research

In the 1980s, on most indicators of race relations, blacks have improved their standing relative to whites. Youth employment for blacks, however, seems to show an opposite trend. In 1954 the difference between black and white unemployment rates for young people between the ages of 16 and 24 was 5.9 percent (with young blacks being less employed). By 1980 this difference had swelled to 14.4 percent. On the surface this suggests that racial prejudice in employment has not only not lessened, it has substantially increased.

This view, however, is perceptively challenged by two statistically sophisticated sociologists, Robert Mare and Christopher Winship.[21] They argue that these statistics are not as depressing as they appear at first because the magnitude of the black-white unemployment differences in the 1950s is actually masked by other aspects of race relations.

To study unemployment rates, one must go to statistics that have been collected by the United States Bureau of the Census in its *Current Population Surveys*. This type of research is known as secondary data analysis. That is, researchers analyze data that was first collected by someone else for another purpose. Such a methodology, of course, is much less costly than doing original research. Large amounts of data that were originally collected for one purpose may be used in numerous other studies. (Only the federal government has the resources to engage in this kind of data collection—a point with which the libertarian would groan in agreement.) The weakness of this approach is that the data have been collected by someone else; thus, the original research may have omitted certain questions that might be crucial. Particularly when using government data there may be a conservative bent to the research in that the questions asked are those that the government in power wishes to know and that the powerful consider to be important. Also, the nature of the massive data collection typically provides little of the detailed information about people that interactionists would insist on to understand how people make their decisions.

Mare and Winship suspect certain changes in the choices made by black youth explain their lower rates of employment. Specifically, Mare and Winship note that black youths are now attending school longer than they had previously and that they are entering the military at rates that are higher than that of whites. Furthermore, once they leave these institutions, they have some difficulty finding a job—not because they are black (or not completely so) but because they have had limited work experience. Finally, the most qualified black Americans attend college and enter the military. As a result, the highly employable black Americans remain out of the job market for many years—a process that Mare and Winship call *creaming*. In the 1950s, blacks would enter the job market immediately after leaving school, and so had a "jump" on whites who completed their schooling. If schooling and military service had been controlled for in the 1950s statistics, the employment difference between blacks and whites would have been much larger.

Such results prove comforting to the conservative, although the authors would disagree that they are sympathetic to conservative views. These data, however, echo the conservative belief that if black Americans become educated, their employment opportunities will open up. Says the conservative, once blacks leave school and the military (and, thus, get beyond their youth), their employment patterns will be much like whites. This is perhaps too rosy a scenario for the immediate future, but Mare and Winship's article does remind us that we must be very careful in analyzing social statistics—what they suggest on the surface may be different than what a careful sociological analysis will demonstrate. This study does not address the type of jobs blacks and whites are able to obtain, nor does it demonstrate that there is no discrimination against middle-aged blacks. Still, we can take some measure of comfort in Mare and Winship's conclusion.

> The growing race difference in employment is, in part, a consequence of otherwise salutary changes in the lives of young blacks, especially increased school enrollment and educational attainment . . . . Our results suggest . . . that worsening labor force statistics for black youths do not denote increasing racial inequality, but rather persistent racial inequalities previously hidden by race differences in other aspects of young adulthood.[22]

Because the authors believe there are still underlying racial differences, they would probably oppose eliminating affirmative

61

action programs. Their analysis, however, might be used by conservatives to suggest that Black-Americans can make it on their own.

Race Relations and Preferential Hiring

The question of preferential hiring—affirmative action (as supporters call it) or reverse discrimination (as opponents call it)—will not disappear until all groups in our society are integrated into the work force in proportions equivalent to their number in the population. As much as any issue discussed in this book, this is a highly personal one because it will affect your success in this world. It is easy for those who already have it made to support affirmative action: it won't hurt them. It is equally easy for those who are racially prejudiced to use opposition to reverse discrimination as a guise for their own bigotry. But it is you who will be applying for jobs and for graduate school, and who will be helped or hindered by these rules.

Despite the fact that some individuals will be affected, we should remember that we are dealing with relatively small numbers; most affirmative action goals will not dramatically limit the opportunity for young white males to advance, nor will they permit minorities to enter into the economic mainstream overnight. They represent a commitment by our society to do better than we have in the past in insuring equitable participation by all. Whether this is the proper means by which we should reach this goal depends on which social policy point of view you find most appealing.

The three views provide different answers to the legitimacy of preferential hiring based on race. The libertarian, who believes in freedom and individual action, suggests that individuals have the right to hire whomever they choose, including hiring only blacks. Yet, the idea of hiring on the basis of race suggests that the supporter of affirmative action wishes that all groups are equally successful, or have equality of outcome. Most libertarians reject this notion as inequitable and which ultimately will weaken an individual's motivation to succeed. Why work hard as an individual, if your group membership will gain those rewards for you?

The social democrat supports preferential hiring, in part from a desire to narrow the group differences between blacks and whites. The social democrat argues that the differences between blacks and whites are not due to innate differences in ability but because the group of which they are a member faces discrimination that is difficult to overcome without extra assistance. Fairness demands that people should not be denied the fruits of society simply because they were born into a certain group.

Although conservatives find discrimination against minorities to be pernicious and immoral, they do not object to the existence of classes in society. Conservatives believe in class mobility, but they do not equate wealth with happiness and goodness, as the other philosophies seem to. Conservatives suggest that there is no reason why a working class family cannot be as happy as a rich one—a comforting belief if you happen to be rich. If we can evolve into a society that judges only ability, everyone will have an opportunity to succeed. A well-adjusted society for the conservative is a stable and orderly one. Seen in this light, conservative social theory has a close resemblance to functional theory in its emphasis on social equilibrium.

Consider one final, difficult question. Why should we not discriminate? What is wrong with wanting to be with people like ourselves and giving them those rewards that we can offer? Today most people reject discrimination, without considering why they should. Why is racial discrimination wrong? Have we created a society in which we have no loyalty to our own group?

The answer ultimately comes down to a question of how we choose to define "our group." As interactionist theory tells us, meaning is not inevitable. Skin color is one very salient way in which people differ, but then so is height, hair color, and regional accent. A person is not "black" or "white", "redheaded" or "blond", but a particular shade. Also we must select which categories are most important to us. Are we "brunettes" or "whites?" If a person is a Russian emigrant, is he or she a Soviet emigre, or a person who escaped Czarist pogroms at the turn of the century? Are Chinese-Americans and Japanese-Americans both orientals or are they two different cultural groups? What about Vietnamese and Cambodian immigrants? Are Floridians and Georgians both southerners, or should they be distinguished?

It is not my intention to end this chapter with a syrupy plea for tolerance; I only suggest that the group you identify with is not carved in stone but is a social decision. Whatever group you see yourself as belonging to, there are some who resent and dislike that group, while others may choose to place you into other groups that may categorize you to your disadvantage. While group loyalty and solidarity has positive aspects, it carries with it the sense that outsiders do not deserve equal treatment.

Questions

1. What does affirmative action mean?

2. Is reverse discrimination ever justified?

3. If there were no discrimination today, should preferential hiring be used to eliminate the remnants of discrimination in the past?

4. Under what circumstances should individuals be treated as members of racial groups?

5. What groups in our society should receive preferential treatment in hiring?

6. Why are most Americans (black as well as white) opposed to preferential hiring?

7. Are numerical racial quotas for hiring ever justified?

8. Should government be involved in insuring affirmative action, or should it be handled voluntarily?

9. Should government contracts be given to companies that do not have many minority workers, even if it can not be demonstrated that they have intended to discriminate?

10. Is racial or ethnic prejudice and discrimination ever justified?

For Further Study

Benokraitis, Nijole V. and Feagin, Joe R. *Affirmative Action and Equal Opportunity: Action, Inaction, Reaction*. Boulder: Westview Press, 1978.

Blackston, William T. and Heslep, Robert D. eds. *Social Justice & Preferential Treatment: Women and Racial Minorities in Education and Business*. Athens, Georgia: University of Georgia Press, 1977.

Cohen, Carl. "Justice Debased: The Weber Decision," *Commentary* 68 (September 1979): 43-53.

Dworkin, Ronald. *Taking Rights Seriously*. Cambridge: Harvard University Press, 1977.

Fullinwider, Robert K. *The Reverse Discrimination Controversy: A Moral and Legal Analysis*. Totowa, New Jersey: Rowman and Littlefield, 1980.

Glazer, Nathan. *Affirmative Discrimination: Ethnic Inequality and Public Policy*. New York: Basic Books, 1975.

Gross, Barry R. *Discrimination in Reverse: Is Turnabout Fair Play?* New York: New York University Press, 1978.

Patterson, Orlando H. "The Socio-Political Question." *Howard Law Journal* 21 (1978): 519-527.

Sowell, Thomas. *Knowledge and Decisions*. New York: Basic Books, 1980.

Notes and References

1. Nijole V. Benokraitis and Joe R. Feagin, *Affirmative Action and Equal Opportunity: Action, Inaction, Reaction* (Boulder: Westview Press, 1978), p. 7, quoting *Federal Register 6*, no. 3109, 1941.

2. *Ibid*, p. 10, quoting *Federal Register 26*, no. 1977, 3 C.F.R., 1959-63, comp. 448, pt. 3, 301(1).

3. The Aleuts are a small group (population of under 2,000) who inhabit the Aleutian Islands, which stretch out to the southwest of Alaska. They have a distinctive language, culture, and racial composition.

4. Thomas Sowell, "A Dissenting Opinion About Affirmative Action," *Across the Board*, January 1981, p. 66.

5. D. Stanley Eitzen, *In Conflict and Order: Understanding Society*, second edition (Boston: Allyn and Bacon, 1982), p. 332.

6. Editorial, *Philadelphia Evening Bulletin*, September 25, 1977.

7. George A. McAlmon, "A Critical Look at Affirmative Action," *The Center Magazine*, March 1978, pp. 45-56.

8. Ronald Dworkin, *Taking Rights Seriously* (Cambridge: Harvard University Press, 1977).

9. Ronald Simon, "Individual Rights and Benign Discrimination," *Ethics* 90 (October 1979): 88-97.

10. "How the Justices Disagreed," *Time*, July 10, 1978, p. 10.

11. 1980 Platform of the Libertarian party.

12. Scott Bixler, "The Right to Discriminate," *Freeman*, 1980, pp. 358-376.

13. William F. Buckley, "Double Thought," *National Review*, August 3, 1979, p. 990.

14. In Harlan's famous dissenting opinion to the case of *Plessy v. Ferguson* in which the court majority legalized "separate but equal" treatment for blacks.

15. William Loeb, editorial, *Manchester (N. H.) Union Leader*, November 22, 1977.

16. Sowell, *op. cit.*, p. 66.

17. "What the Weber Ruling Does," *Time*, July 9, 1979, p. 49.

18. Sowell, *op. cit.* p. 67.

19. Charles Lawrence, "The Bakke Case: Are Racial Quotas Defensible," *Saturday Review*, October 15, 1977, p. 15.

20. Sowell, *op. cit.*, p. 67.

21. Robert D. Mare and Christopher Winship, "The Paradox of Lessening Racial Inequality and Joblessness Among Black Youth: Enrollment, Enlistment, and Employment, 1964-1981," *American Sociological Review* 49 (February 1984): 39-55.

22. *Ibid*, p. 54.

 **Three**

Sex Roles and Sexual Stratification: Should the Equal Rights Amendment Be Adopted?

SIGMUND FREUD ONCE asked, somewhat plaintively perhaps, "What does a woman want?"[1] Although probably not meant in the same way, this question continues to haunt many, if not most, men. The problem seems to be that women are both very different from and similar to men. It is this similarity but difference that makes figuring out what is fair and just so challenging. Even today it takes some effort not to treat women as subtly inferior to men, as in the preceding sentence in which women were being compared *to* men—as if masculinity represented some kind of standard by which all humankind is to be judged. What the role of women should be is hotly disputed, even within the women's movement. Some people argue that women should have the characteristics of men, others that women should remain distinctively feminine, and still others propose androgeny for both sexes, that is, having some characteristics of men and women.[2]

In American society, as in many others, there are distinctively different expectations of women and men. Indeed, how could it be otherwise? Expectations must capitulate to biology. Anatomy is destiny—so said Freud. Only women can become mothers, although both sexes can "mother." Recognizing the limits of our physique and our hormonal equipment, the potential range of human action is quite broad. Both sexes can carry out most of the activities necessary to make a living, yet, in most societies, there is a sexual division of labor with some tasks defined as "female" and others as "male." Some of these tasks are predominantly male in one culture are predominantly female in another.[3] But a division of labor based on physical prowess seems no longer necessary, particularly in Western societies where work is becoming increasingly technological and where women have some freedom from pregnancy through birth control measures.

The weight of scholarly evidence is that most sex-linked behavior typical of men and women is socially, rather than biologically, determined. Although this conclusion may change as we learn more about the subtle effect of genes and hormones, most sociologists feel that the traditional learned patterns of behavior or *sex roles* for men and women are not inevitable.

Numerous institutions direct individuals into what are considered proper sex roles. Women and men are separately socialized through families, the mass media, peers, schools, religion, and even the English language. "Man" still indicates all of humankind, and so girls learn, at least implicitly, that they are a sub-class of "man." While sex role linguists debate furiously whether we need a whole new vocabulary, including neutered pronouns, it is difficult to dispute their basic point that our language communicates important features of society's world view. Most people still feel more comfortable in a world in which men and women are brought up and act differently. A world of people, rather than one of men and women, would be quite a shocking change to anyone who has grown up in this one.

Perhaps as you have strolled through campus you have seen

people wearing buttons that read simply and dramatically, "59¢." When I first read the message, I thought it was the button's price; it is not. The figure is the amount that a white full-time working woman makes for each dollar made by a white full-time working male. This figure, alone, points to a serious inequity between men and women. The figure does not mean, of course, that if a woman and man are employed on the same job, that the woman will only make 59 percent of what the man makes, but rather that women tend to be in lower-paid jobs and have less seniority. Although there are still vestiges of dual pay scales, when people speak of "equal pay for equal work," they are typically referring to *equivalent classes* of work.

Despite women's lower wages, one cannot deny that during the 1970s and 1980s women have made large strides in entering the social, political, and economic mainstream of the United States. There is a greater tolerance for seeing women in a wide variety of jobs; indeed, by 1978 over 80 percent of all Americans claimed to be willing to vote for a woman candidate for President.[4] By 1980 over 60 percent favored efforts to strengthen and change women's status.[5] Clearly a sea change has taken place in American society in terms of women's occupational and political rights, even though it may take sometime to gauge its full effect.

The social side of the "women's revolution" is more difficult to evaluate. As divorce rates rose throughout the 1970s, many Americans began to worry that the family was falling apart and that this was due to the women's movement. People noticed other social trends that emerged at about the same time as the growth of women's rights, such as open homosexuality, increased premarital cohabitation, the decline of religion, and rising abortion rates. Although the causes of these trends are difficult to determine, they were facilitated, whether for good or ill, by the same changes in values that encouraged the women's movement.

Are traditional sex roles functional for society? Sociologists differ on this point. Functionalists argue that the division of labor between the sexes makes sense (or did once) because men are physically stronger and thus better suited to be providers. Women, on the other hand, bear children and are thus better suited to child rearing and family nurturance. The man has the instrumental role in the family and focuses on dealing with the world outside the family and with obtaining resources. The woman carries out an expressive role and focuses on relationships within the family and keeping it functioning smoothly by giving out support and love.[6]

Conflict theorists see the same facts in a different light. Rather than functional for all of society, sex roles are beneficial to some (men), while exploitative of others (women). Men, because of their strength, are able to dominate women and make them work at low-paying demeaning jobs. Women are, in this view, similar to every other oppressed minority group and must revolt to become free.

Question:

Should the Equal Rights Amendment be Adopted?

> Section 1. Equality of rights under the law shall not be denied or abridged by the United States or by any State on account of sex.
>
> Section 2. The Congress shall have the power to enforce, by appropriate legislation, the provisions of this article.
>
> Section 3. This amendment shall take effect two years after the date of ratification.

The Equal Rights Amendment seems on first reading to be simply ensuring justice for all people regardless of their sex. The Amendment's supporters say the surest way to gather support is to have people read it. Opponents add that the way to get people to oppose it is to think about all of its possible effects. The debate on this issue has been marked by torrents of nonsense—on both sides. Those who are pro-ERA suggest opponents are all right-wing bigots or big businesses that are conspiring to keep wages low. They forget that the League of Women Voters opposed it before it passed Congress, and many law professors still oppose it. The opponents of the Amendment claim it is a communist plot. They forget that the Communist

Party of America was opposed to the Amendment's ratification until quite recently.[7] Both sides stereotype their opponents as demons and carry on their debates with a crimson rage and a purple passion.

Despite the claims and counter-claims, no one knows precisely what the effects of the Amendment would be on American life. Amendments to the Constitution are ultimately interpreted by the Supreme Court. Those nine men and women decide what the Constitution means—and these interpretations may change over time. In theory, the court should consider the "legislative intent" of the Congress and the state legislatures. In practice, legislative intent is only one factor that goes into making a judicial decision. The Fourteenth Amendment is a good example. It was passed after the Civil War with the original intent to prevent southern states from enacting laws against freed blacks that would virtually force them into slavery. But the Court has expanded the Amendment, granting poor people the right to be represented by a lawyer, preventing gerrymandering and poll taxes, and extending the Bill of Rights to state legislation. Using this as an argument, an ERA proponent writes, "In short—and this was certainly not foreseen at the time of its passage—the Fourteenth Amendment has become synonomous with protection from government tyranny and discrimination for both blacks and whites."[8] Opponents ask, will the ERA require co-ed bathrooms (presumably with private stalls), the way the Fourteenth Amendment outlawed separate restrooms for blacks and whites, or will it consider the "right to privacy?" No one can be sure until the Amendment passes.

Space does not allow for the discussion of every argument that has been made in support or opposition to the Amendment. Instead, I will examine how peoples' attitudes toward social order affects the way they perceive the Amendment. Before discussing this relationship, however, some history is necessary.

After the passage of the Woman's Suffrage Amendment in 1920, attention turned to assuring broader legal and economic rights for women. On December 10, 1923, the first Equal Rights Amendment was introduced into the Senate by Charles Curtis, a Republican senator from Kansas. Three days later the Amendment was introduced into the House of Representatives by Daniel Anthony, Jr., another Kansas Republican and nephew of the early feminist leader Susan B. Anthony. The early Amendment, called the Lucretia Mott Amendment, in honor of the nineteeth century feminist, stated: "Men and Women shall have Equal Rights throughout the United States and every place subject to its jurisdiction. Congress shall have power to enforce this article by appropriate legislation." (Note that this is broader than the current version which only addresses "rights under the law." At the time the ERA was proposed, the constitutions of many European nations, among them Germany, Austria, and Estonia, had already insured equal rights for women.

Ironically, until only recently the ERA was more forcefully supported by Republicans than by Democrats. The Republicans included support for the Equal Rights Amendment in their 1940 party platform, where it remained until 1980. The Democrats waited until 1944 to endorse it. At first the ERA was supported mainly by business and professional women and was opposed primarily by labor unions, which felt that the ERA would lead to the elimination of protective labor legislation for women (perhaps one reason that it was supported by conservative Republicans). By the late 1960s, after most protective labor legislation had been eliminated, the terms of the debate changed to issues of equal pay and moral equality, and, to some extent, this changed who supported the Amendment.

The ERA, in a weakened form, was passed by the Senate in 1950 and 1953, but it never got through the House of Representatives. In 1970, the ERA was finally brought to a vote on the floor of the House of Representatives, where it was overwhelmingly adopted. The Senate, however, adopted, on a close vote, a provision specifically exempting women from the draft. This move created a stalemate and the Amendment was again put aside. In the 92nd Congress, after some parliamentary wrangling, the Amendment was passed overwhelmingly in both houses and with the support of President Richard Nixon. On March 22, 1972, the ERA was, after nearly fifty years, sent to the states for ratification.

At first it appeared that the ERA would have easy sailing.

The Hawaiian legislature passed the Amendment unanimously on March 22nd. The next day the Delaware and Nebraska legislatures also passed the Amendment unanimously. Within a year thirty of the thirty-eight states required for passage had given their assent. But by February 1975 only four additional states had ratified the Amendment. Indiana ratified the Amendment on a close vote in 1977 bringing the number of states that had ratified the ERA to thirty-five, its final total. By then the anti-ERA activists had become an effective movement. Four states voted to rescind their ratification, and even with a three-year extension (to ten years), the Amendment failed to receive enough support. Now, more than sixty years after its original introduction, the Equal Rights Amendment remains only a hope for its supporters.

The defeat of the Equal Rights Amendment was particularly galling to its supporters because surveys[9] indicated that the public was in favor of it by about a two-to-one margin, with all regional, racial, educational, occupational, religious, and age groups supporting it. Men typically supported the ERA by a slightly wider margin than did women, in spite of it often being labeled as a "woman's issue." Sociologists Andrew Cherlin and Pamela Walters have indicated there are now relatively few differences between males and females in their attitudes toward sex-role equality.[10] Joan Huber and her colleagues have shown that one's perceived consequences of the ERA has more impact on opinion than does one's social position.[11] Others have found that the female opponents of the ERA resemble male religious conservatives; their attitudes are not different because they are women.[12] Despite the popular view that this amendment is a woman's issue, attitudes about the amendment are shared by both sexes.

The Social Democratic Point of View

The social democrat's position on the Equal Rights Amendment is stated elegantly by Riane Eisler in her book, *The Equal Rights Handbook*.

We are today at a branching point. To return to the analogy of history as a train moving forward in time, on one side of that branching is the old track, the patriarchal track that has for so long limited and constrained us all—both women and men. This is the track we choose if ERA and all it represents should fail. At the end of this track, with its premise that we are evil and that we must be controlled, lies the society predicted by futurologists unless we change our course: the authoritarian nightmares foreseen by Orwell in *1984* and by Huxley in *Brave New World*. The other track leads to the humanistic vision in which Eve is no longer the cause of the Fall, a society in which women and men are no longer embattled in dominant-dominated roles. This is the track we choose if ERA passes and is properly implemented. At the end of this track lies the better, more hopeful world which, at this point in history, we can still create.[13]

The social democrat's fundamental concern is with equality; the right of all groups to be treated equally. The fact that many laws, even today, needlessly provide different treatment for men and for women is a source of anger for the social democrat. Although some of these laws are grounded in custom and tradition, the government has not only a right, but a moral obligation to change them. Government should change tradition if the tradition is inequitable.

One of the major results proponents claim the Equal Rights Amendment will have is to insure economic equality. Eleanor Smeal, the past President of the National Organization for Women, has strongly emphasized the economic side of the ERA:

> [The ERA] is profound economically. Essentially, its biggest impact will be on wages and benefits. Elderly women on Social Security would benefit by the ERA, for example, because Social Security is a discriminatory federal program. Really, women are cheated out of millions. So the major reason the ERA is a threat is that it is perceived to be expensive. . . . If there wasn't a dollar factor involved and if the ERA was simply symbolic, as much of our opposition

would like us to believe, then it wouldn't be so great a threat and the opposition wouldn't exist.[14]

Smeal doesn't make clear in these comments which segments of American consumers and taxpayers would have to pay for these profound changes. Clearly every economic benefit has an economic cost, but social democrats believe the benefits to deserving women and men will be worth the cost. It is a case of economic justice.

Supporters of the Equal Rights Amendment frequently point out that benefits would accrue to men as well as to women. Some people, such as law professor Philip Kurland, even believe that men would be the primary beneficiaries of its enactment.[15] Part of the benefit is to "free" men from the dependence of women. ERA-proponent, actor Alan Alda, writes:

> A longer-range benefit . . . is the pleasure we will derive from the companionship of women who finally have the ability to make free choices in their lives and to develop themselves to their fullest potential. A number of men have noticed that those women who have spent years fulfilling the approved submissive role can make men pay for that dependence. (The clinging vine can be a "Venus's flytrap.") Women's independence will set those men free.[16]

This radical restructuring of sex roles and family roles is clearly not going to take place immediately, but as women's opportunities in society expand, so will their personal choices. The ERA is also likely to help men by changing the laws relating to child custody, alimony, and child support. Although the ERA would not eliminate these laws, it would do away with the presumption that the ex-wife will keep the children, while the ex-husband will contribute the money. Even laws dealing with rape will have to be changed to make it clear that a rapist of either sex can be punished. The claims of opponents that rape laws will be eliminated is not accurate, but they will have to become "sex-blind."

Although women now sit on juries, operate their own businesses, and are elected to high office in all fifty states (which was not true in the 1940s),[17] unequal treatment remains. The social democrat claims that, legally, women are still not considered "persons" under the meaning of that term in the Fourteenth Amendment and that this legal fiction denying full personhood to women needs to be eliminated. The government has the right and the obligation to insure that all of its citizens are treated equally, and the Equal Rights Amendment would do precisely this.

The Conservative Point of View

Perhaps the only surprising aspect of the conservative opinion on the Equal Rights Amendment is not that conservatives oppose it, but that it took them so long to realize its implications. The Equal Rights Amendment was well on its way toward enactment before the conservatives became organized and put up such a fierce, and ultimately successful, fight against it. Conservative states like Texas, New Hampshire, Tennessee, and Nebraska had already passed the Amendment before substantial organized opposition developed.

Conservatives believe that the ERA would restructure the relationships between men and women in our society. Dr. Jonathan Pincus, professor of neurology at Yale University, during testimony in Washington, asked, "Is the Equal Rights Amendment to be the Tonkin Gulf Resolution of the American social structure?" His answer to this question was, "I would predict that the Equal Rights Amendment and many of the other goals of its proponents will bring social disruption, unhappiness, and increasing rates of divorce and desertion. Weakening of family ties may also lead to increased rates of alcoholism, suicide, and possibly sexual deviation.[18]

The Equal Rights Amendment, at least as interpreted by

most conservative opponents, flies in the face of what they hold most dear: stability and tradition. They argue that relations between the sexes have proven, over time, to be effective in providing happiness for most women and men and for a smoothly functioning social order. Why fix something that isn't broken? Former Barnard College trustee, Agnes Meyer, wrote in 1950 about working women. Her comments, though extreme for the 1980s, touch the core of conservative attitudes about sex roles. She asks

> What ails these women who consciously or unconsciously reject their children? Surface influences of a competitive, materialistic world have obscured the importance of women's role as the repository of continuity and of purposeful living derived from their biological and social functions. Our technological civilization has atrophied their emotions, and nothing is more horrible than a woman whose instinctive reactions have been destroyed. They are far more egotistical than men, more fiercely aggressive, more insensitive not only to the beauty but to the decency of life.[19]

The fact that no one can be certain how the Equal Rights Amendment will be interpreted frightens conservatives. The social democrat does not see change as necessarily harmful, but the conservative often does. Change should come gradually, and be for a good reason. Conservatives, such as President Ronald Reagan, feel that those laws that unnecessarily discriminate against women can be handled through legislation, rather than a constitutional amendment. Very few people believe that women should not receive equal pay for equal work. Conservatives say, let us decide openly on what needs to be changed, and then change that, leaving the rest of our social system intact.

The effects of the ERA on abortion also pose problems for some opponents. Conservatives point with dismay to efforts to use state Equal Rights Amendments in Hawaii, Massachusetts, and Pennsylvania to argue that there is a constitutional right for abortion to be paid with state funds. The rulings in these cases did not address this argument. Nevertheless conservatives such as Rep. Henry Hyde worry that the same argument might be made if a federal ERA was passed. In order to prevent the possibility of abortion getting help from the ERA, some people would like to amend the next version to ensure that it could not be interpreted in that way.[20]

Another concern of conservative ERA opponents is the possibility of women going into combat. One John Birch Society article is dramatically entitled: "The Proposal to Let Them Shoot Women."[21] This is no idle fantasy of the far right, however, but is something that both the House and Senate sponsors of the ERA in 1971-2 admitted could happen. Thomas Emerson, a leading supporter of the ERA, comments in an influential law review article about the role of the women in the military. "The Equal Rights Amendment will result in substantial changes in our military institutions. The number of women serving, and the positions they occupy, will be far greater than at present. Women will be subject to the draft, and the requirements for enlistment will be the same for both sexes. . . . Women will serve in all kinds of units, and they will be eligible for combat duty.[22] Although not all women would be drafted, and combat assignments would be based on physical ability, it is probable that under the ERA some women would see combat. Conservatives have, so far, been unsuccessful in attaching an amendment preventing women from being drafted. Obviously, women in combat represent a substantial break with the traditional responsibilities of the sexes, and one which conservatives suggest is unnecessary. Much of the conservative objection to the ERA is based on fear; the problem is that it is difficult to assure them that their fears will not come to pass.

The Libertarian Point of View

Most libertarians support the first section of the ERA but oppose the second section. The libertarian accepts that all people, regardless of sex, should be treated equally, and they have no quarrel with insisting all federal and state legislation treat everyone equally. But they worry about a federal power grab in the second section of the Amendment that gives Congress enforcement power. The danger is that Congress may enact laws that go further than simply altering laws that discriminate but will try to *enforce* equality. While libertarians support equality as a matter of policy, they also believe that individuals should, if they wish, be able to discriminate—suffering, perhaps, the consequences of not hiring the best people.

There is some basis for the libertarians' concerns that the ERA will make the government more intrusive into people's lives. Some research links statism (the concentration of power in centralized government) to women's equality. In his study, Francisco Ramirez found that the degree of centralized political power is positively associated with the level of constitutional equality between the sexes.[23] The more powerful the government, the more rights women are likely to be guaranteed. Phyllis Schlafly, the prominent anti-ERA advocate, makes an essentially libertarian argument about this danger of increased federal power:

> The Equal Rights Amendment reminds me of the story about a salmon swimming off the coast. As it sees a succulent piece of fish floating toward it, it says to itself, "High protein content; what's wrong with that? Delicious aroma; what's wrong with that? Just the right size; I can take it in one mouthful; what's wrong with that?" What is wrong with it, of course, is that there is a hook in it. The hook in ERA is Section 2. . . . Any area that Congress has the power to legislate on, the federal agencies have the power to administer and execute, and the federal courts have the power to adjudicate. Section 2 is a big grab for vast new federal power.[24]

Libertarians believe that the power to legislate is the power to destroy. ERA supporters try to point out that Section 2 contains standard language found in many constitutional amendments, but this does not comfort libertarians. They see how the Congress has used essentially the same clause in the Fourteenth

Amendment to extend the reach of government into what had previously been state or private matters. Even worse are the decisions for implementing the ERA that might be made by unelected courts and regulatory agencies, which sometimes go beyond the intentions of both voters and politicians.[25]

Feminism, some libertarians believe, is counter to liberty and is inherently repressive. While not every libertarian would agree with this, the arguments raised by Michael Levin are worth exploring. Levin claims that "the inner logic of feminism is inherently anti-democratic and, indeed, totalitarian. . . . True, it comes packaged in the lang uage of 'liberation,' but so does every other repressive ideology that has achieved any currency."[26] On its surface, Levin's argument makes little sense, but when examined more closely, it is clear he is attacking feminism's implicit statism. Since feminists assume that abilities are randomly distributed throughout the population, any area where there are fewer women than men must be due to social conditioning and discrimination. Levin claims feminists wish to have the government step in to eliminate sexist conditioning and discrimination, something to which he, as a libertarian, is opposed. He suggests that much of the unequal distribution among the sexes results from personal preference and freedom of choice and does not require government action.

Sex Discrimination and Social Research

A wit once remarked that a camel was a horse designed by committee. Despite that warning, many reports on policy are based on the work of committees. Among them is a recent study that examines the question of women's wage discrimination: Do women receive equal pay for work of equal value. The answer to this question is crucial, some say, to the argument supporting the need for an Equal Rights Amendment.

In 1981, the Committee on Occupational Classification and

Analysis of the prestigious National Research Council published a report, edited by Donald Treiman and Heidi Hartmann, entitled *Women, Work, and Wages*,[27] which attempted to answer this question. The committee did not conduct any of the research but, through its staff, sifted through the considerable amount of research that had already been done, and attempted to draw conclusions by means of analyzing and comparing these existing studies.

In a methodology of this kind, one is at the mercy of those studies that have already been conducted. The biases of the original researchers become, in some measure, one's own biases. To the extent most researchers who have conducted research in the area of women's wages have done so out of a concern with women not receiving equitable salaries (a reasonable, if unproven, hypothesis), this will affect those who rely on these studies. Moreover, since the committee itself was drawn from prominent scholars in this area, it is reasonable to assume that they may have expected to discover the conclusions that they found—conclusions that are congruent with the conflict theorist's view of women's place in society. This is not to suggest the panel was being deceptive or dishonest but only to suggest that the vagueness of the question (what is "comparable worth"?) made a value-free stance impossible.

As noted earlier in the chapter, women do earn less than men, but does this mean they are being discriminated against? Perhaps women choose to work in low-paying jobs for reasons other than money, or perhaps women have fewer skills, less "human capital", that would permit them to get better paying jobs. Although each of these factors does affect the job placement of women to *some* degree, Treiman and Hartmann suggest that this does not explain the entire wage differential. Their analysis concludes: "The substantial influence of institutional and traditional arrangements makes it impossible to view current wage rates as set solely by the free play of neutral forces operating in an entirely open market, no matter how attractive such a theoretical formulation may be.[28]

In this study, at least, the libertarian's free market theory is explicitly rejected because of the belief in the existence of *struc-

tural discrimination. It is important to remember that nowhere in this study do the authors demonstrate—or even claim—that some people are consciously discriminating against other people. There is no "smoking gun" of sexism here. Rather, the wage differentials are explained by the percentage of women in a particular occupation. The more women in an occupation, the lower the prevailing wage rate is likely to be. According to this study, this income disparity cannot be completely explained by any other legitimate differences between male and female workers. The committee's report asserts, then, that the present discrimination against women workers is *structural* not *behavioral*. By analyzing previously published data, the committee rejects the belief that women choose low-paying jobs (or at least that this explains most of wage differences) and accepts the view that within companies, women are systematically excluded from high paying jobs and that jobs women hold tend to be underpaid *because* they are held by women. The acceptance of these latter two explanations provides a reason for government intervention.[29]

If we accept as desirable the concept of equal pay for work of equal value, how do we decide what work is worth? Should a doctor be paid as much as a janitor, a secretary as much as a basketball player? Even within a single company, how should work be defined? Ultimately this is a value judgment that rests on ambiguous notions such as skill, effort, responsibility, and working conditions. This report explicitly avoids deciding this question. They make "no judgments regarding the relative value of jobs to employers or to society or the appropriate relationships among the pay rates for various jobs. The concept of intrinsic job worth—whether it exists, on what it should be based, whether there is a just wage—has been a matter of dispute for many centuries. . . . Hierarchies of job worth are always, at least in part, a reflection of values."[30]

This seems to argue against the concept of equal worth, yet, many companies do assess the worth of jobs—and where such methods exist (however inadequate they might be), they should be used to set fair, nondiscriminatory wage rates within a business. Even though some social democrats would argue for setting national standards for equivalent job worth, the committee says that wage setting should be used only where such standards exist for classifying jobs—a social democratic view, but a moderate one. To the extent, however, that we can demonstrate that women are systematically being denied equal compensation for equivalent work *because they are women,* we can argue for the Equal Rights Amendment, which would put teeth into legal efforts to alter these wage differentials. Under an Equal Rights Amendment, courts might well require companies to consider the percentage of women in an occupation to ensure they are not being denied their "fair share." A matter that once might have been handled within a company would become an issue of federal policy.

Sex Roles and the Equal Rights Amendment

The debate between conservatives and social democrats is a central one for understanding the relations between men and women in American society. Over the past twenty years the position of women in American society has changed dramatically and attitudes toward women have changed as well. All this has produced some confusion—particularly in the less monumental but nonetheless significant aspects of life. Should men open doors for women? How should a liberated woman respond when a man offers to pick up the check? When should a gentleman give his seat to a lady? Who should invite whom on a date? Who is grading whom sexually? Many of the once taken-for-granted aspects of sex-role behavior are now openly questioned. These problems do not have the significance that equal job opportunities and pay have, but they may be more problematic since they rely on delicate face-to-face interactions.

Beneath this, there is an even more fundamental question. Should men and women behave identically? Critics of feminism claim that the end result of that social movement will be two sexes of men. By this they mean that there is a danger of women acting like men. They will become aggressive, competitive, smoke more, drink more, have more heart attacks and ulcers, eventually give up their edge in life expectancy. Do we want a world of four billion "men"? Some feminists insist that it does not have to be this way; gaining equal opportunities does not necessarily mean that the traditional masculine styles of work will continue. Women can humanize corporations; with increased attention to personal needs and increased emphasis on interpersonal skills, the workplace can be changed. In this view, women need not stop being women (emotionally) in order to achieve material success. Others suggest that men and women can incorporate the "best" of both sexes—an approach called "androgeny." The difficulty with this is that it is not clear what constitutes the "best" aspects of each sex role. Finally, we might opt for an individualistic approach. Men and women might choose whichever "sex roles" (now no longer sex based) fit them best. According to this "humanistic" view, a person could be feminine, masculine, or androgenous. It is difficult to imagine how children will be socialized in such a situation or how we will learn to react to others with such a bewildering array of social types. But, at least, from this point of view, each person will to their own self be true.

Most Americans believe that men and women should have equal economic opportunities (88 percent in one recent Gallup Poll[31]); however, few Americans would choose a world in which men and women acted identically. Biologically, men and women are permanently distinctive, but even socially there is a belief in the desirability of difference. Although this may constrain some men and some women, and although the gap may need to be narrowed, the difference is likely to remain. In short, economically, most Americans are social democrats on this issue; socially they are, to some degree, conservatives.

Questions

1. Why do you support or oppose the Equal Rights Amendment?

2. Considering the support the ERA had from the American public, why didn't it pass?

3. Does the ERA give too much power to the federal government?

4. Should women have equal job opportunities to men, even if this means fewer job opportunities for men?

5. Should married women with children stay home, as mothers, or should they work outside the home?

6. Should women who are physically able be drafted for combat duty?

7. Why is the ERA such an emotional issue for conservatives?

8. Is the ERA a "radical" proposal or a "simple" matter of justice?

9. Why do men and women support the ERA equally?

10. What will the Equal Rights Amendment do for men?

For Further Study

Boles, Janet K., *The Politics of the Equal Rights Amendment*. New York: Longman, 1979.

Brown, Barbara A., et. al. "The Equal Rights Amendment: A Constitutional Basis for Equal Rights for Women," *Yale Law Journal* 80 (1971): 871-980.

Eisler, Riane Tennenhaus. *The Equal Rights Handbook*. New York: Avon, 1978.

Freeman, Jo. *The Politics of Women's Liberation*. New York: Longman, 1975.

Huber, Joan; Rexroat, Cynthia; and Spitze, Glenna. "A Crucible of Opinion on Women's Status: ERA in Illinois," *Social Forces* 57 (1978):549-565.

Levin, Michael. "Feminism vs. Democracy." St. Croix Review 16 (1983):38-50.

Ramirez, Francisco. "Statism, Equality, and Housewifery: A Cross-National Analysis," *Pacific Sociological Review* 24 (1981):175-195.

Schlafly, Phyllis. *The Power of the Positive Woman* New Rochelle, New York: Arlington House, 1977.

Yates, Gayle Graham, *What Women Want: The Ideas of the Movement*. Cambridge: Harvard University Press, 1975.

Notes and References

1. Ernest Jones, *The Life and Work of Sigmund Freud*, vol. 2: *1901-1919: Years of Maturity* (New York: Basic, 1955), p. 421.
2. Gayle Graham Yates, *What Women Want: The Ideas of the Movement* (Cambridge: Harvard University Press, 1975).
3. George P. Murdock and Caterina Provost, "Factors in the Division of Labor by Sex: A Cross-Cultural Analsyis," *Ethnology* 12 (April, 1973):207.
4. National Opinion Research Center, *General Social Surveys 1972-1982: Cumulative Codebook* (Chicago: National Opinion Research Center, 1982), p. 142.
5. "The 70's: Decade of Second Thoughts," *Public Opinion*, January 3, 1980, p. 33. Based on a poll by Lou Harris and Associates/ABC News, February, 1979.
6. Talcott Parsons and Robert Freed Bales, et al., *Family, Socialization and Interaction Process* (New York: Free Press, 1955), pp.3-9.
7. Riane Tennenhaus Eisler, *The Equal Rights Handbook* (New York: Avon, 1978), p. 34.
8. *Ibid*, p. 4.
9. *Public Support for ERA Reaches New High*, Gallup Report No. 190, July, 1981, pp. 23-25.
10. Andrew Cherlin and Pamela B. Walters, "Trends in United States

Men's and Women's Sex-Role Attitudes: 1972 to 1978," *American Sociological Review* 46 (August, 1981):453-460.

11. Joan Huber, Cynthia Rexroat, and Glenna Spitze, "A Crucible of Opinion on Women's Status: ERA in Illinios, *Social Forces* 57 (December, 1978): 549-565.

12. David W. Brady and Kent L. Tedin, "Ladies in Pink: Religion and Political Ideology in the Anti-ERA Movement," *Social Science Quarterly* 56 (March, 1976): 564-575.

13. Eisler, *op. cit.*, pp. 7-8.

14. "For the E, the R, and the A: An Interview With Eleanor Smeal," *Gray Panthers Network*, July-August 1981, p. 6.

15. Philip Kurland's wire to the Illinois legislature on June 5, 1972 in Phyllis Schlafly, *The Power of the Positive Woman* (New Rochelle, New York: Arlington House, 1977), p. 74.

16. Alan Alda, "Why Should Men Care?: On the ERA," *Ms.*, July, 1976, p. 93.

17. Dorothy D. Crook, "Women in the Eyes of the Law," *Independent Woman* 20 (December, 1941): 209.

18. Phyllis Schlafly, *The Power of the Positive Woman* (New Rochelle, New York: Arlington House, 1977), p. 92; quoting U.S. Senate, Committee on the Judiciary, March 14, 1972, pp. 47-48.

19. Agnes E. Meyer, "Women Aren't Men," *Atlantic*, August, 1950, p. 33.

20. Testimony of Congressman Henry Hyde to the U.S. Senate Judiciary Committee, Constitution Subcommittee, May 26, 1983, reported in the *Phyllis Schlafly Report*, June 1983, p. 1.

21. Susan L. M. Huck, "The Proposal to Let Them Shoot Women," *American Opinion* 21 (April, 1978): 21.

22. Barbara A. Brown, Thomas I. Emerson, Gail Falk, and Ann E. Freedman, "The Equal Rights Amendment: A Constitutional Basis for Equal Rights for Women," *Yale Law Journal* 80 (April, 1971): 978.

23. Francisco O. Ramirez, "Statism, Equality, and Housewifery: A Cross-National Analysis," *Pacific Sociological Review* 24 (April, 1981): 175-195.

24. Schlafly, 1977, *op. cit.*, p. 130.

25. Michael Levin, "Feminism vs. Democracy," *St. Croix Review* 16 (October, 1983): 38.

26. *Ibid,* p. 38.
27. Donald J. Treiman and Heidi I. Hartmann, eds., *Women, Work, and Wages: Equal Pay for Jobs of Equal Value* (Washington, D.C., 1981).
28. *Ibid,* p. x.
29. *Ibid,* p. 167.
30. *Ibid,* p. 10.
31. "Half Say Job Market Bias Still Exists," *The Gallup Report,* No. 203, August, 1982, p. 24.

 **Four**

Culture: Should Elementary School Children Be Taught in Their Native Language?

FEW CONCEPTS HAVE had the longevity and significance in social science writing as has culture. Culture reflects our humanness; it differentiates us from other animals. But what do we mean by *culture*? Among the hundreds, and probably thousands, of definitions that have been put forth, American anthropologist Melville Herskovits defines culture in this general fashion: "Culture is essentially a construct that describes the total body of belief, behavior, knowledge, sanctions, values, and goals that mark the way of life of any people. That is, though a culture may be treated by the student as capable of objective description, in the final analysis it comprises the things that people have, the things they do, and what they think."[1]

This admittedly broad definition suggests that culture is fluid. Within a society, it can include material artifacts (such as the flag or works of art), behaviors (hand-shaking or kissing), or social expectations (the norm of fairness). This last category has two important aspects—*norms* and *values*. *Norms* refer to rules that specify appropriate and inappropriate behavior, the *shared expectations* that people have of each other. *Values* refer to those *shared conceptions* that are used to evaluate the desirability or correctness of objects, acts, feelings, ideas, or events. In understanding both norms and values, however, we should not assume that they are universally accepted, nor need they be completely understood. According to interactionist theory, both values and norms are abstractions. People, say the interactionists, do not behave as they do because they are consciously or deliberately attempting to follow a set of rules, rather they do what seems best in the specific situation they are in. Although the concepts of values and norms are useful for social scientists, who wish to see regularities in behavior (such as, people behave *as if* these things exist), they may not tell us *why* people behave as they do.

Culture is not an innate part of human nature; it has to be learned, even though it is made possible by our biological equipment. *Socialization*, the process of learning a society's culture, is critical to human development. From about age two to about age fourteen, a child goes through a transformation from an egocentric savage to a responsible, civilized human being—a most remarkable change in only a dozen years.

Another remarkable aspect of culture is its diversity. Behaviors and norms that are appropriate in one society can be considered inappropriate in others. Some societies venerate people who are obese; others give special treatment to those who are thin. In some societies the young are revered, in others the old are given deference. In some twins are given a place of honor; other societies see twins as a curse. These marked differences between societies raise an important issue: are there some cultural traditions that are universally moral or are particular cultural traditions right for each particular society. This is the distinction between *cultural absolutism* and *cultural relativism*. Should we say that things like racism or infanticide are absolutely wrong, or should we refrain from making these judgements? If we cannot say that another culture is acting immorally, how can we set any standards for ourselves? If everything is right, then, by implication, nothing is wrong. Although most social scientists would grant that different societies can have different traditions, few eliminate all rules of moral propriety.

No aspect of culture is more important than language. One of the most tragic stories in the Bible is the Tower of Babel, in which the previously monolingual humanity was transformed into hundreds of groups of people who spoke mutually incomprehensible languages. Historically, we have had only modest success trying to understand each other.

The study of language suggests that it shapes the way in which people see the world. This approach to the social effects of language on thought and perception is known as the *linguistic relativity hypothesis,* or the *Sapir-Whorf hypothesis,* after the two American linguists who stated it the most emphatically.[2] Here are some simple examples of how culture and language are related: while most Americans have a limited vocabulary for talking about snow, Eskimos have over twenty words for snow. The Hanunoo people in the Philippines have names for ninety-two different varieties of rice. Even the color spectrum is viewed very differently by different groups.[3] Linguistic relativists suggest people admit some things to their consciousness (they "see" them) while filtering out other things they do not have words for. According to this theory, language is not only a basic means by which culture and information is communicated, but it also structures the way in which we experience the world.

Question:

Should Elementary School Children Be Taught in Their Native Language?

By 1990 it is expected that the largest minority group in the United States will be Hispanics[4]—Americans whose native language is not English but Spanish. Hispanic-Americans, because of their numbers and the seeming unwillingness of many to give up their native culture and become "Americanized," pose special problems for American society. Although many Hispanics can be distinguished from "majority" Americans by their brown skin, perhaps their most distinctive feature as a minority group is their language. The question is should they be encouraged to keep their first language as their primary language or should they be forced to make the transition to English? It is the latter problem that I shall examine.

The problem of language unity in a nation is not unique to the United States. Canada is a good example of the kind of tensions that a battle over language can produce. Likewise, in nations such as Belgium and India language has been a festering problem for years. Some nations (Switzerland, most notably) have several language groups that live in relative harmony, but this is more the exception than the rule. Many people believe that a crucial part of nationhood is a single national language; a common language reflects a common unity. Carll Tucker, editor of the New York-based opinion journal *Saturday Review*, frustrated by his polyglot neighbors, writes:

> If America does have a purpose, as our founders and most subsequent generations have heartily believed, then America has the right and obligation to demand certain contributions and sacrifices from its citizens beyond those that are required simply to maintain the peace and fund government operations. We have the right, for instance, to require a stint of government service, wartime or not. We have the right to require the teaching of American history, the pledging of allegiance, the observance of national holidays. And we have the right to require the learning of our national language in schools.[5]

The controversy of communicating with people who speak a "foreign" language and who share the same country is not new. One of the first books printed in the Massachusetts Bay Colony was a translation of the Bible into the Algonkian speech of local Indians. But by the mid-eighteenth century, Benjamin Franklin was so concerned about the influx of German speakers into Pennsylvania that he wrote: "Why should the [German] boors be suffered to swarm in our settlements and, by herding together, establish their language and manners to the exclusion of ours? Why should Pennsylvania, founded by the English, become a colony of *aliens,* who will shortly be so numerous as to germanize us instead of our anglifying them?"[6]

American's ambivalence toward incorporating foreigners was evident during the War of Independence when the Continental Congress sought support from German-Americans by printing the articles of confederation in German.[7] The tension between those who wanted English adopted as the official language in the United States and those who were willing to grant the legal importance of other languages continued throughout the nineteenth century.[8] In 1840, for example, the state of Ohio explicitly sanctioned German-English schools. Minnesota printed its constitution in German, Swedish, Norwegian, and French; and, prior to the Civil War, Louisiana allowed the use of both French and English in its legislature and courts. Yet, the Congress, on several occasions, refused to publish important public documents in German during this period.

Although the roots of the movement certainly began earlier with increases in immigration from southern and eastern Europe, World War I seems to be the point at which the opposition to second languages in America became more intense.[9] In 1917, former President Theodore Roosevelt drafted and circulated a statement, signed by prominent Americans of a variety of backgrounds, that reflects the sentiment at the time.

> We must have but one flag. We must also have but one language. This must be the language of the Declaration of Independence, of Washington's Farewell Address, of Lincoln's Gettysburg Speech and Second Inaugural. We cannot tolerate any attempt to oppose or supplant the language and culture that has come down to us from the builders of this republic with the language and culture of any European country. The greatness of this nation depends on the swift assimilation of the aliens she welcomes to her shores. Any force which attempts to retard that assimilative process is a force hostile to the highest interests of this country.[10]

At the same time that Americans were becoming more nationalistic and passing restrictive immigration laws, they were limiting education to English. For example, Nebraska outlawed the use of any foreign language in elementary schools, while the town of Findlay, Ohio, imposed a fine of twenty-five dollars for using German on the street.[11] Throughout its history America has been of two minds about the use of second languages in its schools and in its political institutions.

After World War II, and particularly during the last two decades, the United States has accepted a large number of Hispanic immigrants. This immigration is posing problems similar to the immigration of Germans that Benjamin Franklin worried about two centuries earlier. In parts of the United States— southern Florida, southern Texas, New Mexico, and southern California—it is almost as likely for someone to hear a conversation in Spanish as in English. Miami, in fact, has become an international finance center for all of Latin America.

With the large influx of Spanish-speaking people by the 1960s, the pendulum began to swing back toward a greater acceptance of the value of teaching children in their native languages. In 1968 Congress passed Title VII of the Elementary and Secondary Education Act (also known as the Bilingual Education Act). This Act provided funding for projects that would meet the special problems of children (mostly, but not exclusively, Hispanic) with limited English-speaking ability. Many people involved in implementing this act did not see the use of the language children used at home as merely transitional, but rather the use of their first language was a way to promote linguistic and cultural pride by improving their cultural awareness and their native language skills.[12] This act was strengthened considerably by a decision by President Carter's newly appointed Secretary of Education, Shirley Hofstedler in 1980. She handed down a rule that all schools with two or more classes composed of at least twenty-five non-English speaking children must provide classes in the child's native language to help those children learn English and their regular subjects. This federal regulation responded to a 1974 Supreme Court decision in the case of *Lau v. Nichols,* which stated that communities had the constitutional requirement to provide students with appropriate education, despite English-deficiencies. The Court, however, did not specify how this must be done.

There are several ways in which non-English speaking children can learn English. First, as was once common, immigrant children could be thrown in an English language class and allowed to sink or swim. Many swam, of course, particularly when the community shared a cultural value that children should learn the language of their adopted land. But many suffered. A second approach is called English as a Second Language (ESL), in which the student is intensively trained in English without reliance on his or her native language. The child takes instruction in other subjects in English, but he or she has a special class in English-language skills. The third approach is bilingual education (sometimes called bilingual-bicultural education), which has been defined by the director of the U.S. Commission on Civil Rights as: " . . . an instructional program in which two languages—English and the native tongue—are used as mediums of instruction and in which the cultural background of the students is incorporated into the curriculum."[13] This method teaches children in their native language, while slowly teaching them English.[14]

One obvious question is which of these programs works best for the 3.5 million school children whose native language is not English. Unfortunately, the answer is not equally obvious. Some bilingual education programs seem to work, whereas others do not.[15] One U.S. Office of Education study indicates that children deficient in English are not acquiring it through bilingual education and that many of the programs are in fact aimed at maintaining a separate language and culture.[16]

Perhaps not surprisingly, by the late 1970s and early 1980s something of a backlash against bilingualism occurred. In 1980, in Dade County, Florida, voters, by a 3-2 margin, repealed a statute that had established Spanish as the county's *official* second language. In 1981 Reagan's Secretary of Education, T. H. Bell, revoked the Hofstedler bilingual proposals. And later that same year then-California Senator S. I. Hayakawa introduced a constitutional amendment making English "the official language of the United States," which, if passed, would eliminate the possibility of official second languages.

The Conservative Point of View

Surely one cannot deny, argues the conservative, that success in America requires fluency in English. English is part of the tradition and heritage of the United States. America has always been a melting pot—an ethnic fondue—in which immigrants with widely different backgrounds were melted into Americans. Even black Americans have in all important regards left their African roots behind and are culturally Americans (even if they have a distinctive subculture). For the conservative, the existence of two competing languages is devisive and ultimately debilitating.

Nathan Glazer, a leading neo-conservative critic of bilingual-bicultural education, warns against cultural disunity. "Bilingual-bicultural education" comments Glazer, "prevents the development of a common culture, a common loyalty, a common allegiance. . . . It is the unity-divisiveness argument, the belief that this is a better country because people from many countries and with many languages were turned into people having loyalty to one country and speaking one language."[17]

He is further worried about the new Hispanic immigrants who may have only a fleeting and uncertain attachment to this country. Glazer wonders if "undocumented aliens" really wish to become Americanized, or whether they hope to return to their country of birth at some later date.

The conservative suggests that belonging to a society does not diminish a person's sense of heritage or ethnic self-worth; indeed, it may have exactly the opposite result. Consider the comments of Mexican-American writer Richard Rodriguez, who was forced to learn English in parochial school:

> Bilingual educators say today that children lose a degree of "individuality" by becoming assimilated into public

society. . . . [They] do not realize that, while one suffers a diminished sense of private individuality by being assimilated into public society, such assimilation makes possible the achievement of public individuality. . . . Those middle-class ethnics who scorn assimilation seem to me filled with decadent self-pity, obsessed by the burden of public life. Dangerously, they romanticize public separateness and trivialize the dilemma of those who are truly socially disadvantaged.[18]

If someone cannot speak English, Rodriguez suggests, it is inevitable that most people will stereotype him or her as "just another Latino"; speaking the dominant language gives one the opportunity to participate meaningfully in public life—without requesting or demanding special treatment.[19]

The conservative also offers southern and eastern European immigrants as examples of groups that have been successfully "stewed" in the melting pot. The United States public school system was great, according to this view, because it took all these "disadvantaged" children with conflicting cultures, and after twelve years turned them into Americans. Conservatives note that although bilingualism might appear to help immigrants at first, eventually it prevents them from moving into the economic mainstream. "Learning English," says Senator Hayakawa, "has been the primary task of every immigrant group for two centuries. Participation in the common language has rapidly made available to each new group the political and economic benefits of American society. Those who have mastered English have overcome the major hurdle to full participation in our democracy."[20]

While conservatives may overly romanticize the experience of being an immigrant in the public school system, they are arguing against the curious proposal of those who support bilingualism—that we should maintain two separate school systems. Essentially this calls for a segregation of people who speak a different language in a way that would be illegal if they were blacks. Conservatives recognize Hispanics have real and significant problems, but they do not believe these people are unique, nor do their problems warrant the creation of a nation permanently divided by language.

The Social Democratic Point of View

Although many social democrats support bilingual education, others do not. Agreeing with some of the conservative arguments, some social democrats contend that bilingualism is harmful to the nation and to the individual child and is not a "liberal" issue.[21] Indeed, the large majority of the American people oppose bilingualism. In 1980 a Gallup Poll asked, "Many families who come from other countries have children who cannot speak English. Should or should not these children be required to learn English in special classes before they are enrolled in the public schools?" By a margin of 82-13 Americans responded that they should learn English first.[22]

Yet, despite this *vox populi*, there are arguments in favor of bilingualism. It is clear that prior to the emergence of the bilingual movement, public schools were not training Hispanic youngsters very well. Only 30 percent of the Hispanic students in the United States completed high school, and in urban ghetto areas, the dropout rate may have been as high as 85 percent.[23] Most of these students did not have the opportunity to participate in bilingual programs.

The leaders of the Hispanic community typically support bilingual education; some Hispanics feel that in many ways bilingual education is their "civil rights act." Social democrats see no harm in helping groups of people that have special problems; bilingual education is such a case.

Supporters of this program see America consumed by "lingui-chauvinism," an attitude, which in its own way, is as debilitating as racism. Carey McWilliams, the former editor of the liberal opinion journal *The Nation*, writes:

> Whenever a majority has insisted on a rigid monolingualism, it has generally meant that language was

being used as a strategy for keeping the minority in its place. The effect has often been to stimulate the nationalism of minorities. . . . If a majority wants to avoid . . . divisive movements, then it should opt for a policy of intelligent bilingualism as a means, first, of permitting the minority to preserve its cultural heritage and, second, of enabling it to make the best use of the official language as a means of improving its lot. Any attempt to suppress or discourage the minority's language is likely to stimulate separatist tendencies.[24]

Many social democrats feel that a multi-lingual society could be a culturally-rich, free, and happy one. Social democrats question whether it is necessary to maintain cultural imperialism or impose uniformity on a nation; if there is mutual respect for all cultures, people can live in harmony and borrow the best from each culture.

The question is a good one: Why must we enforce cultural uniformity? Sanford Levinson, an instructor in politics at Princeton, lays open the question of whether a society can exist as a collection of dissimilar groups:

It is obviously open to question whether it is legitimate to expect all American citizens to master English, especially if the numbers of Spanish speakers are large enough. . . . Does the government, whether state or Federal, have a duty to print its materials in Spanish as well as English? Does it deny equal protection of the laws by assuming that all American citizens are responsible for knowing English? . . . To accept the premises of strong bilingualism means accepting the fact that large numbers of one's fellow citizens simply have no desire (or ability) to communicate in the most effective manner possible—the speaking of a common language. It means an ultimate rejection of the premise that we are indeed a united nation in favor of the recognition that we are congeries of groups joined together, often uneasily, in a political alliance.[25]

This is a somewhat extreme position, but it is consistent with the view of the American Republic as a confederation of states. It assumes that each group would be given as much freedom as it needed to gain equality for itself and its members. For those who support interest group politics, like the social democrats, the fact that Hispanic leaders tend to support bilingualism is a message in favor of the plan. The assumption that bilingual-bicultural education (even one which is less extreme and does teach English) protects a group's cultural heritage and self-respect is important to the social democrat—the minority group is the best judge of what is necessary to ensure its own equality.

The Libertarian Point of View

Most extreme libertarians are very suspicious about the role of public schools, so more government involvement in this area only serves to increase this basic suspicion. In theory, the libertarian has no objection to any particular form of private education (providing the student is willing to accept the consequences), and since private schools should be free to do as they wish bilingualism is acceptable. Many Hispanics do attend private, Catholic schools that could offer bilingual programs if they wished. Most libertarians are probably dubious about the effectiveness of bilingualism since it removes Hispanics from the mainstream of American social and political life, but they believe that anyone can do what she or he wishes, just as long as it does not infringe on other people's actions.

Libertarians are particularly concerned that this program is a matter of political expediency with little accountability and critical evaluation.[26] The program is seen by some as a sop thrown to Hispanic activists—a jobs program, rather than an educational one. In an article in the *New Republic*, Abigail Thernstrom agrees with this assertion. She writes, "support for bilingual instruction, particularly among Hispanic activists, has not lessened. And the reason is clear: the programs provide both employment and political opportunities, as schools are forced to hire Hispanics without regular teaching credentials, and as students are molded into an ethnically conscious constituency."[27]

Although some defend the hiring of Hispanics on the grounds of providing needed role-models for Mexican-American children, particularly in the primary grades, this disturbs the libertarian who sees another large federal project without clear educational objectives. The estimated cost to taxpayers of the Department of Education's proposed 1980 program ran to one billion dollars over a five year period.

Another concern for the libertarian is that a policy is being developed at the behest of one group (primarily Mexican-Americans) and is being applied to everyone, whether or not they want it. They see some advocates insisting that children be forced into such programs. Nathan Glazer strongly condemns the idea for this reason.

> We suffer from the fact that these policies are being developed and imposed by national bureaucracies, applying their own rules, and by federal courts, and that important distinctions between groups and what they think is best for them will be ignored. One way of taking into account these differences between groups and within groups is to make these programs, in greater measure than they are, voluntary. In the case of the New York City consent judgement, there was an unsettling dispute in which the plaintiff lawyers . . . wanted to *require* students deemed to need bilingual education under the test developed to take it, despite the opposition of some Spanish-speaking parents. Fortunately Judge Marvin Frankel rejected this demand. A true voluntarism will permit each child or its parents to select what they think is best.[28]

If we do need school systems, libertarians believe they should be systems that permit as much freedom of choice as is possible for the students.

Hispanic Education and Social Research

Many Hispanic youngsters do not do very well in school. Why? One explanation is to blame "them" for not having the same values that "we" have. Such a view is convenient—at least if you are one of "us" and not one of "them"—but it may overlook certain crucial pieces of information, such as student perceptions.

How can we find out what these kids "really" think? One method is to spend time with them. This rather obvious technique of sociological investigation is known as *participant observation*. In using this technique, sociologists go into the community and attempt to join the activity they wish to study there. They can either join by pretending to be members of the group (such as getting hired on a construction job or joining a gang of pickpockets) or by informing the group that they wish to spend time with them. Although journalists sometimes observe people or groups, the sociological observer typically is interested in more than merely describing the setting to outsiders; he or she wants to discover some sociological principles that transcend the observational setting.

Sociologists have been observing poor urban communities for many years. Originally, the concern was to examine what was patronizingly called "social disorganization"—this suggested that these people or their communities were "disorganized." Actually, poor neighborhoods are as organized as suburbs; it is just that the organizing is somewhat different. One of the best recent studies of the urban poor is Ruth Horowitz's *Honor and the American Dream*. Horowitz, as a young graduate student at the University of Chicago, spent several years observing the behavior of young Chicano men and women in one of the poorest areas of Chicago, a community that she calls 32nd Street. Horowitz explained to the members of the community that she was interested in the lives of the young people who lived in this area. Eventually she was accepted as someone who could be told things in confidence—even by gang members.

One of the major themes of Horowitz's book is the ambivalence that these young men and women feel toward traditional American values. Horowitz demonstrates that while these Chicanos are *not* hostile toward American values, there are other local community and cultural values that prevent them from capitalizing on the American Dream. Consider this description of the junior high school graduation of some of the gang members:

Wearing their caps and gowns, the more than four hundred eighth grade graduates arrived in yellow school buses at the new downtown auditorium. . . . All were dressed for the occasion, the graduates in new dresses or suits, the family members in their best clothes. Many of the parents took the day off from work. . . . After the speeches and award announcements each student's name was called as everyone clapped. The loudest, and the most prolonged cheers were for each of the graduating Lions. Fifteen of the Lions attended the graduation wearing their gang sweaters. That evening they had a celebration in the park.[29]

Evidently education was valued and supported by these adolescents' peer culture. So how did this positive feeling of education become a set of negative expectations, leading to a 70 percent dropout rate? While the answer is too complex to do justice to here, Horowitz identifies competing pressures that helped assure a high dropout rate among the Chicano youths she studied. First, many of the teachers came from very different cultural backgrounds and expected little from these youths. One teacher, for example, confided in Horowitz that it was her job to "tame the natives."[30] The schools required little homework, and many teachers were satisfied if the students were merely quiet. But the blame was not only placed on the teachers—the world of the streets spilled into the school corridors; guns were a frequent part of the school environment; knives were even more common. Some youths in the community did not respect schooling and charged the school atmosphere with tension and occasionally violence. Most young men felt that defending their "honor" took priority over other cultural values. And the lack of English language skills posed a major problem. Finally, many students questioned whether it made economic sense to graduate from high school—particularly if they were only an "average" student in a poor school. They knew that some high school graduates earned as little as some dropouts. The young women also wondered why they should complete high school if their real goal was matrimony.

Although Horowitz is not concerned with bilingual education as such, she effectively demonstrates some of the problems students have who are ambivalent about the basic values of American education. The Chicano values, which focus on honor and reputation, come easily into conflict with the traditional American value structure, which emphasizes the long-term benefits of education. Supporters of bilingualism are inclined to argue that these other cultural values must be taken into account in any successful educational program, whereas opponents of bilingual education suggest that success in education has always depended upon adopting the traditional values over and above one's own. Traditionalists have not had much success in converting these students because they ask them to reject the values in their community, but neither have bilingual educators been completely successful in demonstrating they can merge the two value systems.

Horowitz's approach to sociology is basically interactionism. That is, she believes that individuals have a large role in shaping their own lives. She also emphasizes that it is improper to lump all of the members of the community together:

> While the failure to finish school does place significant limits on job possibilities, it does not mean that youths have given up completely their hopes of achieving the American dream of economic success. Nor does the school system's failure to provide the mechanisms to develop the competitive ethic mean that youths do not mature into competent and steady workers. The problem that many youths face is the constant gap between their desire to do well and the lack of opportunities. Some confront this problem, while others continue to hedge their bets.[31]

By singling out some as "confronting this problem" and others as "hedging their bets," she seems to emphasize individual freedom. Yet, it would be a mistake to see this as a "hands-off" approach as condemning any public involvement. Horowitz is critical of the educational system and makes it clear that she believes schooling can and should be improved, especially with input from the community. Horowitz sees what occurs in the school as very important for the adult lives that these adolescents will lead. Policy decisions which affect the classroom also affect the streets.

Culture and Bilingualism

Can a society remain stable and free when it has more than one major cultural tradition? Most societies have many cultural strands with one typically predominating. Most nations make a choice (deliberately or by chance) about which symbols and language will represent them to each other and to the outside world. Many countries and organizations that have attempted to be bilingual, such as Canada or the United Nations, have found one language has dominated either in law or in practice, often causing tension for the whole system. Only a few small nations, most notably Switzerland, have shown that harmony can exist within a confederacy of different languages. Likewise, although all nations have within their borders a wide variety of ethnic, regional, economic, and occupational subcultures, there is usually a national "culture" in which most people participate. In the United States such common cultural elements include the concept of America as a melting pot, Paul Revere's midnight ride, the fireworks on the Fourth of July, and the flag. These cultural traditions reflect how we see our nation. A nation's culture reflects its soul; bilingualism raises the question of whether the United States will remain the United States or a nation with two large language communities which cannot—or will not—communicate with each other.

Ultimately, bilingualism raises the question of social cohesion. Sociologists differ over how much consensus of values, beliefs, and culture are necessary in a happy, well-functioning society. Critics of bilingual education (especially when it threatens to produce two different language communities) claim that uniformity is healthy and functional, while conflict is by its nature dysfunctional. Conflict theorists (who tend to be oriented towards the social democratic point of view) see social differences and disagreements as potentially healthy because they prevent a society from becoming static. They much prefer the image of a stewpot to a melting pot.

Everyone agrees that true bilingualism is beneficial. If everyone could speak several languages, Americans would be able to communicate better not only with each other, but multilingualism would permit us to compete better in the world economic market. Although many Japanese businessmen speak English well, few American salesmen can speak Japanese.

But this chapter has not addressed true bilingualism. The real goal of today's bilingual education is not to permit most Americans to speak two languages, but rather to retain and develop the culture and language of an immigrant group. We are not attempting, in any significant way, to have Anglo children learn Spanish. America chooses to define itself as a nation with a single language and a dominant culture; second languages and cultures are welcome only so long as they realize that they are second.

Questions

1. Should the public schools teach children in their native tongues?

2. Are Americans lingui-chauvinists?

3. Why are Hispanics so vehement about bilingual-bicultural education, whereas most other immigrant groups were not?

4. Why is the American public so opposed to bilingual education?

5. How important is learning English for being successful in America?

6. Should parents have the option of deciding if their children should be in bilingual classes or should it be on the basis of language test scores?

7. Is it important for an ethnic group to maintain a sense of its "roots"?

8. Can a multi-cultural, multi-lingual society survive and be stable?

9. Should the government have the obligation to provide an education for students who do not have the ability to speak English?

For Further Study

"Bilingualism: A Symposium," *The Nation* 228 (March 17, 1979): 263–266.

Cummins, Jim. "The Language and Culture Issue in the Education of Minority Language Children," *Interchange* 10 (1979-1980):72–88.

Matute-Bianchi, Maria Eugenia. "What is Bicultural About Bilingual-Bicultural Education?" *The Urban Review* 12 (1980):91–108.

Gilbert Schneider, Susan. *Revolution, Reaction or Reform: The 1974 Bilingual Education Act* (New York: L.A. Publishing Company, 1976).

Ortego, Philip D. "Montezuma's Children," *Center Magazine* 3 (1970):23–31.

Rodriguez, Richard. "Aria: A Memoir of a Bilingual Childhood," *American Scholar* 50 (Winter 1980-1981):25–42.

Symposium on "The New Bilingualism," *Society* 19 (November/December 1981):29–62.

Notes and References

1. Melville J. Herskovits, *Man and His Works* (New York: Knopf, 1948), p. 625.

2. See Edward Sapir, *Selected Writings in Language, Culture, and Personality* (Berkeley: University of California Press, 1949); Benjamin Whorf, *Language, Thought, and Reality* (Cambridge: MIT Press, 1956).

3. Verne F. Ray, "Techniques and Problems in the Study of Human Color Perception," *Southwestern Journal of Anthropology* 8 (Autumn 1952):251–258.

4. Although there are a number of terms used to describe Spanish-speaking Americans, I will use the term Hispanic as the most general but least cumbersome term.

5. Carll Tucker, "English Spoken Here," *Saturday Review*, May 12, 1979, p. 56.

6. Stephen T. Wagner, "America's Non-English Heritage," *Society*, November/December 1981, p. 37.

7. *Ibid*, p. 37.

8. *Ibid*, pp. 36–40.

9. *Ibid*, p. 41.

10. *Ibid*, p. 41.

11. *Ibid*, p. 41.

12. *Ibid*, p. 43.

13. Susan Gilbert Schneider, *Revolution, Reaction or Reform: The 1974 Bilingual Education Act* (New York: L.A. Publishing Company, 1976), p. 2.

14. For a discussion of several bilingual programs see Soledad Arenas, "Innovations in Bilingual/Multicultural Curriculum Development," *Children Today*, May-June 1980, pp. 17–21.

15. Jim Cummings, "The Language and Culture Issue in the Education of Minority Language Children," *Interchange* 10 (1979-1980):72–88.

16. Abigail Thernstrom, "Bilingual Mis-education," *The New Republic*, April 18, 1981, p. 17.

17. Nathan Glazer, "Pluralism and the New Immigrants," *Society*, November-December 1981, p. 34.

18. Richard Rodriguez, "Aria: A Memoir of a Bilingual Childhood," *The American Scholar* 50 (Winter 1980-81):34–35.

19. *Ibid*, pp. 29–30.

20. *The Congressional Record*, April 27, 1981, p. S3998.

21. Thernstrom, *op. cit.*, p. 16.

22. "Crisis of Confidence in Public Schools Continues," *The Gallup Opinion Index*, No. 180, August 1980, p. 13.

23. Isabel Schon, "It is the Primary Job of American Schools to Teach Students the Language of their Country Which Is, After All, English: Con," *English Journal* 70 (February 1981):9.

24. Carey McWilliams, "Bilingualism: A Symposium," *The Nation*, March 17, 1979, p. 263.

25. Sanford Levinson, "Bilingualism: A Symposium," *The Nation*, March 17, 1979, pp. 263–264.

26. Maria Eugenia Matute-Bianchi, "What is Bicultural About Bilingual-Bicultural Education?" *The Urban Review* 12 (1980):91.

27. Thernstrom, *op. cit.*, p. 16.

28. Glazer, *op. cit.*, p. 36.

29. Ruth Horowitz, *Honor and the American Dream: Culture and Identity in a Chicano Community* (New Brunswick: Rutgers University Press, 1983), p. 137.

30. *Ibid*, p. 146.

31. *Ibid*, p. 158.

 **Five**

Social Stratification: Should There be Laws Restricting Inheritance From One Generation to the Next?

FORMER PRESIDENT JIMMY CARTER once remarked: "Life is not fair." In saying this, he was declaring an important sociological conclusion. People are not treated equally, and how they are treated is not entirely a result of anything that they have done. The existence of a system of social stratification in the United States based, in part, on the "accident of birth" gives strong testimony to the fact that there is not complete equality of opportunity and certainly not of outcome.

Social stratification refers to the hierarchical inequality of groups of people. Part of this inequality relates to the fact that groups near the top of the hierarchy have greater access to rewards than those near the bottom. This stratification differs in kind and degree from society to society. In the most extreme case, a society is divided into castes. In this system, as was once true of India and is still largely characteristic of the Republic of

South Africa, status (or socially-defined position) is given at birth, with little opportunity for social mobility among the castes or for intermarriage. A second kind of stratification, and one which generally characterizes the United States, is a class system. In a class system, individuals are still ranked hierarchically, but this position is a function of their economic rank in the status system; even though a person's family may affect his or her class position, there is opportunity for mobility between classes, and marriage is not as restricted. Some societies, such as those that call themselves socialist, have attempted to eliminate the class system and claim to provide for everyone according to their need. Furthermore, expectations of people are supposedly according to their ability, not their social position. Whether because people need to make hierarchical distinctions, or whether they need economic motivation to inspire them to work, or whether those at the top are corrupt, no post-industrial society can truly be considered classless. George Orwell in his book *Animal Farm* gives this cynical comment about class structure: "All animals are equal but some animals are more equal than others."

Sociologists distinguish between two types of status: those that are *ascribed* and those that are *achieved*. Ascribed status refers to those forms of social status that are yours because of some social category that you have no control over. For example, you didn't choose to be female, Chicano, or nineteen years old, nor did you select your parents because they were wealthy. Yet each of these features colors the way that others see you. By contrast, achieved status refers to those positions that you achieve at least partially by your own efforts. If you complete your education, your status as college graduate will be achieved. Likewise, your occupation will be an achieved status. This does not mean that the fact that you graduated from college had nothing to do with external forces (the fact that your parents saved for years, for example), but only that a substantial share of your achievement can be attributed to your own efforts. The greater the extent to which a society relies on achieved characteristics to determine status, the more that society has open social mobility—people, in other words, can slip and climb through social hierarchies.

The dimensions of the class system can be conceptualized several ways. Two of the most widely used are those postulated by Karl Marx and by Max Weber. Marx believed that economic factors were decisive in determining status. Those who own and control the means of production are the dominant members of society. Those who work for those who own the means of production are the proletariet or working class. For Weber determining status was not as simple. Weber divided the idea of class into three closely related factors: power, wealth, and prestige. While these factors often go hand-in-hand, there are some people who may have power without wealth (some politicians), others have wealth without prestige (certain noveau-riche millionaires), and others have prestige but little power (clergymen, for example).

Any reasonably observant person will recognize that America is a stratified society. While we do not have the excesses of wealth of Saudi Arabia nor the depths of poverty of India, we do have many millionaires and many more poor people. Even if few people suffer starvation, all too many fall below the "poverty line."

In a society in which all individuals were nearly equal, we would expect the 20 percent with the lowest income to make nearly as much as the 20 percent who make the most income. Actually as of March 1983 the lowest 20 percent made only 4.7 percent of America's total income, whereas the top 20 percent made 42.7 percent.[1] These percentages have not changed much in the past fifteen or so years, which suggests that American society is becoming neither more nor less stratified. If we examine wealth—that is, assets, including property, stocks, savings, and other capital—we find it is distributed even less equally. The richest 20 percent of all Americans owns 76 percent of its wealth, whereas the bottom 20 percent owns only 0.2 percent of the wealth.[2]

To some people it is not enough to be wealthy; they must also *seem* wealthy. For these people, and this includes all of us to some extent, the symbols of success are important. People wear designer jeans, drive expensive cars, or insist on alligators on their shirts. Sociologist Thorstein Veblen[3] has termed this conspicuous consumption, or the desire for others to know and appreciate how much wealth, power, or prestige a person has. People attempt to shape the impressions that others have of them and their position through material symbols of the self.

Question:

Should There be Laws Restricting Inheritance From One Generation to the Next?

> There is a strange charm in the thoughts of a good legacy, or the hopes of an estate, which wondrously alleviates the sorrow that men would otherwise feel for the death of friends.—Miguel de Cervantes, *Don Quixote.*

As soon as the tide of grief subsides, one of the first questions that many people ask in the aftermath of the death of a loved one is, How much did he leave me. The amount left in a will is often seen as a final measure of affection from the deceased to those who survive. Although inheritances may produce cohesion in families and be related to a norm of reciprocity, according to sociologist Jeffrey Rosenfeld, they may also produce dissention, tension, and discord. It is common for families to be torn asunder by the careless or bitter will of a relative; in some inheritances only the lawyers are the real beneficiaries. Like many social processes, inheritance can have both functional and dysfunctional consequences for those who are a party to it.[4]

Basically there are four patterns of inheritance: First, the deceased may leave his whole estate to members of his family. This is called *familistic inheritance.* In our society spouses are named as beneficieries more often than children. A second type is *articulated inheritance.* In this case, non-kin ties are recognized in addition to family ties. In other wills of this type, money may be put into trusts from which heirs may eventually benefit. This process contributes to the development of American capital and the continued maintenance of the wealth of rich families. Endowments to organizations and other philanthropic gestures also fall under articulated inheritance. A third approach deliberately ignores kinship responsibilities. This, of course, is *disinheritance*. In such situations a person's estate is given to people or entities outside of the family. Finally, there is *escheat*. This occurs when someone dies without either will or family; the deceased expires in a state of social isolation. When this happens the resources revert to the state.

It is frequently said that two things are inevitable: death and taxes. They are not only inevitable, but often go together. The Roman Empire instituted inheritance taxes as a way to pay for its armies, but inheritance taxes have not always been levied. The United States had no such tax prior to the Stamp Act of 1797, and none after its repeal in 1802 until 1916 (with the exception of brief periods during the Civil War and the Spanish-American War). There have been state inheritance taxes throughout American history, and today all states except Nevada have such taxes.[5]

Too high an inheritance tax rate may actually lose revenue for the government. Consider what you would do if you had a million dollars and were told that you had six weeks to live. If the tax rate were 95 percent on inheritances, you would probably not leave much of that wealth to your children since the government would get the lion's share. You might try to avoid the inheritance law by giving gifts, by giving to charity, or by spending the money on yourself. If you chose to live your last six weeks on champagne and caviar, the inheritance tax would not work well as a revenue source. In this case, the government might make more money from a 30 percent rate than from a 95 percent rate. Of course, unless all the various loopholes are carefully closed, it is possible for the official or "nominal" tax rate to be much higher than the actual or "effective" tax rate (that portion of the estate the government receives).

For some people, the issue of how much revenue is collected is not relevant. The issue of inheritance is for them primarily a moral issue—that of insuring fairness. Inheritance taxes may be used for several quite distinct purposes.

Before addressing these issues, consider the importance of inheritance in American life. Does inheritance really make a difference? The answer depends on which category of the rich you examine. If you are interested in the "super-rich," inheritance is a significant factor in wealth transfer. In 1957 *Fortune* magazine studied the richest men in America. Of the seventy-six individuals with wealth in excess of $75 million, forty-one had been recipients of substantial inheritances.[6] Since that time about 50 percent of the names on subsequent lists of the richest people had received inherited fortunes.[7] Another study indicates that only the wealthiest Americans were likely to receive a substantial inheritance (57 percent of those who earned over $100,000 in 1962 received such bequests).[8] For all other income groups, the majority reported no inheritance whatsoever. A Brookings Institute study indicates that gifts and bequests account for at least half of the wealth of the rich.[9] Thus, inheritance does seem to play a role in the amassing of wealth for some families, but obviously not for Americans in general. Despite the considerable opportunities for class mobility, there is almost no opportunity to become one of the truly wealthy unless you have selected your parents with care.

What is the effect of inheriting money? There are two schools of thought about this—one uses the metaphor of "compound interest," the other that of the "gambler's ruin."[10] The first suggests that since the average investment is profitable, all one must do is keep investing one's money. Thus, fortunes continue to grow, posing a danger to equality, and perhaps a need for inheritance taxes. On the other hand, the "gambler's ruin" approach suggests that no one's luck can run forever, and sooner or later the fortune will decline. This is supposedly hastened by the foolishness and extravagance of the children of the wealthy: a group that can hardly be matched for the bad press it receives. As the folk saying goes: "Shirtsleeves to shirtsleeves in three generations." Still, all things considered, most people (though not all) if given the option, would prefer the challenge of keeping a fortune, rather than amassing it from scratch.

As for what inheritance does to the economy, economists disagree. Does inheritance prevent equality and lead to a skewed power structure, or does it lead to the amassing of capital, and, thus, the growth of the economy? To solve this conundrum, we need the legendary one-armed economist: someone who will not say, "But, on the other hand. . . . "

The Social Democratic Point of View

For the social democrat there is something basically unfair about inheritance—something that offends his or her sense of equality, that most basic of social virtues. Inherited wealth destroys equal opportunity. William Greenawalt voices a strong plea for Americans to make opportunity truly equal:

> This is a plea for Americanism; for the principles asserted in the Declaration of Independence; in the State and United States constitutions. It is a plea to put the game of life on the same highly respectable basis as a game of sport or a game of chance—as a foot race, a prize fight, or a game of cards. . . . Most Americans admire fair play and condemn an unfair advantage in any sport, and yet they fail to see that the most essential rules of games of sport are violated in the game of life. . . . No prize fighter would be allowed to enter a ring armed with a knife against an unarmed opponent, and no one with red blood in his veins would care to witness such a contest; yet, where the dollar is concerned, we are so lacking in sportsmanship as to allow one child to enter the game of life, heir to untold wealth, and another, heir to abject poverty.[11]

In a nation that believes in equal opportunity, inheritance may be hard to swallow. And yet, if we believe in equal opportunity, would we not also have to limit the amount that live parents spend on their children? Pushing the logic to its limits, what should we do about inherited traits? People do have different abilities and talents, but heredity, unlike inheritance, cannot be equalized.

When the social democrat criticizes inheritance he or she usually focuses on those who receive it, rather than those who give it. Often the inheritors are pictured as lazy or unworthy, particularly in comparison with most people in society who are not blessed with wealthy parents. Some people suggest that earning money is in itself virtuous. One multi-millionaire was reported to have said: "Too much money is an evil influence for a boy. . . . Money spoils more men than it makes. The inheritance of a great fortune is a bad thing."[12] America is seen as a land of opportunity to make a fortune, not to inherit one.

Because the social democrat sees inheritance as causing poverty for others, he or she also sees the necessity of a tax to try to equalize the situation. The assumption is that one person's wealth keeps another person in poverty; this should be eliminated, especially when it comes about through the "unjust shackles of the dead."

Having wealth laid in one's lap is objectionable for a number of reasons. Social democratic economist Lester Thurow in his "random-walk model" offers one cogent reason: "Under the random-walk model . . . the wealthy are not wealthy because their productive contribution is higher than others, but because they are luckier than others. For most people luck does not command the same respect as productive merit when it comes to determining whether or not individuals should be allowed to retain control over large aggregations of wealth."[13]

Government involvement poses no particular problem for the social democrat, because it will insure equality, the highest social virtue. But some people charge that the social democrat wishes to confiscate inherited wealth to prevent envy, and argue furthermore that inheritance is economically beneficial because it preserves capital for investment and does no one harm. Economist Kenneth Greene says these arguments ignore human psychology:

> If, in the presence of inheritance, those not receiving any inheritance feel worse off because of their envy of others, then one could argue that these people would be made bet-

ter off by confiscatory inheritance laws . . . Envy may often be generated by the belief that others possess something not possessed by oneself and for which the other individual has done nothing which has not also been done by oneself . . . .The neighbors on either side of one's house may display precisely the same material comforts. The one on the east, however, may have let it slip that dad had left a considerable trust fund. Feelings about their third car may be considerably more antagonistic. . . . The student of human capital and the behavioral psychologist may argue that such attitudes are irrational, that the ability to earn income by one's own efforts is no less inherited than a trust, but this does not mean that these attitudes do not exist.[14]

For the social democrats, restricting inheritance is a question of equality and fairness, which to their opponents translates into envy. Envy is the hope that no one has more than you have and a feeling of resentment when they do, whereas a desire for equality is a belief that everyone should at least have equal resources.

The Libertarian Point of View

While the social democrat focuses on those who receive inheritance, the libertarian looks at the generation that makes the bequest. The social democrat suggests that the dead give this money; the libertarian claims that this is true only in a technical sense. A living person wrote and signed the will, and it expresses a living person's choice; it is put into effect after a death. Thus, the libertarian argues that we are not morbidly discussing the rights of corpses, but rather the rights of a productive worker to make economic decisions for the future. Nathaniel Brandon, a close associate of author Ayn Rand, notes, " . . . the crucial right involved is not that of the heir but of the original *producer* of the wealth. The right of property is the right of use and disposal; just as the man who produces wealth has the right to use it and dispose of it in his lifetime, so he has the right to choose who shall be its recipient after his death."[15] The libertarian sees the recipient as secondary and accepts the notion of the "gambler's ruin" in that incompetent heirs can easily lose the wealth that has been left to them. For the libertarian wealth is potentially infinite. Wealth given to one does not prevent others from creating wealth for themselves.

From the libertarian perspective freedom is the key issue, along with its less attractive partner, greed. People should have the right to do what they wish provided it does not hurt another person directly. Gordon Tullock in justifying inheritance relies on the assumption that capital formation (as in large inheritances) does not hurt anyone, but gives to the benefactor freedom of choice. Tullock asks us to

> consider, then, some person who is now alive and realizes that he will die. Clearly, with the confiscatory inheritance tax, he would plan to leave no estate. Clearly, this person has been made worse off by the tax because he has lost one possible degree of freedom. Before the tax was enacted, he could have saved money and left it to his heirs if he wished, and after the tax he no longer can do so. This reduction in his freedom is not offset by any gain to anyone else in society.[16]

Tullock notes that if this tax is set too high, it may actually decrease revenues in that it discourages people from leaving inheritances that might have been left if taxed at a lower rate. Such an inheritance tax would only be justified as a moral concern, not as a means of revenue collection.

Finally, there is the libertarian argument that property is no different from other talents that might be inherited and that cannot be limited. Libertarian economist Milton Friedman puts the issue this way:

> Much of the moral fervor behind the drive for equality of outcome comes from the widespread belief that it is not fair that some children should have a great advantage over others simply because they happen to have wealthy parents. Of course it is not fair. However, unfairness takes many

forms. It can take the form of the inheritance of property, bonds and stocks, houses, factories; it can also take the form of the inheritance of talent—musical ability, strength, mathematical genius. The inheritance of property can be interfered with more readily than the inheritance of talents. But from an ethical point of view, is there any difference between the two?[17]

Libertarians do not deny that some people who inherit money make a botch of their lives (possibly *because* they inherited money), nor do they deny that inheriting wealth makes it easier for those children to remain wealthy. Yet these facts do not outweigh the freedom that is inherent in allowing people to do what they wish with their own property.

The Conservative Point of View

Conservatives, naturally, support the legitimacy of inheritance, even more vigorously than do libertarians. For the libertarian, inheritance is simply something that a person should have the right to give; for the conservative, inheritance makes moral and economic sense.

The conservative respects the orderly and stabilizing force that families have, and inheritance permits the stability of (wealthy) families, preserving moral virtues. Attorney George Alger in a 1924 article, wrote of limits on inheritance as "the new sting of death": "One of the great primary incentives to labor and to thrift is the prospect of being able to leave the savings of a lifetime to the family when the breadwinner passes on; and to continue support and protection after death."[18]

The idea of transferring wealth away from the family it came from is profoundly upsetting to conservatives. Economist Richard Wagner notes with dismay Plato's ill-starred plea for parents to be unaware of which children were theirs. Plato hoped that all parents would act and feel like a parent to all children. Wagner explains:

Aristotle, with a firmer understanding of human nature, both its possibilities and its limitations, noted in his *Politics* that such a practice would merely result in all parents' acting with equal indifference toward all children. . . . The responsibility of one parent for all children and the absence of particular responsibility for any individual child would produce universal indifference, as Aristotle detected, not universal love, as Plato hoped. An extension of the Platonic idea would support the taxation of bequests, with the ultimate objective being to socialize or to prevent them. Parents would leave wealth not to particular children, but to all children. The Artistotelian perspective suggests the tragic dimensions of this policy: the present generation would transmit little wealth to the next.[19]

One of the major groups that is fighting to decrease inheritance taxes is named the National Committee to Preserve the Family Business, a name indicating their concern with preserving the status of the (wealthy) family. As the spokesman for one family-owned business (worth some $20 million) told a Senate committee recently: "For a family that wishes to maintain a certain unity and which is proud of its achievements, the implications are not only financially momentous, but emotionally traumatic as well."[20]

Conservatives further argue that inheritance is valuable for the society as a whole. A society that did not value capital formation and saving (reflected in low taxes on inheritance) would be worse off than a society that did—at least in the long-run. Wagner proclaims that there is survival value in permitting inheritance:

> Without inheritance, characteristics compatible with the accumulation of wealth would have less survival value in our society relative to such characteristics as pleasing superiors, scoring well on examination, and appearing personable in public. . . . Yet in a free-enterprise economy, those who have become relatively wealthy are to a considerable extent those who have been relatively more successful in producing services valued highly by other people. . . . The characteristic of providing valuable services to others has

higher survival value in a social order that permits inheritance than in one that does not, and it would seem quite important to promote the survival of this characteristic rather than to promote its extinction.[21]

This is essentially a social Darwinist argument, emphasizing the economic survival of the fittest. From this point of view, a social order which does not promote those traits that it needs to survive, surely will not survive. In short, capital accumulation is related to the nation's productivity. While some economists suggest that this is not necessarily the case,[22] it is an article of faith of the conservative capitalist who accepts the legitimacy of the class system.

Wills and Social Research

Although wills have not been used as much as they might be to understand family dynamics and wealth transfer,[23] one recent study focused on their sociological implications. Although Jeffrey Rosenfeld's book, *The Legacy of Aging*, does not explicitly address the moral virtue or economic cost of laws restricting inheritance, his is the most detailed sociological treatment of this topic.

Rosenfeld's interest in the topic was piqued, as is the case for much sociological research, by a personal experience. Rosenfeld's wealthy bachelor uncle passed away shortly before he was to be married. This death threw the family into an emotional crisis. Had Uncle Julius left his estate to his fiancee? What could be done to keep his wealth within the "family?" When his will was probated, these fears were for nought. The wealth stayed in the family. Yet Uncle Julius's will was not without its surprises. For example, he left his sociologist-nephew a portion of his estate, while some other nephews received nothing. A unified family was brought to the edge of conflict. Wills, Rosenfeld observes, can have severe repercussions on family relations.

As noted earlier, Rosenfeld distinguishes among four types of inheritance: familistic, articulated, disinherited, and escheat. He was curious to learn how different settings of old age affect the type of bequest. To explore this, Rosenfeld selected three "communities" on New York's Long Island: a retirement community (Golden Village), a hospital specializing in long-term geriatric health care (Brookdale), and an oceanside community in which the elderly were relatively integrated with their families (Beachside).

To examine this question, Rosenfeld coded the contents of 226 wills of people sixty-five years of age and older who resided in one of the three communities and who died between 1967 and 1971. Because this was archival research, Rosenfeld did not interview the elderly who made wills to find out why they did what they did, nor did he interview the lawyers who had helped the elderly complete wills or the recipients who had received the inheritance. By examining the wills filed in Surrogate's Court, Rosenfeld has an "objective" record of what these people wrote. What he does not know is *why* they wrote it. Motivation can only be glimpsed at through an occasional comment. Although this archival analysis has the advantage of providing systematic evidence (especially systematic evidence about the past), it does not permit an interactionist understanding of the writer's position as it was experienced.

Rosenfeld discovered that in Beachside, where the elderly were more integrated with their families, over 70 percent left everything to their kin, as compared to nearly 60 percent in Brookdale Hospital, and less than 50 percent in the Golden Village retirement community. Apparently the existence of a strong peer-community at Golden Village was sufficient to weaken the inheritance ties to one's family, although no one in this group disinherited their families. Within such a community there was more likely to be "articulated inheritance"— inheritance to those outside the family circle as well as to those within it. Apparently the elderly were making conscious choices about whom they wished to thank, rather than simply relying on custom.

Both disinheritance and escheat were found most commonly in the geriatric nursing facility, Brookdale, and was particularly common among those with relatively small estates. These individuals were presumably more likely than those in the other subsample to be cut off from their families and without social support. In some cases, the elderly left their estates to the hospital; in other cases, they simply did not leave a will. Since these people were the least well off, it might be suspected that members of their families felt, coldly perhaps, that there was little to be gained in maintaining family ties or in befriending them. Rosenfeld speculates that as more elderly are put into nursing homes and other hospital facilities, the number of disinheritances and escheats may increase, although this would only seem to apply to those without many resources.

This research does not have any direct implications for inheritance taxes, but it does indirectly suggest that preventing inheritance is harmful. Although Rosenfeld points to the conflict that may be caused by wills, they are also a means by which the elderly can maintain some power in their relationships. The fact that those without many resources leave money outside the family or to the state, suggests the possibility that although blood is thicker than water, cash is thicker than both. A state that removes this incentive might weaken family relations, a point that is congruent with conservative thought. Wills are functional for the elderly in binding their kin to them. This assumption is only implicit from Rosenfeld's archival data because we do not know the specifics of the deceased's family relations, but some functional implications are present.

Stratification and Inheritance

Inheritance combines the sociologist's concern about the equitable distribution of material rewards with the importance of family ties. The disagreement between the conservative and the social democrat is a disagreement between those who support the primacy of the family (and, thus, tradition) and those who think that equality and equal opportunity are more important. The libertarian's focus on the rights of the property owner to distribute his property reflects a traditional concern with freedom.

It is a matter of philosophical judgement as to what kind of society one prefers—one with sharp class distinctions or one in which these distinctions are blunted as much as possible. As I mentioned at the beginning of this chapter, some societies are sharply hierarchical, the extreme being societies with systems that assign people at birth to social positions they cannot leave. Other societies strive for classlessness in which all are equal. Still other societies allow for considerable social mobility between economic classes—a person can move up or down the scale.

The caste society is, at least in theory, highly stable and orderly. People know where they stand, and if socialization has been successful, they should be satisfied with their lot in life. The danger is that at some point in this "Brave New World", the lower castes will learn how poorly they are being treated and will rise up in revolt.

The classless society enforces equality, but in so doing, may eliminate motivation to do better. The desire to avoid poverty may fuel the productivity of capitalism. If individuals do not have an internal motivation to work, then a classless society does not work well.

The socially mobile society seems to have the best of both worlds: motivating people to succeed, while eliminating unfair hurdles. In such a system, however, opportunity has replaced stability. The world becomes a battleground for each individual; it is a world of total, and brutal, competition. It is a society of successes and failures. In the other social systems you can attribute your social and economic position to external forces, in the mobile society, it is up to you.

These three societies, although extreme types, represent ways in which a social order might arrange for rewards to be distributed. Inheritance adds a twist to this distribution in that it brings kinship connections into the equation. Should family ties be one means of wealth transfer in a society? The conservative, who is enamoured of the positive role of the family, says that in-heritance is an important means of holding families together. Money provides a cement between generations. Parents *do* work hard in order to provide the best lives for their children; they may even sacrifice what they really want and need for the sake of their children. The social democrat points out this would be fine if all families had equal opportunities, but some families oppress other families in order to gain or maintain their wealth. It is one thing for us to let every individual succeed on the basis of merit, it is quite another to let superior financial resources slop over from generation to generation. The social democrat believes that in such a situation the government may be a more responsible dispenser of a family's revenue than members of the family itself. Only the libertarian would argue there is a right to inheritance; the others frame the issue as either financially wise or morally unwise. Even though the transfer of funds from gen-eration to generation may be of questionable fairness, it is the rare child who requests that he or she be disinherited in the name of his or her less fortunate peers.

Questions

1. Should inheritance be permitted between generations?

2. Should family businesses be saved through changes in in-heritance laws?

3. Should the dying have the right to leave their property to whomever they choose?

4. Should spouses be allowed to receive inheritances tax-free? Should children?

5. Would confiscating wealth destroy capital formation and saving?

6. If you made a will now, who would you leave your property to? Why?

7. Is inheritance fair to poor families?

8. Is inheritance a gift from the dead or a decision made by the living?

9. What would a society in which there was no inheritance be like in terms of spending?

10. Is the inheritance of property and money the same as the inheritance of talent?

For Further Study

Chester, Ronald. *Inheritance, Wealth, and Society.* Bloomington: Indiana University Press, 1982.

Friedman, Lawrence M. "The Law of the Living, The Law of the Dead: Property, Succession, and Society," *Wisconsin Law Review* 1966(1966): 340–378.

Friedman, Milton and Rose. *Free to Choose: A Personal Statement.* New York: Harcourt Brace Jovanovich, 1980.

Rosenfeld, Jeffrey. *The Legacy of Aging: Inheritance and Disinheritance in Social Perspective.* Norwood, New Jersey: Ablex, 1979.

Thurow, Lester C. *Generating Inequality: Mechanisms of Distribution in the U.S. Economy.* New York: Basic Books, 1975.

Tullock, Gordon. "Inheritance Justified," *Journal of Law and Economics* 14 (1971): 465–474.

Wagner, Richard E. *Inheritance and the State: Tax Principles for a Free and Prosperous Commonwealth.* Washington, D.C.: American Enterprise Institute, 1977.

Notes and References

1. U.S. Bureau of the Census, *Current Population Reports*, series P-60, No. 140, reported in U.S. Department of Commerce, *Statistical Abstracts of the United States 1984*. (Washington, D.C.: Dept. of Commerce, 1984), p. 465.

2. Executive Office of the President, Office of Management and the Budget, *Social Indicators, 1973* (Washington, D.C.: U.S. Government Printing Office, 1973). p. 182.

3. Thorstein Veblen, *The Theory of the Leisure Class* (New York: The Macmillan Co., 1899).

4. Jeffrey Rosenfeld, *The Legacy of Aging* (Norwood, New Jersey: Ablex, 1979), pp. 3–4.

5. Richard E. Wagner, *Inheritance and the State* (Washington, D.C.: American Enterprise Institute, 1977), p. 1.

6. Richard Austin Smith, "The Fifty-Million Dollar Man," *Fortune* November 1957, p. 176.

7. Lester Thurow, *Generating Inequality* (New York: Basic Books, 1975), p. 130.

8. Dorothy Projector and Gertrude Weiss, *Survey of Financial Characteristics of Consumers*, Federal Reserve Technical Paper (Washington, D.C.: Government Printing Office, 1966), p. 148.

9. Cited in Michael Kinsley, "High on the Hog III: Triumph of the Will," *New Republic*, August 22 & 29, 1981, p. 18.

10. *Ibid*, p. 18.

11. William Greenawalt, *What Democracy Must Do To Be Saved* (Denver: Bowen, 1934), pp. 1, 4.

12. George W. Alger, "The New Sting of Death: On Limiting Inheritance," *Atlantic*, March 1924, p. 297.

13. Thurow, *op. cit.*, p. 197.

14. Kenneth V. Greene, "Inheritance Unjustified?" *Journal of Law and Economics* 16 (1973): 417–419.

15. Nathaniel Brandon, "Common Fallacies About Capitalism," *Capitalism: The Unknown Ideal*, Edited by Ayn Rand (New York: New American Library, 1966), p. 85

16. Gordon Tullock, "Inheritance Justified," *Journal of Law and Economics* 14 (1971): 471.

17. Milton and Rose Friedman, *Free to Choose* (New York: Harcourt Brace Jovanovich, 1980), p. 136

18. Alger, *op. cit.*, p. 291.

19. Wagner, *op. cit.*, pp. 20–21.

20. Kinsley, *op. cit.*, p. 17.

21. Wagner, *op. cit.*, p. 84.

22. Paul L. Menchik, "The Importance of Material Inheritance: The Financial Link Between Generations," *Modeling the Distribution and Intergenerational Transmission of Wealth,* Edited by James D. Smith (Chicago: University of Chicago Press, 1980), p. 180.

23. Clifton D. Bryant and William E. Snizek, "The Last Will and Testament: A Neglected Document in Sociological Research," *Sociology and Social Research* 59 (1975): 219–230.

 **Six**

Religion: Should Religious Property Be Taxed?

CYNICS OFTEN PROCLAIM that man made God in his own image. From this sociological insight, it should not be a surprise that in Western societies God has traditionally been pictured as a powerful, adult, white male. Since no one has seen Him, this belief has come from the popular imagination and from secondary sources such as the *Holy Bible,* the *Book of Mormon,* and the *Koran.*

Religion poses problems for the modern social scientist because it is impossible to *prove* the truth of a religious belief. Religious beliefs rest on faith, and social science requires the testing of assumptions that might otherwise be accepted without proof. For this reason, sociologists refrain from attempting to determine the accuracy of religious beliefs.

Nevertheless, sociologists do recognize that religion is an important social institution. Among the key components of religion that concern social scientists are the following:

1) Religion deals with issues of life and death, providing

answers to questions about where the individual stands in the universe.

2) Religion provides rules for what individuals should do and what will happen should they break these rules.

3) Religion provides a set of beliefs for adherents and a set of rituals by which they can express those beliefs.

4) A religion has a community of believers—a social group that shares beliefs, values, and customs.

Sociologists distinguish between two types of religious organizations: *churches* (or denominations) and *sects*. Churches include the larger, wealthier, more established denominations, such as, Episcopalian, Methodist, Lutheran, and Roman Catholic. These denominations are large organizations with an extensive hierarchy open to dealing with the secular world in a flexible way; they are willing to tolerate others who disagree, recognize the inevitability of popular vices, and believe, for the most part, that scripture is to be accepted metaphorically. Recruitment to a church is likely to occur at birth; that is, a person is born into a family that belongs to a church. In contrast, a sect is typically a small group, maintaining a set of beliefs that differ considerably from mainstream churches; often these beliefs include a literal interpretation of the Bible and rigid ethical restrictions. Typically, believers reject the views of others, and require people to be converted (that is, consciously and voluntarily accept the beliefs) before being accepted. Unlike churches, sects typically do not have formal hierarchies; ministers are selected from among the congregation. Many Pentacostal churches have the characteristics of sects. Between sects and churches fall institutionalized sects; these groups have some of the characteristics of each, and include religious groups such as the Mormons or Southern Baptists.

A crucial issue that dates back to the early years of sociology is the role of religion in a community. Emile Durkheim,[1] the prominent French sociologist writing in the early twentieth century, argues that religion is universal because it is necessary for the continued existence of society. A society's values and beliefs are reaffirmed through a shared religion. Furthermore, religious institutions socialize people into the beliefs of the society. Religion, thus, promotes unity and consensus within a society; it matters little what the specifics of that religion are.

Other social theorists, such as Karl Marx, viewed the consensus caused by religion as undesirable. Religion is, for Marx, "the opiate of the masses" because it blinds them to their "true" condition, which is oppression. Religion tends to prevent change by making existing social arrangements seem right and proper. The structure of society is given religious sanction, even when that society is doing evil things. We know that religions have, on occasion, supported wars, prejudice, or even slavery. Religion may teach people that they should meekly accept their lot in life ("The meek shall inherit the earth"), ignoring the fact that their lot may be unjust. For social conflict theorists, religion may stand in the way of progress and social justice, despite the fact some religious leaders do fight actively for social change.

One of the most remarkable features of religion in America is its almost total separation from government. The First Amendment to the Constitution enforces considerable distance between church and state. Yet there *is* a relationship between religion and government in the United States; it is just not in the usual sense of the state annointing a particular church. Rather, it is what sociologist Robert Bellah terms *civil religion.*[2] This paradoxical phrase refers to the generic religion that is sanctioned and endorsed by the government. Although the government is supposed to be entirely separate from establishments of religion, it stamps "In God we trust" on coins, citizens recite "one nation, under God" in the Pledge of Allegiance, and most legislatures begin each session with a prayer (an act illegal in public schools). The key to understanding the acceptability of the civil religion is that it does not refer to any specific religion. The god of the civil religion is non-sectarian and appeals to most Americans. Among the key elements of this civil religion are: 1) the belief that God has a special destiny for the American nation, 2) the belief that citizens should work within the system to make whatever changes seem desirable and not rely on revolutionary violence, and 3) Americans should share moral principles, including freedom, faith, and equality. These beliefs are so general that virtually anyone with a belief in a supernatural power could accept them without offending their fellow citizens. The existence of the civil religion may have eliminated some need for the traditional, mainline denominations (for example, the Episcopalian, Methodist, Presbyterian churches) which, along with church attendance, have declined in recent years. Although over 90 percent claim to believe in God,[3] Americans do not take their religion as a matter of life and death, as is true in Iran, Lebanon, or Northern Ireland.

Question:

Should Religious Property Be Taxed?

> We also notify you that it shall not be lawful to impose tribute, custom or toll upon any one of the priests, the Levites, the singers, the doorkeepers, the temple servants, or other servants of this house of God.—*Ezra* 7:24

Perhaps it is not surprising that there is biblical authority for tax exemptions for churches. From the establishment of Christianity as the official state religion of the Roman Empire by Emperor Constantine I, churches have received special treatment at the hands of the taxman. With very few exceptions, church property has been exempt from taxation in the United States, and most Americans agree that this is fair and just. In a mid-1960s Gallup Poll 77 percent of the respondents said that church property used for religious purposes should be excluded from taxation.[4]

Aside from this majority opinion, there has been some sentiment in the United States for taxation. The state of Virginia taxed church property until 1840. Presidents James Madison and Ulysses S. Grant publically declared their support for taxation of churches. Even some churchmen have supported taxation of religious property in the interest of fairness.

Non-taxable property makes up a significant portion of our

tax rolls. As of 1983 there were 851,000 non-profit organizations in the United States. Of the fifty billion dollars given to charity, 46 percent of it went to church-related organizations.[5] In 1974–5, it was estimated that there was $814 billion dollars worth of tax-exempt real estate in the United States; about $118 billion was religiously exempt property (approximately evenly split between Protestants and Catholics). Assuming an average tax of 3.5 percent, the elimination of this tax exemption on religious property would bring in approximately $4 billion (undoubtedly considerably higher by now) in revenue. The estimated direct and indirect cost of church privileges came to $10 billion in 1975.[6] Regardless of whether these figures are too high or too low, it cannot be denied that the elimination of church tax exemptions would raise considerable revenue.

What does the Constitution say about this issue? The First Amendment to the Constitution reads, in part, as follows: "Congress shall make no law respecting an establishment of religion, or prohibiting the free exercise thereof." Since 1940, this passage has also been extended to the states. The first clause is known among legal scholars as the "establishment clause;" the second as the "free exercise clause"—neither one provides a clear answer to the question of taxation. Would a law that taxed churches be a law "respecting an establishment of religion?" Would a law that exempted churches be the same?

In the 1947 case of *Everson v. Board of Education*, Justice Hugo Black writing for the Supreme Court majority notes:

> Neither a state nor the Federal government can set up a church. Neither can pass laws which aid one religion, aid all religions, or prefer one religion over another. Neither can force nor influence a person to go to or remain away from church against his will or force him to profess a belief or disbelief in any religion. No person can be punished for entertaining or professing religious beliefs or disbeliefs, for church attendance or non-attendance. No tax in any amount, large or small, can be levied to support any religious activities or institutions, whatever they may be called, or whatever form they may adopt to teach or practice religion. Neither a state nor the Federal government

can, openly or secretly, participate in the affairs of any religious organization or groups and vice versa. In the words of Jefferson, the clause against establishment of religion by law was intended to erect "a wall of separation between church and state.[7]

Clearly, this was not intended to mean that there could be absolutely no contact between church and state. No one would argue, for instance, that city fire departments should allow churches to burn down. It seems reasonable for the police to provide traffic guards at crossings used by parochial school children. The government pays medicare funds to church-owned hospitals. The wall is not without its chinks. Still, there is disagreement on the size of those chinks. Legal scholars fall into two categories: the accommodationists and the separationists. The accommodationists believe the state should try to accommodate the needs of the churches in an even-handed, neutral way. The separationists believe the government should, as much as possible, attempt to avoid any kind of direct or indirect connection with religious institutions. Those who wish to provide tax credits for parents of parochial school children are among the first group, whereas those who wish to ban Christmas decorations from government buildings are among the second.

With regard to the issue of taxation of church land, the U.S. Supreme Court decided in the 1970 case of *Walz v. Tax Commission of the City of New York* that tax exemptions for religious property did not violate the Constitution. Chief Justice Warren Burger (in a 7-1 decision) ruled that the exemptions for religious organizations constituted only a minimal and remote involvement between church and state and, in his view, constituted less of an involvement than would the taxation of churches.

There are some limitations on the ability of churches to avoid taxation. At one time churches could run competitive businesses tax-free. That was changed with the Tax Reform Act of 1969. However, there remains a certain gray area as to when the use of a church is secular and when religious. Robert Schuller's Crystal Cathedral is often used for secular concerts, for example. Does that church use constitute a competitive business? The Internal Revenue Service claims it does. Churches are also not supposed to get involved in politics to any significant degree, but what constitutes a significant degree has never been fully specified. In at least one major case, the Court of Appeals ruled that conservative, anti-Communist preacher Billy James Hargis's Christian Echoes National Ministry did not qualify for tax deductions because of its lobbying. Finally, despite what you may have read, not anyone can turn his home into a church, simply by becoming a mail-order minister. Most such cases are decided in favor of the Internal Revenue Service, and may result in large penalties for the homeowner-cum-minister. Forget the idea of setting up the Church of the Holy Sociologist. Although the boundaries of what constitute a church are not precise, those over the boundary are likely to suffer the consequences of the noncollective nature of their beliefs.

The Conservative Point of View

The conservative believes that the church is the cornerstone of society, and that no action of the government should undercut its strength. A strong society is one that has a strong moral system and religious heritage. In 1906 President Charles W. Eliot of Harvard University extolled the value of separating morality from the taxman by noting: "The things that make it worthwhile to live in Massachusetts, to live anywhere in the civilized world, are precisely the things which are not taxed."[8] Or as one minister asked a wealthy man who refused to contribute money for a new church: "What was the real estate worth in Sodom?"[9]

Generally speaking, conservative support for tax exemption falls under what is called the "quid pro quo" theory. The church does something for the government and the government does something for the church. The church helps provide for the malnourished and homeless, and teaches moral virtues. The government in turn does not tax the church. John Godfrey Saxe, a prominent New York attorney, comments that the justification for tax exemption for churches, colleges, hospitals and similar institutions

. . . is that their service is a public service and, therefore, the people, through their government, cooperate to the extent of a limited tax exemption, in maintaining these public-service institutions in the field of liberty. The reason of this public policy is apparent. The principle has been accepted as axiomatic that *private* property necessary to the essential support of government ought not to be the subject of taxation. . . . It is based primarily on the theory of the general benefit resulting from an increase of religious, educational or charitable uses. . . . To tax such property would tend to destroy the life which produces a constant increase of taxable property as well as other benefits infinitely more valuable.[10]

Besides charitable work, the conservative would point to the church's role as the protector of a moral society. Although some cynics might scoff at the beneficial power that churches have over their congregations, for conservatives this is a very real feature of religion. It has been seriously suggested that without churches we would have to spend more money on law enforcement.[11] Dean Kelley, a leading advocate of religious tax exemption, contends.

religion is entitled to special civil treatment, not just because it deals with the most intense and sensitive commitments of the human heart, but also because it performs a special function in society—one that is of secular importance to everyone—and its special treatment is the best way of insuring that that function is performed. The provisions made in American law for protecting freedom of religion are not just a matter of sentimentally indulging those individuals who are quaintly disposed to such archaic behavior, but a very sensible, hard-headed, present-day way of trying to make available to those who need it, in as many forms and varieties as possible, the crucial ingredient for their lives that religion provides. . . . What each religion is doing for its adherents—regardless of what shape "salvation" takes within it, or what deity or deities it calls upon (if any)—is to help them to "make sense" of life, especially their own lives which are both unsatisfactory and

unalterable: failure, handicap, defeat, loss, illness, be-
reavement, and the prospect of their own death.[12]

Of course, the approximately 60 percent of the population who
do not attend church during any given week might disagree
about the need to exempt organized religion, and the approximately 6 percent of Americans who profess to disbelieve in God,
might be even more passionate in rejecting this argument.[13]

Conservatives also believe tax exemption provides for a
separation of church and state, in that it removes religion from
the sometimes heavy-handed reach of the Internal Revenue
Service. This, says the conservative, constitutes a clear separation of church from the control of government. Since the church
is of more significance than the state in the mind of the conservative, this separation is important. The conservative is less concerned with the government acting like a church, supporting,
for example, prayer in school, than for the church to aid the government in providing tax revenues, which may lead to government intervention in the affairs of religion. As Supreme Court
Chief Justice John Marshall observed: "The power to tax involves the power to destroy."[14] And Supreme Court Justice
Brennan states in the Walz tax decision, "The symbolism of tax
exemption is significant as a manifestation that organized religion is not expected to support the state; by the same token the
state is not expected to support the church."[15] By separation of
church and state the conservative means that the church should
be separate from the state but the state not always separate from
the church.

The Libertarian Point of View

The libertarian believes in a total separation of church and state,
just as he or she believes in a total separation of the state from
almost every aspect of society. The 1980 Libertarian party platform presented the issue of religious tax exemptions in a rather
extreme light: "In order to defend religious freedom, we advo-

cate a strict separation of church and state. We oppose government actions which either aid or attack any religion. We oppose taxation of church property for the same reason that we oppose all taxation."[16] Implicit in this statement is the assumption that if there is to be taxation of any property, religious property should be treated like any other piece of land.

The libertarian believes tax exemption provides a benefit to churches just as certainly as if they were given a direct cash handout. Hope Eastman, a lawyer who opposes exemptions for churches, strongly proclaims that such tax breaks do aid churches.

> Contrary to what many people think, a tax exemption *does* afford an economic benefit to a religious institution. It is not a direct benefit in the sense that a taxpayer's money is taken and transferred to a church, in the manner of subsidy. However, to the extent that a religious institution is free from the tax-paying burden, imposed on all kinds of other institutions and, as a result, has that extra money to spend on its own functions, it has received a benefit—a government benefit conferred on a religious institution.[17]

Note the difference between this view and that of the conservative's "quid pro quo" theory. The libertarian believes that religious tax exemption *costs* citizens money. The conservative, on the other hand, believes that for this subsidy, citizens are receiving something in return. The libertarian objects in principle to the fact that the non-religious are forced to support a church. Even if the church provides benefits, these benefits are given within the context of the establishment of religion. Whether or not a person attends a church, tax exemption forces him or her to support it. Supreme Court Justice William O. Douglas in his dissent in the Walz case makes a cogent argument in defense of the nonbeliever.

> The question in the case, therefore, is whether believers— organized in church groups—can be made exempt from

real estate taxes merely because they are believers, while nonbelievers, whether organized or not, must pay the real estate tax. . . . A believer and nonbeliever under the present law are treated differently because of the articles of their faith. Believers are doubtless comforted that the cause of religion is being fostered by this legislation. Yet one of the mandates of the First Amendment is to promote a viable, pluralistic society and to keep government neutral, not only between sects, but also between believers and nonbelievers.[18]

Ultimately for the libertarian, the church is a player in the great capitalist economy. If it can survive by itself, fine; the church deserves to survive. But libertarian theory does not believe that a church, like any other economic organization, deserves to survive through a subsidy. *Nation* magazine asked the question in 1929: "Would the taxation of churches be an ecclesiastical disaster? We think not. Hundreds of half-used churches would be closed if their members were compelled to pay taxes upon them, but the gains in efficiency and vigor among the remaining churches probably would outbalance that loss. Denominations divided by petty quarreling would be forced to unite or die."[19] This perspective suggests that churches follow the same law of supply and demand as do other business ventures.

Finally, libertarians note that churches use taxpayers' money and should pay their fair share of the services they use. Churches need sewers, street cleaning and upkeep, and police and fire services. These services are provided to them without their giving anything in return. Although some churches have contributed token "conscience money" toward payment for services, most are willing to accept the benefits of receiving something for nothing. Even though it is not immediately apparent whether a church's "fair share" should be based on how much they use or how much they can afford to pay, libertarians argue that there is no doubt that a fair social order would require churches to contribute to the same extent as other citizens and businesses. If the church had no special standing, it would clearly be separated from the state.

The Social Democratic Point of View

Like the libertarian, the social democrat gives no special place to religion in the construction of a social order. Yet, unlike the libertarian, whose primary concern is freedom, the social democrat's concern is justice. Of course, like most members of the American public, many social democratic politicians support tax exemption as a practical matter of separation of church and state. Yet there is something about the arrangement that troubles many social democrats.

Churches, when viewed as a group, are wealthy; and yet, many churches seem more concerned with amassing wealth than with helping the needy. This is compounded by the fact that few churches publish detailed accounts of their holdings, so it is difficult to determine how much a church owns. The image of church wealth can be quite disconcerting. In an article in *Look* magazine, author Kenneth Gross describes a scene in front of a church. "One August afternoon, a green truck parked outside St. Patrick's Cathedral in Manhattan. While two armed men kept a hair-trigger vigil, another heavily armed pair loaded the armored car with sacks of cash: Sabbath receipts for deposit in secret bank accounts."[20] Any organization with so much wealth and so little public accountability will inevitably raise suspicion, even if their actions are scrupulously moral. Not surprisingly, churches have been accused of a variety of sins. One Michigan state representative accused churches of being slum landlords.[21] Certain churches are, by every reasonable measure, big businesses.

These issues become more complicated when churches become involved in important social issues. When the Boston Archbishop warned his parishoners not to vote for two House candidates who supported abortion, the National Abortion Rights Action League threatened to seek repeal of the archdiocese tax exemption.[22] Civil rights issues have been particularly thorny in this respect. According to David Alpern and Howard Fineman, authors of an article in *Newsweek* concerning taxes and the church, a "proposal has been made that tax-exempt privileges be withdrawn from those churches which will not integrate their congregations. The argument is that exemption, based upon the expectation of mutual services rendered, is voided if the governmental policy and legal requirements of impartiality among races are not respected."[23] From this point of view, there are some moral issues that are of such overriding social significance that the rights of any given church pales beside them. Although no church has lost its tax exemption because of its social policies, some religious schools have. In 1983 the Supreme Court, in the case of *Bob Jones University v.United States*, ruled by a vote of 8-1 that Bob Jones University *can* practice racial discrimination (prohibiting interracial dating), but it is not entitled to federal tax benefits if it does. The Court felt that there are certain policies that are so compelling that the government can rightfully penalize a religious institution. While many greeted the decision with pleasure, approving of the government's action to take whatever steps necessary to fight racism, others wondered if this might also be extended to the social policies of churches that the state finds objectionable. For example, could the Catholic Church find its tax exemptions revoked because women are not allowed to be priests? Once the wall of separation between church and state has been breached, can it ever be healed? However, such reasoning is not particularly troubling to many social democrats because each social issue is a separate case, and *some* social issues *are* worthy of government intervention.

Ultimately, the issue is state over private control. The social democrat points to the role of the state in insuring justice for all of its citizens and argues that decisions of public welfare can best be made by the representatives of the people. Lucy W. Killough, for example, wonders whether morality should be financially supported by government aid to a select group of institutions. She comments, "Who knows whether the increase in public morality due to a stained glass window is more or less desirable than the community benefits of a snow plow? If the promotion of morality is ground for tax exemption, it might be wise to exempt the home."[24] The *"quid pro quo"* argument does not hold weight for social democrats because they feel all welfare services should be financed and administered by the state. Ultimately the state is responsible for insuring that these welfare services are provided in a just and equal manner. The attitude toward government takeover of private charity is a reflection, in part, of how much someone trusts the state.

Religious Fund Raising and Social Research

Conducting research on the financial structure of religious groups is nearly impossible. Most religions feel an obligation to shield their economic status from the public—perhaps out of a desire to keep the barrier between church and state strong; perhaps from a desire to hide from the public how wealthy they really are. We know almost nothing about the wealth and fund-raising techniques of our major religions. Many of the "new" religions are slightly more penetrable—not in terms of the total amount they earn, but in how they make it. Paraphrasing a stock brokerage advertisement, these religions make money the "old fashioned" way—they solicit handouts on the street.

David Bromley and Anson Shupe, two Texas sociologists, spent two years in the late 1970s studying the Unification Church in the Dallas-Fort Worth area. By using participant observation and in-depth interviewing techniques and researching what others have written about the church, they attempt to answer the question of how "new" religions (particularly the Unification Church and the Hare Krishnas) finance themselves.[25] While these groups have somewhat unsavory reputations, they both own considerable property. The Unification Church owns a number of large businesses as well. The hostility toward Reverend Sun Myung Moon's Unification Church is particularly intense, leading otherwise tolerant Americans who would never consider using offensive epithets when talking about Jews, Catholics or Protestants to call members of the Unification Church "moonies." Bromley and Shupe suggest that this hostility, which has made the church a whipping boy, is derived from: 1) its radical reformulation of Christianity, which alienates conservatives, 2) its anti-Communist and cold-war ideology, which angers social democrats, and 3) its requirement that individuals give up their personal life for a life in the Church, which troubles libertarians and others who believe in the sanctity of the individual.[26]

Since Bromley and Shupe are interested in the question of how these religions finance themselves, they are essentially asking a "functional" question—that is, how is activity organized so as to permit the continuation of the religion? They openly observed and interviewed members of the Unification Church in an attempt to understand their organizational perspective. The study implicitly supports the right of the organization to exist and to earn money, but it ignores the issues of whether these organizations should behave as they do, or whether they should be taxed. Also, by looking into the techniques that church solicitors use to gain support in face-to-face contact with the public, the study has an interactionist flavor.

The theoretical model that explains the fund-raising techniques of these new religions is "resource mobilization" (also discussed in chapter 9 on social movements). This approach focuses on how organizations mobilize the resources—material and human—available to them in order to achieve their goals. New religions, such as the Unification Church, have one major advantage: the time and enthusiasm of their members. Members are totally committed to their religion, and so the church has no labor costs, other than what it costs to provide for their expenses. Believers approach the general public and try to get contributions, either directly or indirectly. For example, they say they are collecting money for a "worthy" cause without mentioning who is sponsoring that cause. Members are convinced that religious fundraising is a profoundly moral and devout activity. "Fund raising" says one believer, "is probably the most amazing way to know God. It is not salesmanship or personality that brings in contributions—it is God. Hence, fund-raising is successful when God is there and not when He is gone."[27] The Reverend Moon points out that the inscription "In God We

Trust" on U.S. currency means that our cash ultimately belongs to the divine. Even if one needs to lie or shade the truth to get a contribution, this need not be a sin, since you are really helping people by doing it. This is a particularly sensitive issue because outsiders might refuse to contribute to the Unification Church if they were not deceived or pressured.

According to Bromley and Shupe, fund-raising of new religions is successful because

> (1) it is made a central component of the member role and so can justifiably occupy a major share of each member's time and energy; (2) it is made *congruent* with the movement's ideology and the communal group structure in such a way that the intense moral commitment generated in such groups is displaced into fund-raising activities; and (3) the ideology self-accorded special status of the movement allows members to neutralize any normative constraints which might otherwise restrict their maneuvers.[28]

Bromley and Shupe estimate each fund-raiser can contact 120 people (two each minute) in one hour. If only one in six contributed, say, an average of $.50 (perhaps just to be left alone), this would be $100 in a ten-hour day. If we assume 1,000 solicitors work fifty, five-day, weeks a year, this raises twenty-five million *tax free* dollars. With low labor and overhead costs, this is quite a pile of dollars.[29] This allows the Unification Church to buy businesses and will perhaps lead to income-generation and fund-raising more in line with traditional churches.

Bromley and Shupe do not take any political stance in this article, but by portraying these new religions as operating within the constraints of their resources, as traditional religions do, they seem to provide *implicit* support for a hands-off approach. New religions do differ from traditional religions, but these differences may be primarily a consequence of different resources available to them. If one has poor "parishioners," one needs to go outside the flock for support. Certainly there is no suggestion here that these new religions should be subject to laws different in scope from religions which were once new but are now traditional.

Religion and Tax Exemption

In some ways, the American Constitution is a strange document for sociologists because it refuses to enforce moral consensus on its citizens. Most governments go to considerable lengths to ensure that their citizens share the same beliefs, sometimes through a state church, or at least, a state sanctioned religion. In America, atheists are supposed to be treated the same as Scientologists, Hare Krishnas, Black Muslims, Roman Catholics, and Baptists. Whatever sense of unity Americans possess, it is not derived from sharing a common faith but rather from an ideal that people should be free to choose a religion if they wish. Similarly, the Bill of Rights eliminates the possiblity of a government newspaper, or any controls on speech or press. America cultivates a bewildering garden of intellectual flowerings. Although civil libertarians emphasize the need to permit still more freedom and diversity, compared to most societies America is remarkable for its reluctance to impose order on its people.

Is this lack of consensus real and, if it is, should it concern us? As was noted at the beginning of the chapter, most Americans have a common civil religion. Even though our private religious beliefs are diverse, we share a view about the special qualities of America. With the possible exception of the late 1960s, most Americans have had no doubt that America is one of the greatest, most moral nations on earth. Our diversity and our freedom to be different strengthen and unify us. Add to this the belief that America is under God's special protection, and we have a widely shared public theology that binds Americans together, even in the face of a diversity that could break us asunder.

We might also wonder whether religion is necessary for a society. Could a nation of atheists find happiness, unity, and freedom? Most of the states within the orbit of the Soviet Union are officially atheistic. Yet, the Soviet Union, like the United States, has a civil religion. In the case of Mother Russia, this religion is much stronger than in the United States, to which the impressive rallies in Red Square in Moscow give testimony. Second, there is comparatively little personal freedom in the Soviet

Union, at least in the terms valued by Americans. Freedom of speech, religion, and the press are routinely ignored by the Soviet government. Could this be a consequence of the absence of religion? Could Marx have been right, that religion serves as the opiate of the masses, a force that causes individuals to accept their lot in life in the hope of a better afterlife? Without such a pacifier, the government must step in with repressive measures. Religion from this perspective limits political protest and decreases the need for repressive measures.

It is very difficult, if not impossible, to demonstrate the role of religion in our society. Like the belief in God, a person's decision about the effects of religion on society are, in some measure, a matter of faith. The decision a person makes about the effects of religion are likely to spill over into his or her attitude toward the legitimacy of tax exemptions for churches. Do churches deserve to be indirectly subsidized? Should the government tax collectors ignore church wealth, as they ignore charity? And, if there is to be tax exemption, do churches have a moral responsibility to help the poor, even if these poor are not members of their congregation or even of their faith? Finally, is morality the sole province of government, or should it be delegated to private organizations with their own, individual concepts of what constitutes moral action? These are some of the problems that result when a society must make a decision about the role of the secular state and the religious community.

Questions

1. Should religious property be taxed?

2. Should churches be forced to disclose their wealth and holdings?

3. Does taxing churches violate the separation of church and state?

4. Does exempting churches from taxation violate the separation of church and state?

5. Should tax exemptions be taken away from churches that do not follow government policy? If so, what policies shall be used to determine church tax exemptions?

6. Is tax exemption equivalent to a tax subsidy?

7. Does religion improve the moral climate of a community?

8. Does a society need religion? Why?

9. Is it fair to atheists for churches to have tax exemptions?

10. What would likely happen if tax exemptions for churches were to be eliminated tomorrow?

For Further Study

Baker, John W, ed., *Taxation and the Free Exercise of Religion*. Washington, D.C.: Baptist Joint Committee on Public Affairs, 1978.

Bellah, Robert and Hammond, Phillip. *Varieties of Civil Religion*. New York: Harper and Row, 1980.

Bittker, Boris I. "Churches, Taxes and the Constitution," *Yale Law Journal* 78 (July 1969): 1285–1310.

Kelly, Dean. *Why Churches Should Not Pay Taxes*. New York: Harper & Row, 1977.

Larson, Martin A. and Lowell, C. Stanley. *The Religious Empire*. Washington, D.C.: Robert B. Luce Co., 1976.

Robertson, D. B. *Should Churches Be Taxed?* Philadelphia: Westminster, 1968.

Tussman, Joseph. *The Supreme Court on Church and State*. New York: Oxford University Press, 1962.

Notes and References

1. Emile Durkheim, *Elementary Forms of Religious Life* (New York: Collier, 1961).
2. Robert Bellah and Phillip E. Hammond, *Varieties of Civil Religion* (New York: Harper & Row, 1980).
3. George Gallup, Jr., "U.S. in Early Stages of Religious Revival," *Journal of Current Social Issues* 14 (1977): 53–55.
4. D. B. Robertson, *Should Churches Be Taxed?* (Philadelphia: Westminster, 1968), p. 34.
5. Orr Kelly with Barbara Quick, "Nonprofit Groups: Are They Worth Their Tax Breaks?" *U.S. News & World Report*, January 31, 1983, p. 38.
6. Martin A. Larson and C. Stanley Lowell, *The Religious Empire*. (Washington, D.C.: Robert B. Luce Co., 1976), pp. 18–19.
7. *Everson v. Board of Education*, 330 U.S. 1 (1947).
8. Robertson, *op. cit.*, p. 194.
9. *Ibid*, p. 196.
10. "Ministers Propose Taxing Churches," *Literary Digest*, December 30, 1933, p. 19.
11. Robertson, *op. cit.*, p. 194.
12. Dean M. Kelley, *Why Churches Should Not Pay Taxes* (New York: Harper & Row, 1977), pp. 47–48.
13. D. Stanley Eitzen, *In Conflict and Order*, 2nd ed. (Boston: Allyn and Bacon, 1982), pp. 416–417.
14. *McCulloch v. Maryland*, March 6, 1819, in Bergen Evans, *Dictionary of Quotations* (New York: Avenel Books, 1968), p. 681.
15. *Walz v. Tax Commission*, 397 U.S. 691 (1970).
16. David Bruce Johnson, comp., *National Party Platforms of 1980* (Urbana: University of Illinois Press, 1982), p. 88.
17. Hope Eastman, "Why Churches Should Be Taxed," in *Taxation and the Free Exercise of Religion*, John W. Baker, ed. (Washington, D.C.: Baptist Joint Committee on Public Affairs, 1978), p. 37.
18. *Walz v. Tax Commission*, 397 U.S. 700, 716 (1970).
19. "Saintly Profiteering," *The Nation*, May 15, 1929, p. 577.
20. Kenneth G. Gross, "Should We Tax Church Wealth?" *Look*, May 19, 1970, p. 25.

21. Hugh McDiarmid, "Why the Secrecy on Church Property?" *American Atheist*, September 1979, p. 8.
22. David M. Alpern with Howard Fineman, "Churches, Politics and the Tax Man," *Newsweek*, October 6, 1980, p. 46.
23. Robertson, *op. cit.*, pp. 31–32.
24. *Ibid*, p. 198.
25. David G. Bromley and Anson D. Shupe, Jr. "Financing the New Religions: A Resource Mobilization Approach," *Journal for the Scientific Study of Religion* 19 (1980): 227–239.
26. David G. Bromley and Anson D. Shupe, Jr., "Evolving Foci in Participant Observation: Research as an Emergent Process," in *Fieldwork Experience*, William B. Shaffir, Robert A. Stebbins, and Allan Turowetz, eds. (New York: St. Martin's, 1980), p. 193.
27. Bromley and Shupe, "Financing the New Religions," *op. cit.*, p. 232.
28. *Ibid*, p. 233.
29. *Ibid*, p. 236.

 **Seven**

Bureaucracy and Organizations: How Should Welfare Be Distributed?

THE TERM "RED TAPE" started out very innocently. When British government workers needed to keep related documents together, they tied them up with a red ribbon, called tape. From this harmless start, we all became ensnared. Few social organizations have as unsavory a reputation as bureaucracies. They are seen as impersonal and out-of-touch with the needs of those they are supposed to serve. Bureaucrats have been derided by critics of all political hues as having "pointy-heads" and "cold hearts." We have even had to coin a euphemism—social service providers—for those in welfare agencies.

Despite this bad image, human beings have probably always felt it in their interest to form groups to achieve some goal.

Groups of people can achieve things that a single person cannot. In some cases, such as hunting bands, several people may be required to accomplish a single task; in other cases, such as sailing a ship, there is a need for people to do different tasks for a common end. On a ship, the captain makes the final decisions and takes the ultimate responsibility, while officers below him or her take on other specific tasks and responsibilities. This organization of group activity into specialties is referred to as a *division of labor*. Such a system is highly functional for a society. Since a person cannot usually be a jack-of-all-trades, he or she develops expertise in fewer areas. As groups, and the tasks facing them, become increasingly complex, the division of labor also becomes more intricate.

As some societies became more complex, the local, face-to-face groups (churches, farms, villages) that dominated a person's dealings with other people were replaced by large organizations. One of the major differences between the small groups of the past and the large organizations of the present is size and all that size implies. In a small group, a person is known personally and knows those who provide him or her services. In a large organization, people are clients, and the people serving them are likely to be anonymous and impersonal. Yet, large organizations are necessary to achieve some desirable social goals. What large organizations lose in friendliness, they make up for in efficiency or *economy of scale*. This phrase refers to the idea that it is often cheaper per unit to produce many objects than only a few. The small widgit maker must purchase the same machine as the large widgit maker, yet the small widgit maker uses the machine only part of the day, while the large widgit maker uses the machine constantly. Since the machine costs the same for both manufacturers, it is easy to see why producing many widgits is cheaper than producing a few.

If it is impossible for large organizations to be personal, then perhaps they should just try to be more efficient. Sociologists refer to these large organizations as *formal organizations*. They have a consciously planned structure that is organized to achieve socially valued goals. Often these organizations have detailed *organizational charts* showing how employees are connected to each other. These plans, in effect, describe the rights and responsibilities of members of the organization and suggest the proper patterns of communication among the parts of the organization. These charts show in detail the "vertical" hierarchy (who reports to whom) and the "horizontal" divisions (activities in which organizational personnel are engaged).

Interactionists have correctly emphasized that an organization rarely functions in exactly the manner specified in an organizational chart. Rather an informal structure exists that is used to get things done through agreements and tacit understandings. Interactionist sociologist Anselm Strauss refers to this as the *negotiated order*[1] to set it apart from the formal structure.

Many organizations strive to become bureaucracies, in the formal sense that sociologists use the term. A *bureaucracy* is a system of administration that has specialized roles, a hierarchical authority structure, and explicit rules and procedures. A bureaucracy is supposed to achieve organizational goals more efficiently and effectively. It is the ultimate "rational" organization. According to Max Weber,[2] the early twentieth century German sociologist who insightfully studied the dynamics of bureaucracy, the ideal bureaucracy has the following characteristics: 1) work is divided into small tasks performed by specialists, 2) a clearly defined hierarchy of authority exists, with well-defined responsibilities and duties, 3) decisions are made on the basis of technical knowledge, and not because of personal ties, and 4) members are judged on ability, with discipline fairly enforced.

The bureaucracy should treat everyone fairly and equally. Imagine going to some government agency to make a request and learning that the person behind the desk was uncooperative because he or she did not like your race or ethnic background. If you are treated well, a bureaucracy might seem like a pretty good system, but if you are treated unfairly, it might seem like a very poor one. Treating everyone identically may seem to be the ideal, but in doing this, people's unique situations cannot be considered. In fact this is the reason bureaucracies seem officious, stagnant, and unresponsive. This very vice, however, is also a virtue—an effort to be fair to everyone.

Question:

How Should "Welfare" Be Distributed?

The New Testament reminds us that the poor will always be with us.[3] Perhaps more to the point is American humorist Abe Martin's comment: "It's no disgrace t' be poor, but it might as well be."[4] Most Americans are ambivalent about "the poor."[5] They believe that America is the land of opportunity, that anyone can get ahead, yet, they also recognize that many people are at the mercy of a capricious economy. They are realistic enough to understand that the vagaries of circumstances often make it easier for some people to be more financially successful than other people.

In a 1978 New York Times-CBS News poll, 58 percent of those surveyed opposed "most government-sponsored welfare programs," while 31 percent supported them. Fifty-four percent agreed that "most people who receive money from welfare could get along without it if they tried." When the questions became more specific, support for welfare grew: 81 percent supported food stamps for the poor and aid to poor families with dependent children; 82 percent agreed that free health care should be provided for people who cannot afford it.[6] In a 1977 Gallup poll, only 2 percent of the American public believed that welfare was fine as it is, and only 2 percent felt that we should eliminate welfare entirely. Most of the respondents felt a need for the welfare bureaucracy to investigate and screen applicants better[7]—an expensive idea.

Picture in your mind the typical welfare recipient. Is he a muscular youth lounging around some street corner with his buddies; is she a young mother trying to control her brood of screaming youngsters; is she an old woman hobbling around on a cane? The image you have of welfare recipients and their motivations for getting welfare will color your attitudes toward the welfare system, and how—or if—aid to the needy should be distributed.

Welfare is a very broad term. The United States government offers various types of aid programs to its citizens: Social

Security, unemployment compensation, food stamps, Aid to Families With Dependent Children, Medicare, Medicaide, farm subsidies, and veterans' benefits. We might consider college loan programs as welfare, and some would include government aid to struggling industries—such as Chrysler or Boeing. For purposes of our discussion welfare is government payments in cash or its equivalent to individuals who are defined as in need. This chapter will focus on those welfare programs that aid the poor or, in the political rhetoric of today, the "truly needy." It will ignore the various welfare-type programs specifically for the middle-class or even for the rich. Within this framework, two types of programs will be discussed: "income-tested" programs that only give aid to those people who make less than a particular income (for example, in the food stamp program recipients can have incomes at 130% of the official poverty level) and programs that give aid to anyone who falls within a particular group, such as Social Security or unemployment compensation. These latter non-income based programs or entitlement programs typically have greater public support than those that aid only the needy. When most middle-class Americans refer to the "welfare mess," they are typically referring to those programs for which they do not qualify.

Although poor people have always existed, large-scale government welfare programs have not. In 1888 German Chancellor Otto von Bismarck introduced the first European program of social insurance for the needy, giving workers protection against accidents, sickness, and old age.[8] While most governments in the nineteenth century had poor laws for the destitute, these programs often required people to live in "poorhouses" provided by the government, a degrading prospect. In the United States, it was not until the Great Depression in the 1930s that aid programs at the federal level (some state programs existed) were created. Before the economic upheaval of the Depression, people could argue that if someone was poor it was somehow his or her fault. The Depression, which threw many millions of Americans out of work, was clearly not the "fault" of those who became unemployed. Under these circumstances, President Hoover began some relief programs, but it was not until the administration of Franklin Roosevelt that a full fledged effort to help people was put into effect.[9]

It should be remembered however, that during the 1920s the federal government provided only a few welfare-type programs. It was not until Lyndon Johnson's Great Society that welfare began making up a large segment of the federal budget. According to one expert on social welfare, the proportion of the gross national product spent on income security and welfare programs (excluding education) increased from 1.5 percent in 1929 to 15.2 percent in 1976.[10] In 1982 the government spent 91 billion dollars on welfare programs alone, compared to 8.8 billion dollars in 1964. This is despite a decrease from 36.1 million officially classified as poor in 1964 to 29.3 million in 1982. The food stamp program in 1964 provided aid to 360,000 people at a cost of 30 million dollars; now 23 million people receive aid at a cost to taxpayers of 11.1 billion dollars.[11] But even President Reagan's proposals do not involve cutting food stamps or other welfare programs to their 1964 levels. Indeed, despite the attempts by President Reagan to cut (trim or slash, depending on your view) welfare programs, the major programs (Social Security, Medicare, and Medicaid) have been substantially increased from 1980 to 1983. The Reagan administration claims to have cut only the "richest of the poor" from eligibility.[12] The much heralded "Reagan revolution" does not seem to have succeeded in dismantling the "welfare state," despite the "horror stories" that have been reported.

One thing seems indisputable; we now have a large federal welfare bureaucracy in the United States. To provide aid to so many, large numbers of people must be involved. Our welfare system is a classic bureaucracy that attempts to treat people equally and that has formal rules, an authority structure, and impartial enforcement (often through the courts). Because of the nature of the welfare system, it is sometimes frustrating both for the poor and for those who wish to change it. For example, the welfare bureaucracy makes it difficult to eliminate fraud. To eliminate or greatly reduce fraud one would have to investigate those who seem "suspicious." Such a system would mean treating people individually rather than as members of a group.

This could raise costs beyond a tolerable level and could raise issues of invasion of privacy.

The Libertarian Point of View

The extreme libertarian point of view, as stated in the 1980 party platform, is simple: "We oppose all government welfare, relief projects, and aid to the poor programs. All these government programs are privacy-invading, paternalistic, demeaning, and inefficient. The proper source of help for such persons is the voluntary efforts of private groups and individuals."[13] Even if a welfare program could be set up that was not privacy-invading, paternalistic, demeaning, and inefficient, many libertarians would continue to oppose it. Government welfare flies in the face of the basic libertarian theory of human nature and government responsibility. The primary reason that a person is poor is, to be blunt, because he or she chooses to be. This person believes there is more to be gained by continuing to remain indigent than by working hard. According to libertarians, this is more likely to occur in a society in which the poor are taken care of by the government supplying a "safety net." Being a welfare cheat from this perspective makes sound economic sense; why work if you can get something for nothing? While the libertarian's attitude may strike you as cold-hearted and cynical (and even wrong), there is no doubt that some people do cheat the system.

Many people on welfare have made life choices that make it more likely that they will be poor. Young people drop out of high school or do not attend college because of immediate economic concerns. Women may decide not to use birth control methods or use them incorrectly. The elderly spend their money before retirement, saving nothing. These people will come to the middle-class taxpayer and say "bail us out." To some libertarians this seems like the fable of the thrifty ant and the foolish grasshopper. Unlike welfare cheats, these people do not deliberately try to get a free ride. But the libertarian contends that they should be responsible for their own mistakes in judgment, even if they suffer. Such an argument is put forth in an article by libertarian John Semmens on the failure of unemployment compensation:

> Implicit in the decision of an individual whether to accept a given job is the issue of compensation. If a person turns down a job because the pay is too low he is expressing a preference for leisure at that price. Is the economy failing because it does not provide a job at the desired wage? Or is the individual to be castigated for withholding his labor. . . . If taxpayers are to be required to make up the difference between desired wage and offered wage, the destruction of productive output will be the end result. . . . The availability of alternative sources of income. . . supports the willingness and ability to withhold labor. The payment of unemployment compensation abets the preference for leisure among those eligible for benefits.[14]

These positions are fairly extreme, and even some libertarians would not accept them entirely. Yet most libertarians do wish to decrease or eliminate the government's role in providing welfare. Most would agree that there are some people who do need help, even if they are partially to blame for their own situation, but they question whether government is the best provider of welfare services? Many libertarians believe that charity should be primarily voluntary. They point to the long tradition of private, voluntary charity in this country. Furthermore, they argue that if taxes were drastically reduced by cutting the welfare budget, this would, perhaps, lead to the growth of more private welfare agencies. The libertarians believe government charity fosters dependency, and some even suggest that the "welfare establishment" perpetuates dependency to maintain its own power. Welfare, they assert, is as addictive as heroin; it teaches people to be helpless. While this is obviously too extreme to be taken as a general statement of fact, once one has received public charity, continuing to receive it becomes easier and easier. Private charity, on the other hand, fosters independence since it has no vested interest in maintaining a poor person's dependency on welfare.

The libertarian also feels welfare programs often grow like cancer. Consider the 1966 projection by Howard P. Davis, the Department of Agriculture's deputy administrator of food programs: "Ultimately, when the program reaches maximum expansion, we've been figuring on 4.5 million people, covering half the counties in the nation, and involving somewhere between $375 million and $400 million a year." The actual figures for fiscal year 1982 are nearly 23 million citizens receiving food stamps at a cost of $11.1 billion dollars.[15] The libertarian's response to this is that it is obviously much easier to start a government program than it is to stop one. Because of their philosophy of human nature and government, libertarians are extremely suspicious of federal welfare programs, believing that charity, if it is to exist at all, should begin at home.

The Social Democratic Point of View

The social democrat and the libertarian stand diametrically opposed to each other on this issue. The social democrat believes welfare is the *minimum* responsibility of a government to those it governs. President Franklin Delano Roosevelt, the architect of the New Deal, remarked in his Second Inaugural Address in 1937 that "The test of our progress is not whether we add more to the abundance of those who have much; it is whether we provide enough for those who have little."[16]

The social democrat assumes that the vast majority of people who request government aid sincerely need that help and are not trying to "get something for nothing." For many social democrats, the social programs that grew out of the New Deal and the Great Society constitute, in the words of President Franklin Roosevelt, "a second Bill of Rights," which includes "the right to a useful and remunerative job," "the right of every family to a decent home," and "the right to adequate medical care."[17] This view transforms what libertarians or conservatives might see as gifts or charity into rights.

Because of their belief in the basic goodness of human beings, many social democrats find the suspicion that is directed toward welfare recipients unfair and demeaning. They are willing to accept on face value most people's request for help, and resent, for the most part, the checks made on recipients. The *New Yorker* Talk of the Town comments that suspicion towards welfare poses moral dilemmas for reasonable people:

> The reason welfare runs the way it does, in this city and probably in other cities, is that as a nation we have ceased to regard it as a matter of social justice, or even as a matter of the least-we-can-do sort of charity, and have decided that it is a nasty, if perhaps obligatory, chore. . . . Such an approach robs the welfare process of all dignity and brotherhood, not only for poor people forced to spend thirty days without cash but also for those of us whose taxes foot the bill for welfare. It turns them into cadgers and the rest of us into suspicious, sneering cads, and that is sad, even when it saves a little money.[18]

Social democrats believe welfare is more than simply a humanitarian gesture. They claim an effective welfare system is in the interest of the whole nation. They agree with Nobel Prize winner and Swedish economist Gunnar Myrdal that "well-planned social reforms are a profitable investment, for they improve the quality of life and thus the productivity of people and also preclude future public and private expenditures."[19] This philosophy says people are "human capital," and an efficient society will attempt to develop this capital. Cutting welfare programs to levels that would only aid the most desperately poor may actually force welfare recipients to quit low-paying jobs in order to qualify for the newly tightened welfare requirements. Welfare restrictions, rather than promoting strong families, may break them apart, in that single or abandoned mothers will receive more aid than those with stable marriages. Although, in one sense, people who work part-time and those with spouses may need help less than others, by excluding them, the social democrat argues, it makes it more likely that they will become divorced or choose to be unemployed. The point is that too often cuts in welfare may actually cost more money, rather than less—all the while destroying the nation's human capital.

Unlike conservatives and libertarians, social democrats are much more likely to approve of *federal*, as opposed to state, welfare programs. They contend that there are advantages to a centralization of services and the equity that this brings to the welfare system throughout the nation. If power is centralized, then responsibility is centralized. Rather than fifty different welfare systems, a federal system, with increased power, makes it immediately apparent where failure lies. (As things currently stand in the United States, a mishmash of federal, state, and local systems operate.) If states and localities have different policies, potential recipients may choose to live in those areas that offer the most generous programs. Thus, New York and California, which are relatively generous, may be forced to provide for emigrants from Texas and Mississippi, states that are less generous. States and localities are thus being penalized for their generosity. A federal welfare system would distribute the burden more equally.[20] An editorial in the *Minneapolis Tribune* underscores this point, "Only the federal government can provide equitable access to a minimum standard of living for all of America's poor. Poverty is a national problem, unequally distributed and tied closely to national economic policies. It requires a national response."[21]

Social democrats do not fear a centralized bureaucracy. Bigness does not necessarily mean badness; it can mean systematic compassion for those who cannot get by any other way.

The Conservative Point of View

Unlike libertarians, conservatives do not have an instinctive hatred of government charity. It is true that most conservative politicians oppose most welfare proposals at the time they are enacted, but this seems to be due more to their dislike of large-scale social change. Once a program, such as Social Security, proves workable, it will gain the conservative's endorsement.

Nevertheless, government welfare programs, particularly those on the federal level, are considered methods of last resort. Particularly troubling to the conservative are welfare programs that are administered through large bureaucracies.

Remember that, for the conservative, although government is not an object of hatred, it is an institution of secondary importance, except for preserving the peace. Thus, the conservative would be more pleased if institutions, like the church or the neighborhood or the family, could accomplish the same results. There is a presumption that whenever possible poor people should be given support within their community, through their church, or by asking their extended family. The conservative is profoundly troubled that these primary institutions have been eclipsed by big government.

Nathan Glazer, in describing Reagan's attitude toward government power, comments, "Their [members of Reagan's administration] aim is not to *increase* the authority of lesser, centrally appointed administrators, but to *reduce* it; they seek to increase the power and weight of people outside the administrative chain altogether, those on whom administrators operate— whether they be beneficiaries, clients, the "people," the public, or the taxpayers.[22]

Those programs that the conservatives like best are those that are set up by private or religious agencies. They look with alarm when these agencies are "taken over" by the federal government and "bureaucratized." Glazer presents several troubling examples of successful local programs that have been brought under federal auspices. One example is the "meals-on-wheels" programs, which take food to the elderly at meal sites. Once these programs receive federal funding, they are pressured to change. Prior to federal intervention, "meals-on-wheels" was a cost-effective program that had volunteers carry food to the elderly living in their own homes.[23] According to one study, it is likely that the federal government will enforce the following regulations:

> Each service must provide more than 100 meals daily, that they provide auxiliary social services to meals recipients,

that they cooperate with area-wide comprehensive planning agencies for the elderly, that they train their staffs and send them to seminars provided by the Administration on Aging, that they provide evidence the areas they work in have suitable concentrations of the aged poor, and that they have full-time directors. . . . [N]utrition education must be provided. . . . A project council must be organized, and there are elaborate regulations as to how it must be constituted and what its powers will be. The project must give employment preference to persons over sixty and members of minority groups. . . . Another regulation specifies in detail what a government-funded meal must consist of (which can scarcely take into account regional or ethnic tastes).[24]

These may be reasonable regulations theoretically, but when applied to a small, local program, they can cripple it. If such small food programs reject government help, there are welfare entrepreneurs eager to move into the food service "business" and push the volunteers out with the aid of government funding. What may begin as valuable government aid can become so bogged down in red tape that it kills the very spirit of community involvement that the aid was supposed to foster.

Such examples point to the problem that conservatives see with welfare programs—over-centralization, inflexibility, and removal of responsibility from the people to be served. It should be no surprise that the 1980 platform of the Republican party and the welfare pronouncements of Ronald Reagan emphasized the need for decentralization of welfare and, wherever possible, making welfare both voluntary and private. An editorial in the *Charleston Evening Post* romantically recalls a time when charity was based in the local community: "Welfarism was not always as big in this country as it is now. There was a time, before Washington began providing solutions to people's problems, individuals and institutions joined hands to look out for the needy and the sick. There was a time when neighbors rallied round to help the family down the block, when churches met spiritual and material needs, when the more fortunate aided the less fortunate by giving money through such agencies as community chests."[25]

The removal of personal responsibility for giving charity is troubling to the conservative because government, a secondary institution, takes control away from the primary institutions that reside in the local community.

Government Welfare Programs and Social Research

As noted earlier, governmental welfare programs are not inevitable. Some theorists argue that the development of these programs is a direct result of industrial development and urbanization—two forces that increased both the need and the demand for welfare services. Recent research also suggests political variables, including the nature of the state, affects the growth of welfare.[26]

In a paper entitled "Why Not Equal Protection?: Explaining the Politics of Public Social Welfare in Britain and the United States, 1880s-1920s," two Marxian sociologists, Ann Orloff and Theda Skocpol, ask why social welfare legislation came so late to the United States as compared to Great Britain.[27] The methodology they use is both historical (focusing on the four decades bracketing the start of the twentieth century) and comparative (analyzing the differences between two political units). Studies of this type are becoming increasingly common, as sociologists recognize the benefits that can be gained from viewing concepts over time and space. Yet in research of this kind, as in any archival research (see chapter 5), one is at the mercy of the data that has been collected. Decisions about what data to collect are often made by the powerful. So, for example, there has been relatively less documentation of the lives of women than men, or of the poor than the rich. Still, when a researcher's hypothesis corresponds to issues for which data has already been collected, this methodology can be of great value.

Orloff and Skocpol's methodology does not necessarily imply a specific perspective, but by focusing on state power, they ignore the individualism inherent in interactionism and libertarianism, and in doing so lean heavily toward conflict theory. The study focuses more on the needs of the dominant forces in society than on the needs of those people with less power or control. Orloff and Skocpol suggest that what happens in an industrial, capitalist state is largely a function of the desires of the powerful. The study does, however, acknowledge that both Britain and the U.S. are democratic, liberal systems, not conservative dictatorships.

Orloff and Skocpol select two political systems for study: The whole of Great Britain and the state of Massachusetts although they also examine welfare programs in America on the national level. Since America is a federal system, with most of the power residing in the states, the states passed most of the early welfare legislation. This contrasts with Britain where welfare decisions are made at the national level. Massachusetts was specifically selected for analysis because crucial variables, such as percent of elderly, proportion of the population residing in towns, percent of the population in manufacturing, mining, and construction, and trade union membership, were very similar to Great Britain. These similarities, however, did not lead to similar welfare systems. Massachusetts did follow the British model in passing laws that regulated industries, but was several decades slower than Britain in passing welfare laws, such as the Workers' Compensation laws, which involved state spending.

In reviewing the historical evidence, Orloff and Skocpol make a surprising discovery. Although "officially" the United States government did not have any welfare programs before the Depression, in effect it did—and a very large program at that. This was the Civil War pension system. This "welfare" program began as a means to compensate soldiers for wounds suffered during the Civil War, but over the course of a few decades, it became a means by which any Union soldier who was disabled for any reason could receive a pension, and the widow of a Union soldier was also entitled to a pension for the rest of her life. This pension system was expanded largely for political gains, particularly by the Republican party in the late nineteenth century. Although it was ostensibly to aid soldiers, the system was also rife with patronage and corruption. When the pensions "naturally" expired (along with those who received them), they were not extended to other groups. Thus, Orloff and Skocpol claim that the United States had a welfare system that it dismantled.

The crucial differences between the patterns of welfare legislation in Britain and the United States are differences in state formation and in how parties and administrations operate. Specifically, Orloff and Skocpol note that in Britain democratization (in the form of extending the vote to workers) and bureaucratization (in the form of a professional civil service system) occurred together. Thus, political parties felt a need to propose programs for their constituents. This was particularly true of Britain's Liberal Party, which tried to shore up working people's allegiances against the inroads of the left-wing Labour Party. The bureaucracy was used to institute these programs efficiently—at least so it was believed.

In the United States (and in Massachusetts as a case study) the situation was quite different. Democratization had occurred long before the growth of the government bureaucracy. Furthermore, there was no significant labor party to push the other parties toward making expensive welfare promises. Americans looked at the expansion and corruption of the Civil War pension system and saw how government could mishandle welfare. The United States and individual states did not have professional civil service systems necessary to institute a program of this kind. The welfare programs that did exist were typically controlled by the courts rather than by the executive branch.

Underlying this analysis, of course, is the belief that these programs represent a significant advance for workers. For Orloff and Skocpol, the primary forces that prevented the expansion of welfare in America were the lack of a civil service system, the absence of a workers' party, and the corruption of the Civil War pension system. While the authors make the point that it should not be concluded that the establishment of a welfare system will inevitably occur, noting that the Civil War pensions were not replaced, the underlying unstated assumption is that there *should* be progress in the growth of public welfare. By emphasizing how welfare systems help and protect workers, they make a social democratic argument but deflect attention from the harm that others suggest develop from this same system.

Bureaucracy and Welfare

Is it the responsibility of government to force charity from one group of citizens to another? In other words, should government become involved in the redistribution of income? If it should, what is the proper form for this redistribution to take? Remember that every penny a poor person receives is taken from a person not so poor—welfare comes from government revenues, largely, though not entirely, taxes.

There is a school of thought that suggests that the most efficient answer is simply to give every poor person enough money to make them non-poor. Black economist Thomas Sowell offers some support for this idea. "A few years ago, someone calculated how much it would cost to lift every man, woman and child in America out of poverty by simply giving them money. It was one third of what was being spent on poverty programs."[28] But there is something offensive about this efficient solution. It smacks of rewarding people for being poor. If a person is poor, he or she wins the government lottery. Most people would suspect that such a system would only serve to increase the number of poor people the following year. Yet, such a solution would trim the bureaucracy; once a person's level of poverty was determined, the government would only have to peel off the cash and say goodbye.

Despite our distaste for the occasional inflexibility and arrogance of the bureaucrat, we should give the devil his due. Welfare bureaucrats must deal with insistent clients, not generally the sort of people "respectable" bureaucrats enjoy spending their time with. Participant observation indicates that welfare workers can be crudely manipulative, deceptive, or "bureaucratic."[29] But, a survey of welfare clients finds that most of them are satisfied with the service they receive.[30] Welfare workers, like the rest of us, act as they do because of organizational constraints; they are neither angels of mercy nor vampires. Likewise the bureaucratic system attempts to insure that everyone is treated equally—even if equally sometimes means inhumanely. Once we introduce the option of a welfare worker using his or her own judgment, the possibility of favoritism and discrimination arises. A bureaucracy permits us to check the legitimacy of the clients' claim for services, to deliver those services, and then to follow-up, which helps insure, to some degree, that the services are used properly.

The welfare system, as it is currently structured, is not entirely satisfactory to any of the three points of view. The libertarian sees the system as a means for government to gobble up control of people's lives, with its primary purpose to keep the government bureaucrats in power and muzzle the free-enterprise system. The conservative sees the welfare system as usurping the proper role of local forms of government and the more primary, personal forms of organizational charity—the church, community, and family. The social democrat finds the welfare system demeaning to those citizens who need a helping hand. The large, impersonal agencies serve as bastions of suspicion and mistrust, offering only another obstacle to a life with dignity. Each point of view sees the welfare bureaucracy as undermining those values they see as most important in a just and happy social order. But in the end one could say that if everyone finds the welfare system wanting, it must be a fair compromise.

Questions

1. Is a federal bureaucracy the most effective means of distributing welfare?

2. Are most people who receive welfare benefits responsible for their own poverty?

3. Should we be doing more than we are to eliminate fraud? What should we do?

4. Does the government have a moral obligation to help the poor?

5. Is it in the economic interest of the country to provide welfare?

6. Should able-bodied people on welfare be forced to work for assistance?

7. Is private charity preferable to government welfare?

8. Would you, under any circumstances, accept government welfare? Is there any type of aid that you would not accept?

9. Should welfare be provided by the federal government or by states and localities?

10. How can a bureaucracy be humanized?

For Further Study

Berkowitz, Edward and McQuaid, Kim. *Creating the Welfare State: The Political Economy of Twentieth-Century Reform*. New York: Praeger, 1980.

Blau, Peter. *The Dynamics of Bureaucracy*. Chicago: University of Chicago Press, 1963.

Glazer, Nathan. "Towards a Self-Service Society?" *Public Interest* 70 (Winter 1983): 66–90.

Goodsell, Charles T. "Conflicting Perceptions of Welfare Bureaucracy," *Social Casework* 61 (1980): 354–360.

Jacobs, Glenn. "The Reification of the Notion of Subculture in Public Welfare," *Social Casework* 49 (1968): 527–534.

Meenaghan, Thomas and Washington, Robert. *Social Policy and Social Welfare: Structure and Applications*. New York: Free Press, 1980.

Novak, Michael. "The Rich, the Poor and the Reagan Administration," *Commentary* 76 (August 1983): 27–31.

Semmens, John. "Make-Work Won't Work," *The Freeman* 33 (1983): 561–569.

Max Weber, *The Theory of Social and Economic Organization*, trans. Henderson, A. M. and Parsons, Talcott. New York: Free Press, 1947. Originally published in 1922.

"Welfare in America and Europe," *Editorial Research Reports* 2 (December 9, 1977): 935–952.

Notes and References

1. Anselm Strauss, *Negotiations* (San Francisco: Jossey-Bass, 1978).
2. Max Weber, *The Theory of Social and Economic Organization*, trans. A. M. Henderson and Talcott Parsons (New York: Free Press, 1947), pp. 329–341. Originally published in 1922.
3. *Matthew* 26:11.
4. Frank McKinney Hubbard, Abe Martin's Sayings and Sketches, 1915, quoted in John Bartlett, *Familiar Quotations*, 14 ed. (Boston: Little, Brown, 1968), p. 895.
5. William Ryan, *Blaming the Victim*, revised ed. (New York: Random House, 1976).
6. "Welfare in America and Europe," *Editorial Research Reports* 2 (December 9, 1977): 937–938.
7. "Single 'Welfare Chiselers' Are Prime Target of Public's Reforms," *Gallup Opinion Index*, No.144, July 1977, p. 23.
8. "Welfare in America and Europe," *op. cit.*, p. 942.

9. Edward D. Berkowitz and Kim McQuaid, "Bureaucrats as 'Social Engineers': Federal Welfare Programs in Herbert Hoover's America," *American Journal of Economics and Sociology* 39 (1980): 321–335.

10. Eveline M. Burns, *Social Welfare in the 1980s and Beyond* (Berkeley: Institute of Governmental Studies, 1977), p. 3.

11. David A. Lips, "How to Get Out of the Food Stamp Trap," *Reason*, August 1983, p. 25.

12. Michael Novak, "The Rich, the Poor & the Reagan Administration," *Commentary*, August 1983, pp. 29–30.

13. David Bruce Johnson, comp., *National Party Platforms of 1980* (Urbana: University of Illinois Press, 1982), p. 94.

14. John Semmens "Make-Work Won't Work," *The Freeman* 33 (1983): 561–562.

15. Lips, *op. cit.*, p. 25.

16. John Bartlett, *Familiar Quotations*, 13th ed. (Boston: Little, Brown & Co., 1955), p. 919.

17. Jeremy Rabkin, "The Judiciary in the Administrative State," *Public Interest* 71 (1983): 62.

18. "Notes and Comment," *The New Yorker*, June 6, 1983, p. 30.

19, Gunnar Myrdal, "Welfare in America: The View From Sweden," *Saturday Review*, December 11, 1976, p. 47.

20. Lewis Walker and Chester L. Hunt, "Welfare Reform and the Possible Demise of White Paternalism and Black Flight in Mississippi," *Journal of Sociology and Social Welfare* 8 (1981): 70–82.

21. Editorial, *Minneapolis Tribune*, January 29, 1982, printed in *Editorials on File*, vol. 13, January 16–31, 1982, p. 65.

22. Nathan Glazer, "Towards a Self-Service Society?" *Public Interest* 70 (1983): 67.

23. *Ibid*, p. 80.

24. *Ibid*, pp. 80–81.

25. Editorial, *Charleston Evening Post*, October 21, 1981, printed in *Editorials on File*, vol. 12, October 16–31, p. 1187.

26. Ann Shola Orloff and Theda Skocpol, "Why Not Equal Protection? Exploring the Politics of Public Social Welfare in Britain and the United States, 1880s–1920s," unpublished manuscript, 1984. Presented by Theda Skocpol, faculty colloquim, University of Minnesota.

27. *Ibid.*
28. Stone, *op. cit.*, p. 72.
29. Glenn Jacobs, "The Reification of the Notion of Subculture in Public Welfare," *Social Casework* 49 (1968): 527–534.
30. Charles T. Goodsell, "Conflicting Perceptions of Welfare Bureaucracy," *Social Casework* 61 (1980): 354–360.

 **Eight**

Education: Should Books in Public Libraries Be Censored?

Mine eyes have seen the glory of the burning of the school.
We have tortured all the teachers,
We have broken every rule,
We are marching down the hall
To hang the principal,
Our gang's marching on.
Glory, glory hallelujah,
Teacher hit me with a ruler;
I hit her on the bean
With a rotten tangerine
And she ain't no teacher any more.[1]
(Sung to the tune of "The Battle Hymn of the Republic")

As the preceding ditty suggests, school and learning need not be synonymous. President Reagan's National Commission on Excellence in Education in their 1983 report, *A Nation at Risk: The Imperative for Educational Reform*, notes that 13 percent of all seventeen-year-olds are functionally illiterate (as high as 40 percent among minority youth), College Board Scholastic Aptitude Test scores have declined consistently from 1963 to 1980, and only one-fifth of all seventeen-year-olds can write a persuasive essay.[2] Schools are neither necessary nor sufficient for education and, in fact, many people become educated outside of a formal school setting. Nevertheless by educating children in large groups and processing them through a formal organization, schools are efficient. Despite the problems that plague our public schools, they have managed to educate many more students than they have failed to educate.

School is neither heaven nor hell. It is an environment where once someone knows the rules, he or she can get by. The avowed goal of schooling is to educate the student. To some extent education also involves teaching the moral prescriptions of our society, along with the family and the church. It is also supposed to transmit technical information that is necessary for students to become successful functioning citizens. By the time a person completes high school, he or she is expected to: know how to read and write, know how to solve basic mathematical problems, be aware of the greatest artistic achievements in our culture, and be physically fit. Finally, and not least important, the person has learned how to get along with his or her peers. But there is also another level of education that goes on within schools. This "hidden curriculum"[3] consists of things like sexual education, drug use, dirty jokes, how to deceive parents— things that children have taught each other through the ages.

In America education is taken very seriously. For well over a century Americans have been committed to providing an education to every child. This progressive view of mass education was not accepted in Europe until much later. This difference can still be seen in regard to post-secondary education. Most Americans assume that all young adults should have the opportunity to attend a college or technical school if they wish. (The many grant and loan programs that are available also seem to support this.) In other nations only a small minority attend any kind of post-high school program, and there is no general sentiment that they should be entitled to.

Given America's intense commitment to mass education, it

may seem strange that schools are not primarily controlled on the federal level, rather than on the local level. Even with the federal government's increased involvement (for example, the regulations local school boards must follow if they wish federal aid), most decision-making still occurs within local school districts.

Obviously a school system that aims to educate its entire child population necessarily must have several levels of emphasis, unlike a school system that only trains the elite. American education has tried to meet this challenge with "technical education." In addition to learning the Three Rs, many students are also taught a trade. This vocational emphasis is also found on the post-secondary level.

Schooling can be seen as a functional social institution that unifies the society by teaching similar values and knowledge to the mass of young people. Some people see schools as a melting pot in which students with different backgrounds are treated in nearly identical fashion; thus, producing a common national culture among the graduates.

In contrast, those people who adhere to a more conflict point of view of society see other outcomes of schooling. They do not see education as a homogeneous process. There are real differences among schools, particularly those that have a more middle-class set of values. The question of the effects of school facilities on educational achievement is, perhaps, debatable. The 1966 Coleman report[4] found that the characteristics of the school had only a slight effect on a child's achievement. On the other hand, within schools, children from different backgrounds do get treated differently. Teachers who expect particular children to do well often find that these children actually do better than their peers. This disturbing example of a self-fulfilling prophecy is known as "the Pygmalian effect,"[5] after the Cockney flower girl in George Bernard Shaw's play *Pygmalian* (later turned into *My Fair Lady*) who recognizes that what she could be depends on how she is treated. Children who are poor, black, or who have reputations as being disciplinary problems may find themselves with at least one strike against them.

Conflict theorists take the functionist view of schools as a mechanism by which society can continue to be stable and turn it on its head. They see schools as a means by which a class system reproduces itself. The children of those who are dominant will be dominant themselves, while the children of factory workers find themselves directed toward the factory and even receive hidden messages that they should drop out.

As was noted at the beginning of the chapter, education does not occur only within school. Many talented people continue their education after they leave school, and some people leave school early to create their own education. Some people even charge that a school as currently formulated is not a good place to become educated.[6] While schools (including college) are able to teach masses of facts, other life experiences may be equally effective in producing insight and creativity. Schools are learning institutions from the top down; that is, they are bureaucracies founded on the authority of degrees. For some people, that degree is an important credential; for others, the truth can be found on a summer breeze.

Question:

Should Books in Public Libraries Be Censored?

Few among us would like to be known by that rather pejorative title "the censor." This phrase dredges up images of the blue-nosed Puritan, the little old lady in tennis shoes, the dour dowager, or the extremist crank who finds Communists under everyone's bed. At the same time, most of us would like to be known as people of discerning judgment. We wish to be known as people who can separate the wheat from the chaff, the trash from the genius, the pearls from the swine. This is part of the paradox of the debate on censorship. It is the difference between "censorship" and "selection." Censorship is what the other guy does; selection is what we do.

What would a library without "selection" look like? It would either purchase every book that is published or, more feasibly, it would purchase books by random selection. Imagine the chaos in the library system if books were chosen by sticking pins in the pages of book catalogs. Clearly someone must make decisions, but how?

Political scientist Harold D. Lasswell defines censorship as: "the policy of restricting the public expression of ideas, opinions, conceptions and impulses which have or are believed to have the capacity to undermine the governing authority or the social and moral order which that authority considers itself bound to protect."[7] This definition takes the motivation of the "censor" into account. In this definition a librarian who decides not to purchase the autobiography of the chairman of the American Communist party would be engaging in censorship, while one who decides not to purchase the autobiography of Gerald Ford would be only making a selection. It is easy to see how such a definition systematically favors those books that challenge the system, as opposed to books that support it.

The selection process is supposedly designed to insure that a library purchases the "best" books, those that the community would be most interested in and most "needs," and those books that provide a diverse collection. Yet these criteria may lead librarians to purchase some books over others on ideological grounds. Favored styles and subject matters pass in and out of favor, definitions of what the "community" is interested in depend on a librarian's perceptions and stereotypes, and what makes for a diverse collection is a matter of judgment. (How well represented should Communist, racist, Nazi, or fundamentalist Christian works be?). A librarian has considerable leeway in such matters, and it is this latitude that makes some argue that censorship and selection are synonymous. While we might be willing to concede, in some cases, that different motivations are involved, selection and censorship have precisely the same result—certain books are not put on the shelf.[8] If censorship consists of removing books already purchased, we must admit that librarians do this all the time for such "appropriate" reasons as a work becoming outdated. Even this can be a matter of ideology—for example, what constitutes scientific progress is never certain.

Crucial to the definition of censorship is the role of the librarian. Some see librarians as dedicated professionals striving, despite inadequate budgets, to provide a diverse array of knowledge to the public; they are in constant battle with outsiders who wish to limit what people can read. Contrast this to the view that librarians are government bureaucrats, responsive only to those political functionaries who appointed them and to the universities that trained them. These librarians try to enforce a particular set of views. When a member of the public (who supports the library through their taxes) objects to a particular book, the librarian is unwilling to understand that in a democracy citizens have a legitimate right to help select books. These two images give widely different views on the legitimacy of selection and censorship. Librarians, like members of most white collar occupations, think of themselves as professionals, with the authority of doctors and lawyers. Those outside the occupation see librarians as government employees whose primary function is to serve the wishes of the public. Library selection, from this viewpoint, is always government censorship, because a government employee is doing the choosing of what the public will have access to read. The question of censorship then becomes a question of who has the power to make decisions.

The idea of censoring library material is not new and is parallel to other attempts to suppress material thought to be immoral or subversive. The first major flowering of moral crusaders in the United States occurred in the aftermath of the Civil War,[9] with the establishment of Anthony Comstock's New York Society for the Suppression of Vice in 1873. To this day Comstockery refers to the vigorous suppression of material deemed to be obscene or immoral. Similar societies grew in number and in influence throughout the latter part of the nineteenth century, and they managed to pass legislation that significantly limited what could be sent through the mails.

During the twentieth century, censorship attempts have continued. The list of authors whose works someone has wanted to ban is impressive: William Faulkner, James Joyce, Mark

Twain, J. D. Salinger, William Shakespeare, and Theodore Dreiser to name a few. Although it is fair to say that the mood is more tolerant now than earlier in the century, cases still arise in which some citizens wish to have materials taken off library shelves. In 1981 Judith Krug, head of the American Library Association's Office of Intellectual Freedom reported that in about six months 148 books were challenged.[10] Of course, this statistic alone does not tell us much since the seriousness of the challenges is not indicated (you could, if you wish, challenge the Bible). It does suggest, however, that there are still people who would like to see books removed from libraries.

Knowing that they might be challenged makes some librarians more careful about the controversial titles they purchase. A 1959 study found that nearly two-thirds of the librarians surveyed in California said that controversy about a book or author resulted in a decision not to purchase the book.[11] For good or ill, librarians engage in self-censorship in the name of selection. Political scientist Oliver Garceau describes how the issue of censorship becomes obscured: "The censorship of library holdings does not often become a public issue, largely because it is an intramural activity. As a member himself of the white collar middle class that uses his library, the librarian has a green thumb for cultivating those books that will be popular and an equal knack for weeding out what will be considered dangerous."[12]

There are far too many books published for librarians to read even a small portion of them, so they rely on book review journals. In 1970, thirty-six thousand books were published, but the *Library Journal,* the widest read book review journal, reviewed only about nine thousand of these,[13] and one would guess that fewer than half of all the books published are reviewed anywhere. Thus, these book review journals serve as *gatekeepers*—a mechanism that provides entry (or rewards) to selected things or persons. If a publisher does not get his books reviewed, for all practical purposes they are shut out of the library market. To the extent that such journals do not review religious literature, radical political tracts, racist books, or pornography, it is easy to see why, despite the proclamation of diversity, libraries actually reflect mainstream thought.

The Libertarian Point of View

The extreme libertarian believes the government has no business running libraries since these institutions do not provide for the common defense or internal peace. For them, the issue of public library censorship is moot.

Leaving aside this extreme position and recognizing that there will be libraries and librarians who will make decisions about books, the libertarian is deeply offended by any hint of limits to public access to any type of writing. For the libertarian, the library is a free market place of ideas; those ideas that are offensive or incorrect will fall by their own weight. Consider the comment made by the nineteenth century libertarian philosopher, John Stuart Mill:

> The peculiar evil of silencing the expression of an opinion is that it is robbing the human race: posterity as well as the existing generation; those who dissent from the opinion still more than those who hold it. If the opinion is right, they are deprived of the opportunity of exchanging error for truth; if wrong, they lose what is almost as great a benefit, the clearer perception and livelier impression of truth, produced by its collision with error. [14]

Some believe that there should be a "freedom to read"—a right as vigorously upheld as any. For libertarians this right follows directly from freedom of speech and the press. Thus, there is a right to be a passive recipient of ideas and not just an active disseminator of them. The American Library Association has articulately expressed this in a document adopted in 1953 and revised in 1972:

> The freedom to read is essential to our democracy. It is continuously under attack. . . . We trust Americans to recognize propaganda, and to reject it. We do not believe they need the help of censors to assist them in this task. We do not believe they are prepared to sacrifice their heritage of a free press in order to be "protected" against what others think may be bad for them. We believe they still favor free

enterprise in ideas and expression. . . . Every silencing of a
heresy, every enforcement of an orthodoxy, diminishes the
toughness and resilience of our society and leaves it the less
able to deal with stress. . . . We believe that free communication is essential to the preservation of a free society and
a creative culture.[15]

The image of the marketplace of ideas is a central metaphor for
the libertarian, and they support the free market here as elsewhere. Libertarian economist Milton Friedman sarcastically
proposes that the government may wish to do with books what
they have already done with cigarettes—require a warning label
on them: "Reading is dangerous to mental health and may cause
death from revolution and other disturbances."[16]

In addition, there are many technical problems with censorship. What is obscene to one person is not so to another. Attitudes of acceptability keep changing. Defining what is offensive
or obscene is impossible. And how do we prevent censorship
from leading to thought control. Libertarians often argue that
any censorship will lead to all censorship; as one porno shop op-
erator commented: "If they succeed in [censoring] pornography,
you'll see all future Pentagon Papers and all future Watergates
suppressed."[17]

Are there really to be no limits? Some librarians and other
libertarians believe that a free and open library should have
hard-core pornography and other sexual material in its open
stacks. The American Library Association's Task Force on Sex
Related Media is attempting to provide reviews to librarians on
materials dealing with sexuality.[18] Radical political scientist
Mulford Q. Sibley opts for a totally open library purchasing policy in order to picture the world more perfectly:

Perhaps a certain proportion of supposedly obscene literature, other things being equal, should not only not be excluded but rather positively included as indispensible in
every library collection. . . . Our grasp of reality is imperfect and if it is ever to approximate "truth," all forms of expression must not only be tolerated but encouraged. Once
we begin making exceptions—for obscene or other suppos-

edly evil literature—we have given up the quest for understanding and have in effect arrogantly set ourselves up as those who know what is absolutely true and right.[19]

For the libertarian, a library will not be entirely free of censorship until all types of published material are included—pornographic, fundamentalist, racist, and that written by ignorant, illiterate people. That day has not yet arrived.

The Conservative Point of View

Although conservatives are more likely than others to support censorhip,[20] not all conservatives totally support it. For example, when the Boston Public Library was under attack in the 1950s for carrying Communist literature, Herbert Philbrick, a leading anti-communist, telegraphed: "Shocked to hear that the Boston Public Library has under consideration the suppression of vital information concerning the methods, nature, and extent of the Soviet conspiracy against the United States. Such suppression would be directly in line with the current policy of the Communist Party in the United States to conceal the true aims of the Party from all except its trusted members."[21] He argues that it is important to know about those you abhor, as does John Stuart Mill.

Other conservatives, however, see a justification for controlling what is provided in libraries. Librarians often argue that "good books" can have positive effects on their readers, and for this reason reading is important. The conservative carries this one step further by saying, if good books have beneficial effects, does it not logically follow that "bad books" have negative effects and shouldn't we do something about it?

After all, conservatives note, citizens subsidize libraries through their taxes; should they not have some right to say what is in them? Why should government-employed librarians not be held accountable to the people who pay their salaries; are they always above reproach?[22] Whereas libertarians are likely to emphasize the part of the First Amendment that mentions freedom of speech and the press, conservatives stress the last phrase: "the right of the people. . . to petition the government for a redress of grievance." Surely removing an objectionable book from a library constitutes a "redress of grievance." While citizens only have the right to *petition*, objections to books fall under the First Amendment.

The conservative believes that access to some books may have significant negative effects, which a government may legitimately wish to control. Control may increase the level of civility in a society since some writings may lead to a debasement of moral standards. Harry Clor, an advocate of some forms of censorship, argues: "We know of no civil society which has yet established its fundamental law or ethical code upon the affirmation that any man may do just as he likes and live just as he please as long as he avoids 'violence, constraint or fraud.' This is hardly a mere accident of history, for the human community is always interested in something more than the prevention of violence, constraint, and fraud."[23] Some books, particularly those that are felt to be obscene, weaken the bonds of civilized society. Some theorists believe that society needs consensus and moral agreement in order to function and reject the argument that a wild diversity of opinion makes for a stronger, freer social system. Some beliefs may undermine the basic institutions of society: the church, the family, and the community. The *Dallas Times Herald* editorializes that pornography may blunt our moral sense:

> Pornography is not morally neutral. It has to do with man the savage, man the naked ape (to borrow C. S. Lewis' phrase), man shorn of the restraints and inhibitions which alone make possible civilized existence. The danger is that we should cease to think of this sort of man as abnormal. That which we hear and see again and again and again, we become inured to. But do we wish to become inured to behavior which runs counter to Judaeo-Christian tenets?[24]

Unlike libertarians who reject the notion of moral or cultural absolutes, conservatives believe that such absolutes exist. They worry about a society that is eager to separate religion from education but is willing to allow anything in the name of freedom of the press. Conservative columnist George Will, in discussing the removal of prayer from school, presents this unfortunate paradox this way: "It is, by now, a familiar process: people asserting rights in order to extend the power of the state into what once were spheres of freedom. And it is, by now, a scandal beyond irony that thanks to the energetic litigation of 'civil liberties' fanatics, pornographers enjoy expansive First Amendment protection while first graders in a nativity play are said to violate First Amendment values.[25] The paradox is even more ironic to the conservative when it is remembered that both the schoolhouse and the library are paid for by taxes and are run by government functionaries. The conservative sees no reason why the people's institutions cannot express popular values.

The Social Democratic Point of View

Most people who adopt "left" or "liberal" stands in American politics agree with the basic thrust of the libertarian point of view on library censorship. This may be the case because in the past, most of the censors have been conservatives and much of what has been censored has appealed more to the left or liberal social principles. *The Wall Street Journal* sees censorship as a battle between the proponents of the traditional culture, "the bedrock Americans" (conservatives), and the "cosmopolitan Americans" (libertarians and social democrats).[26]

Despite this, some social democrats believe that censorship is justified to prevent attacks against minority groups and the disadvantaged. It is this set of arguments that will be examined here.

The social democrat, unlike the libertarian, does not accept freedom as an absolute. People do not have the right to discriminate, nor do they have the right to deceive or to harm others (cry fire in a crowded theater). Morris Ernst, a prominent civil liberties lawyer, makes a distinction among ideas, sedition, and merchandising words.[27] Only the first of these is protected, claims Ernst. But some would go further and ask, since we do not permit libel of individuals, should we allow libel of groups? Why should we permit literature that attacks Jews, blacks, or women in our libraries? To give such works a place on the shelf gives them a legitimacy they do not deserve. While Hitler's *Mein Kampf* deserves a place as a historical document, contemporary Nazi tracts do not deserve any recognition. This, of course, presumes we are able to distinguish among those writings that are politically correct and those that are not. While this may seem troubling, the social democrat contends that librarians continually sell those books that are considered outdated and wrong. Just as a fact can be shown to be wrong, so can an opinion.

Among the groups that have made a special attempt to indicate their disapproval of certain types of literature are the National Organization for Women and the Council on Interracial Books for Children. They condemn such books as *The Story of Doctor Doolittle, Mary Poppins,* and *Hansel and Gretel* on grounds of racism, enthnocentrism and sexism. These groups justify their position based on the Fourteenth Amendment's guarantee of "equal protection of the law" Author Melvin Berger warns that books can have real (and harmful) effects: "If a book presents a poor image of some group of people, it deprives them of equal protection and may lead others to treat the group in a different way, which also violates the Civil Rights Act of 1964. . . . Books that show such bias are contributing to discrimination. . . . and are thus justly criticized."[28] Although these groups do not support censorship as such, they recommend that the books chosen and purchased present desirable images.[29] This directly affects publishers and means that fewer "incorrect" books will be published. In a recent incident, a supposedly racist children's book, *Jake and Honeybunch Go To Heaven,* was refused by many libraries, even though they had other books by this popular children's author.[30] Raising the consciousness of librarians so they self-censor books has also long been a tactic of the conservative.

Radical feminists who are concerned about the effects of pornography recently have made one of the more interesting ar-

guments in the debate over censorship. Andrea Dworkin, author of *Pornography: Men Possessing Women*, ably presents the
feminists' view that pornography sends an ideological message
to women. Dworkin writes,

> The major theme of pornography as a genre is male power,
> its nature, its magnitude, its use, its meaning. Male power,
> as expressed in and through pornography, is discernible in
> discrete but interwoven, reinforcing strains: the power of
> self, physical power over and against others, the power of
> terror, the power of naming, the power of owning, the
> power of money, and the power of sex. These strains of
> male power are intrinsic to both the substance and produc-
> tion of pornography, and the ways and means of pornogra-
> phy are the ways and means of male power.[31]

While feminists and conservatives both oppose pornography,
they do so on quite different grounds. The conservative sees the
obscene as undermining morality, whereas the feminist sees
pornography as an affront to the civil rights of women. Indeed,
the City of Minneapolis recently passed an ordinance (subsequently vetoed by the mayor) that defined pornography as a
form of sexual discrimination against women, violating their civil
rights. Under this ordinance a person could sue those who
display pornography (which could include libraries).[32] The of-
fense is to a minority group, as opposed to an attack on the moral
fibre of the society as a whole. Ironically, defining pornography
in terms of its ideological components seems to give it additional
dignity and makes it fall clearly under the rubric of the First
Amendment.

Pornography and Social Research

As actors in the political drama, pornographers do not have too
many admirers. Nevertheless, until quite recently, there was no
substantial social scientific research that demonstrated that this
"art form" could have negative consequences. At one time, aca-

demics were among the most vocal opponents of censorship, arguing that there is little evidence that pornography leads to violence against women. Although the major battle about library censorship is not about the purchase of explicitly pornographic materials, libertarians believe that such materials should be included.

Discovering the effects of sexually explicit material on public behavior is not easy. Rapists are surely different from lawful persons on more than their reading and viewing habits. Nor are potential rapists likely to reveal candidly their inner secrets to prying social scientists. As a result, most of the research on the effects of pornography has been laboratory experiments conducted with college students. Perhaps the leading advocate of this approach to studying pornography is Wisconsin social psychologist Edward Donnerstein. Donnerstein's research is especially concerned about the relationship of pornographic films to violence on women.[33]

The basic methodology in Donnerstein's numerous experiments[34] uses a male student in an introductory psychology course who signs up to particiate in an experiment to earn extra credit toward his final grade in the course. When he arrives at the laboratory, he meets a second subject, who is actually a confederate of the experimenter. He is told by the experimenter that the research is designed to study performance under stress. The student is asked to write an essay that is to be evaluated by the other "subject" who may shock him if the essay is a poor one. After completing the essay and regardless of the quality of the writing, the student is shocked a set number of times. Presumably he believes this judgment has been made by his fellow subject. Then, in a "break" in the experiment, the subject is asked to rate and provide physiological measures about a film that is supposed to be used for a future experiment. Some of the films are pornographic, some are not. After the film, the original experiment begins again. The subject now gets to shock the experimental confederate after the confederate performs a task. Finally the subject is given a short questionnaire, and the real purpose of the experiment is explained.

Among the conditions tested in this methodology is

whether there is a different response to a male or female confederate, whether the amount of shocks received by the subject (his level of "anger") affects his response, and whether the content of the film (pornographic or not) affects his behavior. This is supposed to measure aggression, which is measured by the level of shock he decides to give to the confederate when it is his turn to punish, which is supposed to be a surrogate for rape.

Laboratory experiments sometimes seem to compete with the best of the Broadway stage in the intricacy of their plotting. We never learn exactly what the subject *believes* he is experiencing, only that he reports being angry when expected to be and aroused when that is called for. These "manipulation checks" suggest that the experimental manipulations are having some effect, presumably the one that is intended. The control the experimenter has over the situation is one of the most potent advantages of this methodology. Nevertheless, we cannot be certain how the subject is defining the events he is experiencing. By focusing on the experimenter's view of the world, this methodology is alien to interactional methods, yet is congruent with functionalism and conflict theory. Since Donnerstein is examining the feminist issue of the relationship between pornography and violence toward women, we can tentatively label this body of research as falling within the conflict theory approach.

In a forthcoming book Donnerstein describes eight of his most recent experiments in this area, a style of presentation that is often found among experimental social psychologists. The assumption is that each experiment leads to the next as the experimenter tests related questions. The results of one study provide questions for the next. Each experiment further refines the experimenter's theory and eliminates hypotheses that are demonstrated to be false. Thus, experimental social psychology may be closer to the model of "natural science" than any other methodology described here.

It is not possible to describe Donnerstein's whole series of experiments. The following only briefly summarizes some of his most significant conclusions. Basically, his findings support the view that viewing pornography, even for short periods of time, even by "intellectual" college students, can increase the level of violence toward women. This is not, however, the case with all pornography, only that which also shows aggression toward women—such as a film in which a man rapes a woman and in which she appears to enjoy it. In such a situation, Donnerstein suggests that the male's inhibitions against violence toward women are lowered. Angry male subjects are particularly likely to shock female confederates after seeing a film that is both aggressive and pornographic. Even films that are "merely" aggressive toward women (with no overtly sexual content) can, in some instances, provoke higher levels of shock to females. Aggressive pornography does not appear to produce heightened aggression toward other male subjects.

Such experiments provide troubling indications that potentially material found in libraries (in this case films, not books) can have unsavory effects. Even though Donnerstein does not argue for censoring such materials, it is significant that the proponents of the recent anti-pornography ordinance in Minneapolis brought in Professor Donnerstein as a witness to testify about his research. His approach is perceived as being supportive of feminist activists who wish to limit pornographic violence. These findings certainly add weight to those social democratic arguments that claim pornographic material is an assault on women.

Censorship and Education

In part, the arguments raised in this chapter boil down to questions about trust. How much should we trust ourselves? How willing should the government be to trust its citizens? Americans believe that education can have positive effects on those who are educated. Few people would ever question this belief. But, if there is positive education, is there also negative education? Are there some things that are harmful to us as individuals and to the society we are part of? Is learning some particularly kinky sexual technique likely to make us or our partners immoral? Are there some things that would be better for us not to know? Those who see individual human beings as naturally good and rational (the libertarians) argue that a person can make his or her own choices. But, if we agree with the conservatives that human nature is basically fallible, we might wish to opt for some measure of control.

The long-term effects of communication are very difficult to determine. If we could somehow arrange a random group of subjects that had been exposed only to pornography (or televised violence or comic books) and compare them to another random sample that had no exposure, we could better understand the nature of cultural effects. Unfortunately this is not possible. People who choose to read pornography are different from people who do not in many ways, so it is virtually impossible to get any definitive effects of long-term exposure. Also, the effects of pornography may be so subtle that it would require very large groups to notice any difference. Perhaps only 1 of 1,000 people are affected by pornography in a harmful way.

A second set of questions concerns who should do the controlling? We can expand this question from the issue of library censorship to that of education as a whole. Is it right and proper for the government (even a local government) to run schools? How can these institutions, populated by government employees, help but pass on the government line? While this line may not be inflexible, the very fact that teachers are certified by the government and are paid through public taxes, makes them prone to accept the rightness of state power. Can you imagine a school that kept as much distance from the state as public schools must keep from the church?

Education in a free society is a dangerous business. Education implies the teaching of beliefs, ideas, norms, and values. But in a democracy, what should be taught? We want to teach our children the truth, but we cannot always agree on what the truth is. Do we agree sufficiently on a political or moral system to permit one truth to be taught? Should we teach our children that communism is wrong, even though some of us think it is right? Should we teach them to respect their fellow citizens, even though we may feel some do not deserve respect? Should we only teach evolution, or should we also teach creationism? And what should we do with sex education: strictly teach it as fundamentals of human plumbing? The more the members of a society share a view of the world, the more agreement there will be on the content of education. Perhaps, then, we should relish our disputes about what children should learn; surely it indicates we are still free.

Questions

1. What is the difference, if any, between selection and censorship?
2. Should librarians have the sole responsibility for deciding which books to purchase?
3. What kind of input should citizens have in the book selection process?
4. On what basis should books be purchased for a small public library?
5. Is there a "freedom to read?"
6. Should obscene works be censored by the government?
7. Should hard-core pornography be purchased by libraries?
8. Should children be prevented from reading some books?
9. Does a diversity of opinion lead to freedom or the breakdown of order?
10. Should libraries purchase books that are racist or sexist?

For Further Study

Berger, Melvin. *Censorship*. New York: Franklin Watts, 1982.

Boyer, Paul S. *Purity in Print: The Vice-Society Movement and*

Book Censorship in America. New York: Charles Scribner's Sons, 1968.

Busha, Charles H. *Freedom Versus Suppression and Censorship*. Littleton, Colorado: Libraries Unlimited, 1972.

Clor, Harry M. *Obscenity and Public Morality: Censorship in a Liberal Society*. Chicago: University of Chicago Press, 1969.

Dworkin, Andrea. *Pornography: Men Possessing Women*. New York: Perigee, 1981.

Office for Intellectual Freedom of the American Library Association, *Intellectual Freedom Manual*. Chicago: American Library Association, 1974.

Thomas, Cal. *Book Burning*. Westchester, Illinois: Crossway Books, 1983.

Zurcher, Jr., Louis A. and Kirkpatrick, R. George. *Citizens for Decency: Antipornography Crusades as Status Defense*. Austin: University of Texas Press, 1976.

Notes and References

1. Mary and Herbert Knapp, *One Potato, Two Potato . . . : The Secret Education of American Children* (New York: W.W. Norton, 1976), p. 173.
2. The National Commission on Excellence in Education, *A Nation at Risk: The Imperative for Educational Reform* (Washington, D.C.: U.S. Department of Education, 1983), pp. 8–9.
3. Barry Glassner, "Kid Society," *Urban Education* 11 (1976): 5–22.
4. James Coleman, et al., *Equality of Educational Opportunity* (Washington, D.C.: U.S. Government Printing Office, 1966).
5. Robert Rosenthal and Lenore Jacobson, *Pygmalion in the Classroom* (New York: Holt, Rinehart and Winston, 1968).
6. Ivan Illich, *Deschooling Society* (New York: Harper & Row, 1971), pp. 1–24.
7. Harold D. Lasswell, "Censorship," in *Encyclopedia of the Social Sciences* (New York: Macmillan, 1930), vol. 3, p. 290, quoted in

Charles H. Busha, *Freedom Versus Suppression and Censorship* (Littleton, Colorado: Libraries Unlimited, 1972), p. 83.

8. Leon Carnovsky, "The Obligations and Responsibilities of the Librarian Concerning Censorship," *The First Freedom*, Robert B. Downs, ed., (Chicago: American Library Association, 1960), p. 312.

9. Paul S. Boyer, *Purity in Print* (New York: Charles Scribner's Sons, 1968), pp. 1–5.

10. James Mann, "Books and TV—New Targets of Religious Right," *U.S. News and World Report*, June 8, 1981, p. 45.

11. Marjorie Fiske, *Book Selection and Censorship: A Study of School and Public Libraries in California* (Berkeley: University of California Press, 1959), cited in Busha, *op. cit.*, p. 89.

12. Oliver Garceau, *The Public Library in the Political Process* (New York: Columbia University Press, 1949), p. 132 in Busha, *op. cit.*, p. 87.

13. Busha, *op. cit.*, p. 75.

14. John Stuart Mill in Carnovsky, *op. cit.*, p. 313.

15. Office for Intellectual Freedom of the American Library Association, *Intellectual Freedom Manual* (Chicago: American Library Association, 1974). Part 2, pp. 14–15.

16. Milton Friedman, "Book Burning, FCC Style," *Newsweek*, June 16, 1969, p. 86.

17. Editorial, *Arkansas Gazette*, June 27, 1973, printed in *Editorials on File*, vol. 4, January-June, 1973, p. 844.

18. Gordon McShean, *Running a Message Parlour: A Librarian's Medium-rare Memoir About Censorship* (Palo Alto: Ramparts Press, 1977), pp. 229–232.

19. Mulford Q. Sibley, "Intellectual Freedom, Suppression, and Obscenity," *Intellectual Freedom in Minnesota: The Continuing Problem of "Obscenity,"* Nancy K. Herther, ed., (Minneapolis: Minnesota Library Association, 1979), pp. 14–15.

20. Louis A. Zurcher, Jr. and R. George Kirkpatrick, *Citizens for Decency: Antipornography Crusades as Status Defense* (Austin: University of Texas Press, 1976), pp. 242–243.

21. James Rorty, "The Attack on Our Libraries," in Downs, *op. cit.*, p. 304.

22. Cal Thomas, *Book Burning* (Westchester, Illinois: Crossway Books, 1983), p. 80.

23. Harry Clor, *Obscenity and Public Morality* (Chicago: University of Chicago Press, 1976), p. 199.

24. Editorial, *Dallas Times Herald,* June 22, 1973, printed in *Editorials on File,* vol. 4, January-June, 1973, p. 838.

25. George Will, quoted in Thomas, *op. cit.,* p. 22.

26. Editorial, *Wall Street Journal,* June 27, 1973, printed in *Editorials on File,* vol. 4, January-June, 1973, p. 841.

27. Clor, *op. cit.,* p. 103.

28. Melvin Berger, *Censorship* (New York: Franklin Watts, 1982), p. 65.

29. *Ibid,* pp. 64–65.

30. "Black Folklore Controversy Erupts: Farrar Questions Selection Policies," *School Library Journal,* vol. 29 (March 1983): 68.

31. Andrea Dworkin, *Pornography: Men Possessing Women* (New York: Perigee Books, 1981), p. 24.

32. Jean Bethke Elshtain, "The New Porn Wars," *New Republic,* June 25, 1984, pp. 15–20.

33. Edward Donnerstein, "Pornography: Its Effect on Violence Against Women," *Pornography and Sexual Aggression,* Neil M. Malamuth and Edward Donnerstein, eds. (New York: Academic Press, 1984, in press).

34. Edward Donnerstein and Gary Barrett, "Effects of Erotic Stimuli on Male Aggression Toward Females," *Journal of Personality and Social Psychology* 36 (1978): 182–183.

 **Nine**

Social Movements/ Collective Behavior: Can Civil Disobedience Be Justified?

"WE SHALL OVERCOME," says an old Negro spiritual, which in time, has become the anthem for the civil rights movement. This song recognizes the important role that groups of citizens have in our social system. People have the right, perhaps the obligation, to protest when they feel that injustice is being practiced by the government, social institutions, or their fellow citizens.

Although Americans like to think of themselves as having a representative democracy, this represents only part of how policy is made. Elections are not the only means by which citizens influence their government. The First Amendment to the Constitution, the right to assemble peaceably and to petition the government for redress of grievances, is also a way to bring about change. It is a valuable tool in a free society. Throughout our history, citizens have attempted to change government policies through social movements and collective behavior—topics much examined by sociologists.

A *social movement* is a collection of individuals who organize together to achieve or prevent some social or political change. Obviously, social movements differ considerably in their structure, tactics, ideology, and goals. Some social movements are centrally organized with a strong and effective hierarchy. This hierarchy may be open or secretive, democratic or authoritarian. Social movements may engage in persuasion, letter writing, voter registration, civil disobedience, or violence. Depending on a perceived need and effectiveness, people within a social movement may change their approach. Thus, some terrorist organizations may renounce terrorism when they perceive it is in their interest to do so; other groups may become frustrated within the political sphere, and choose to become more violent. There is some evidence that in America groups engaging in forceful action (violence or civil disobedience) are more successful in responding to repressive treatment than "meek" organizations.[1]

Throughout American history a remarkable array of social movements has existed: from the International Workers of the World to the National Association of Manufacturers, from the Students for a Democratic Society to the Women's Christian Temperance Union, from the American Nazi party to Bnai B'rith. These movements reflect libertarian, conservative, and social democratic ideologies, and others not as compatible with democratic ideals. The goals and ideas these groups choose to fight for are extremely diverse. Some groups organize to promote change and others (called *counter-movements*) oppose it. Sometimes after change occurs (as after the 1973 Supreme Court decision that legalized most abortions) the role of opposing movement organizations switch. The pro-abortion groups are fighting to keep things the way they are while anti-abortion groups are fighting to change the situation.

Sociologists have proposed a number of theories to explain what causes the emergence of social movements. An early approach suggests that members of social movements have psychological characteristics in common. These theorists, such as

Gustave LeBon,[2] see social movements as fundamentally irrational, as are their participants. Other theorists emphasize that social movements meet a need for the individual member. These approaches, however, ignore what the movement is fighting for in their haste to characterize the participants. While it seems reasonable to suggest that people who choose to be active in social movements may have different preferences than those who do not, this does not explain why a movement exists or why it arises when it does.

One explanation is the existence of "strain" in society. When a problem (a strain) is recognized, groups are likely to coalesce to deal with it. This strain may be an "objective" problem (such as the existence of guns), or a "perceived" problem (such as people feeling relatively deprived compared to others). Such a theory has considerable appeal, because it recognizes that social movements are a response to what is occurring in society. Yet, some charge that strain theories rely too heavily on a simple cause-effect analogy. The problem exists and then a social movement arises to meet it. The difficulty here is there are many problems but only a few social movements. For example, one of the most active social movements is attempting to obtain a nuclear freeze. It is by no means clear, however, that the proliferation of nuclear weapons is a recent problem or even that it is the most pressing problem.

Resource mobilization theory[3] has been formulated to explain why some movements succeed and others do not. As the name suggests, access to resources is crucial to an aspiring movement. No social movement can grow until there is a committed group of individuals who are willing to acquire and use resources. In the broadest sense, these resources need not only be material objects, but can also include mobilization of the press, recruitment, and use of members' social networks. These mobilizers may, at first, be outsiders, with the expertise and resources to assist in the mobilization of a movement, such as the members of the Communist Party of America who went down south during the 1930s to help organize southern workers.

Typically, social movements that are oriented toward change will not have the material resources of governments or those in favor of keeping the status quo. But one potential advantage they do have is their ability to use "bodies" in collective behavior. *Collective behavior* is the behavior of large numbers of people, which typically is unstructured and relatively unplanned. Crowds, mobs, demonstrations, sit-ins, and picketlines are instances of collective behavior. While social movements may not have much cash, they have supporters, and these supporters can make a strong argument by their mere presence.

Some people argue that crowds are, by their nature, irrational (they have a "group mind") and subject to contagious mass behavior,[4] but an alternate view sees collective behavior in a more positive light. According to the emergent norm theory,[5] crowds are not as uniform as they might appear from a distance. For example, participants may have different motives for being present: from some looking for violence to others hoping to meet a member of the opposite sex; a few hope to pick a pocket, while still others express a deeply held conviction. This approach to collective behavior suggests norms develop through the interaction of the group. A crowd situation is usually ambiguous, with most of its members not certain what they should be doing. As a result, a few outspoken members can define proper behavior. Even though the majority of the crowd may not feel strongly, it will typically go along because at the moment it seems the proper thing to do. This approach to crowd behavior is set squarely within the interactionist tradition because it assumes what is happening will be uncertain until it is defined through the dynamics of social contact.

Whether social movements and collective behavior are functional or harmful depends on how you evaluate their methods and goals. Functional sociologists are more cautious than conflict sociologists about endorsing the idea of collective behavior as such, because it may indicate a radical restructuring of the relationships within a social system. Conflict theorists are more enthusiastic about such behavior and hope for the radical restructuring of relationship among classes and social institutions—something that would disturb functionalists.

Question:

Can Civil Disobedience Be Justified?

Does true freedom mean the right to say "No!" whenever one feels like it? For some this is precisely what freedom means and, for those individuals, civil disobedience comes easy. The issue of what constitutes civil disobedience has always been a difficult definitional problem for philosophers, political theorists, and jurists. I will use a simple and rather straightforward definition of the term: "Anyone commits an act of civil disobedience if and only if he acts illegally, publicly, nonviolently, and conscientiously with the intent to frustrate (one of) the laws, policies, or decisions of his government."[6] Obviously no society can long exist if every citizen chooses the laws he or she will accept or disobey. Of course, civil disobedience is different from disobeying laws generally; it is a subset of all law-breaking. Among the criteria usually proposed to differentiate civil disobedience from other criminal activity are that in addition to being performed in public view, it is: derived from moral principles, avoids harm to others, and usually the case that the lawbreaker willingly accepts the punishment given out by the courts.[7] It is this last feature of civil disobedience that may differentiate some recent American protestors from the tradition of true civil disobedience since many of these people have attempted to avoid the punishment they otherwise would have received.

The history of civil disobedience is a lengthy one, populated with numerous distinguished names. Socrates and Antigone both refused to obey the state on what they believed to be moral grounds. Saint Augustine points to the Gospels as justification for civil disobedience to immoral laws. More recently the example of Mahatma Gandhi in the campaign for Indian independence has proven to be an attractive model for many pacifists. Gandhi was able to free India from British rule with a minimum of violence; he succeeded because he had moral authority on his side and was backed by millions of nonviolently protesting Hindus and Moslems.

In America, too, civil disobedience has had a long history.

In 1755 Pennsylvania Quakers opposed taxes levied by the British to fight the French and Indian Wars. Some might consider the Boston Tea Party to be an act of civil disobedience although, in this case, the protestors were not arguing that a law was immoral but that it was passed without the representation of the colonists. Throughout the Revolutionary War there were acts of civil disobedience aimed at the British. Even after Americans had their own government, protests continued. Throughout our history, some people of conscience have refused to pay taxes for wars they considered immoral or unjust. Perhaps the most sustained period of civil disobedience during the nineteenth century concerned the opposition to acts that condoned slavery. Many northern abolitionists who strenuously opposed the fugitive slave act aided and abetted slaves in winning their freedom.

The twentieth century has also witnessed considerable disobedience. The civil rights movement, and its leader, the Reverend Martin Luther King, used the inspiration of Gandhi to organize nonviolent civil disobedience. Civil disobedience continued throughout the decade with protests against the war in Vietnam, including sit-ins, draft card burning, and tax protests. Although the amount of civil disobedience declined during the mid-1970s, by the end of the decade and into the 1980s protest aimed first at nuclear power plants and then at nuclear arms production increased. In the six-month period of March to September 1982, 3,481 persons were arrested for protesting the nation's nuclear weapons policy. Many of these people were arrested at large-scale demonstrations at the United Nations and at the Lawrence Livermore Laboratory, near San Francisco. Of these, nearly 1,500 spent some time in jail.[8] Tax protest, also grew in number in the latter part of the decade, though it apparently did not reach that of the Vietnam peak. During 1971, the IRS recorded a peak of 1,740 returns from war tax resisters (and a remarkable 70,000 households resisted the federal excise tax on telephone bills in 1972 and 1973). In 1979, the IRS estimated between 1,000 and 2,000 Americans were war tax resisters.[9]

Most of the social movements mentioned so far are considered liberal causes, but the right also participates in this kind of activity. During 1981, as many as five thousand auto workers participated in a tax-resistance movement with ties to the extreme right.[10] Likewise, fundamentalist ministers disobeyed the laws when Nebraska courts shut down a fundamentalist religious school. Reverend Jerry Falwell's Moral Majority endorsed civil disobedience in such cases. Remember that anyone can claim a moral objection to laws he or she dislikes.

Civil disobedience is often an effective means of achieving change. Even if people do not gain immediate satisfaction, they get publicity for their cause exposing the ideas of the social movement to other citizens who would not otherwise know about it. This represents, in the words of the Russian revolutionary Pyotr Kropotkin, "the propaganda of the deed." The act, whether or not effective in achieving the group's ends, does communicate a message to the public.

The Libertarian Point of View

Libertarians believe individual freedom is the ultimate value in society; as a result, they see civil disobedience as a profoundly moral act. It is moral, not so much because it prevents the application of an unjust law, but because the individual stands up to an oppressive government. Although libertarians do not support random or continual law-breaking, the content of the law that is broken is not as critical as it is to social democrats.

Probably the greatest theorist of civil disobedience from a libertarian perspective was Henry David Thoreau, the nineteenth century Massachusetts transcendentalist. Following the lead of his friend Bronson Alcott, Thoreau refused to pay the Massachusetts poll tax as a matter of principle. Thoreau's immediate objection to the tax was Massachusetts's indirect support of slavery and the U.S. goverment's expansionist war with Mexico. These were only symptoms of something larger, however. Thoreau made clear that his opposition was really an opposition to all government. In July 1846, he was stopped in Concord by the local constable who asked him to pay the tax he had not paid for three or four years. When Thoreau refused to pay, the constable jailed him. By the following morning, an anonymous friend had paid his tax and Thoreau went on his way. His night in jail led to Thoreau's 1848 lecture to the Concord Lyceum, "The Relation of the Individual to the State," now better known as "Civil Disobedience." Thoreau rejected the coercive power of the state, writing:

> I heartily accept the motto, "That government is best which governs least;" and I should like to see it acted up to more rapidly and systematically. Carried out, it finally amounts to this, which also I believe—"That government is best which governs not at all;" and when men are prepared for it, that will be the kind of government which they will have . . . . It is for no particular item in the tax-bill that I refuse to pay it. I simply wish to refuse allegiance to the State, to withdraw and stand aloof from it effectually. I do not care to trace the course of my dollar, if I could, till it buys a man or a musket to shoot one with—the dollar is innocent—but I am concerned to trace the effects of my allegiance. In fact, I quietly declare war with the State, after my fashion, though I will still make what use and get what advantage of her I can, as is usual in such cases.[11]

What, then, is Thoreau's theory of government; are we truly to live in a state of blissful anarchy? Thoreau's idealistic answer is that the individual conscience must always take priority over the state. For Thoreau the consent of the governed depends on each individual law and can be withdrawn at will:

> The authority of government, even such as I am willing to submit to . . . is still an impure one: to be strictly just, it must have the sanction and consent of the governed. It can have no pure right over my person and property but what I concede to it. The progress from an absolute to a limited monarchy to a democracy, is a progress toward a true respect for the individual. . . . Is a democracy, such as we know it, the last improvement possible in government? Is it not possible to take a step further toward recognizing and organizing the rights of man? There will never be a really free and enlightened State until the State comes to recog-

nize the individual as a higher and independent power, from which all its own power and authority are derived, and treats him accordingly.[12]

The ultimate power in a social system for the libertarian is the individual, and some libertarians even claim that their theory of government is profoundly anti-war because it rejects the need for collective force. Libertarians note that many nuclear war protestors see no contradiction in government forcing individuals to support other programs. That is, many of these hypocritical protestors accept government power as essential. Frederick C. Foote, a libertarian law student, argues that a weak state is not a warlike state: "Laissez-faire capitalism, in contrast [to socialism or a welfare state], is the only social system that consistently upholds individual rights and bans the use of force against peaceful citizens. It is the only system under which no group, however large, can use force against another group, however small. *In theory and in practice, Laissez-faire capitalism is the only social system fundamentally opposed to war*."[13]

The extent to which libertarians disobey laws varies; some, despite their rhetoric, are model citizens. Others try to do whatever they can to remain free of government entanglements in this complex world. While the voluntary compliance to the Internal Revenue Service is extraordinarily high, the IRS has methods for enforcing its will. It takes a brave, committed, masochistic, or foolish person to stand up to this might.[14] Yet, despite the difficulty, libertarians believe it is the mark of free citizens to pick and choose which laws they will obey,[15] and on occasion to say, "I won't." While you may pick and choose which laws you will obey, other free citizens may choose to isolate you if they think you have made poor decisions; this threat produces cooperation and social order.

The Social Democratic Point of View

Civil disobedience is a problem for social democrats because they believe in the power of the state to do what is morally right and to enforce equality. Whereas libertarians believe self-motivated civil disobedience is morally justified, the social democrat examines the goal of the disobedience and the nature of the government involved. Moreover, the social democrat is likely to welcome a collective social movement more than the libertarian, who focuses more on individual moral actions.

The nature of the government is critical to social democrats. Political scientist Hanna Pitkin writes, "If it is a good, just government doing what a government should, then you must obey it; if it is a tyrannical, unjust government trying to do what no government should, then you have no such obligation. . . . Legitimate government acts within the limits of the authority rational men would, abstractly and hypothetically, have to give a government they are founding. Legitimate government is government which deserves consent."[16]

This sense of moral absolutes is found throughout social democratic writing. They believe equality and justice are concepts worth protesting for. The social democrat does not like all governments, only moral ones. Consider the words of Yale University Chaplain William Sloane Coffin, an outspoken supporter of civil rights and opponent of the war in Vietnam:

> Too often we forget that majority rule can never be equated with the rule of conscience. After all, the majority of our citizens have in the past supported slavery and child labor, and today still support various forms of racial discrimination, sex discrimination, slums, and a penal system far more punitive than curative. . . . [W]e must recognize that justice is a higher social goal than law and order. . . . Rarely do the powerful ask which side is struggling for greater justice; rarely do the powerful see what is clear to me, that a conflict for the emancipation of a race or a class or a nation has more moral justification than a law to perpetuate privileges. In other words, the oppressed have a higher moral right to challenge oppression than oppressors have to maintain it.[17]

In war-tax protest this issue is sometimes phrased as the hypocrisy of "praying for peace and paying for war." The problem with this approach is who defines what is moral? Consider the comments of the Reverend Martin Luther King, Jr.: "A just law is a law that squares with a moral law. It is a law that squares with that which is right, so that any law that uplifts human personality is a just law. Whereas that law which is out of harmony with the moral is a law which does not square with the moral law of the universe. It does not square with the law of God, so for that reason it is unjust and any law that degrades the human personality is an unjust law."[18]

King suggests that to disobey an unjust law reveals deep respect for *law*. But such a belief does not really solve anything. As we know from the history of religious strife, God's law is not easily interpreted by human beings. Some churches discriminate against blacks because of their interpretation of the Bible; should those churches engage in civil disobedience to prevent integration? Should those citizens who are against abortion act from their moral principles and stand in the doorway of abortion clinics or prevent them from being built, as others do at nuclear plants? These are difficult questions for social democrats to answer since presumably not all forms of disobedience are justified from their position. If citizens share a belief in what is moral (for example, the abolition of slavery or the prevention of nuclear war) and they can agree on which tactics help them reach that goal, then civil disobedience is morally right—both in provoking the government to act and in raising moral issues in the minds of others.

Social democrats see civil disobedience as a moral drama—an action designed to persuade and to lead to further action. David Carlin, Jr., a Rhode Island State Senator, sees civil disobedience as a form of political theater.

> Civil disobedience is essentially a theatrical performance, a public action carried out in full view of an audience and with that audience in mind. Like a good play, it will exhibit character as well as plot. That is, actors will make the audience understand not simply the significance of their act of disobedience, but the significance also of the characters performing the act; for unless we understand the characters, we will not be able to appreciate their actions. In this

particular play the characters, of course, will be those of exceptionally good persons—the saints or moral heroes.[19]

From this perspective it is not surprising that religious people are frequently publicized for their activity in civil disobedience. Religious leaders give the movement moral credence by indicating that the protest is founded on justice and human values and not in selfishness.

The Conservative Point of View

Because of their love for order, civil disobedience presents a troubling moral issue for conservatives. A government must lose all shred of moral authority and democratic process before the conservative will concede the right to disobey laws. Laws in a democracy are enacted with the consent of the governed. If citizens oppose the laws, they can elect different politicians in the next election and operate within the accepted political channels. Because a political democracy allows us to change leaders, some legal authorities, such as Alexander Bickel, see all civil disobedience as coercive in its ultimate attempt to sidestep the electoral process.[20]

As one judge comments that, "Every time that a law is disobeyed by even a man whose motive is solely ethical, in the sense that it is responsive to a deep moral conviction, there are unfortunate consequences. He himself becomes more prone to disobey laws for which he has no profound repugnance. He sets an example for others who may not have his pure motives. He weakens the fabric of society."[21]

If someone believes the legal process is sacred (or nearly so), then any disruption becomes a very serious breach of order. Those people who civilly disobey the law may wish to define their action as obeying a higher law, but Cornell University philosopher Stuart Brown, Jr. contends that lawbreaking is lawbreaking:

> The very notion of a justified case of [civil disobedience] seems to imply a contradiction. It seems to imply the possi-

bility of a legally permitted case of lawbreaking. For if civil disobedience, which is lawbreaking, can be justified, then surely the law ought to permit it where justified. But the law logically cannot permit lawbreaking. It logically cannot take the position that in the course of a public protest the breach of a valid law is no breach. . . . The moral beliefs and convictions of a man absolve him from obedience to the law only where the law itself allows.[22]

The conservative emphasizes the responsibility that citizens have to abide by the laws they, through their votes, helped to enact. It is too tempting for people to structure their sense of outrage and impassioned morality on the basis of whether their side has prevailed in a fair political struggle. Just as the majority may not always be right, it need not always be wrong, and there should be a strong presumption that it is correct. The conservative is likely to reject claims that the United States is not truly a democracy and not worthy of support from its citizens. Philosopher Sidney Hook sees the social democratic vision of civil disobedience as "sour grapes." He writes, "It is characteristic of those who argue this way to define the presence or absence of the democratic process by whether or not *they* get their political way, and not by the presence or absence of democratic institutional processes. The rules of the game exist to enable them to win and if they lose that's sufficient proof the game is rigged and dishonest."[23] Of course, if a person believes he or she is fighting for basic moral principles, a defeat would only support his or her questioning of the legitimacy of democratic institutions.

Conservatives also maintain that civil disobedience affects everyone in the society in that it costs the taxpayers money that could be spent elsewhere. Consider tax protests. If tax protesting ever reached significant levels, non-protesting taxpayers might have to make up the difference that the government loses by not being able to collect taxes from everyone. Rather than preventing the government from spending money on military weapons, these protestors might only insure that everyone else's taxes will be proportionally higher. At the present time such redistribution of the tax burden has little practical effect, but it could. Likewise, protests of all kinds, and particularly those that involve civil disobedience, cost taxpayers money for police, court proceedings, jailing, and sanitation. One protest in Minneapolis in 1983 against the Honeywell Corporation, which makes guidance systems for nuclear missiles, resulted in the arrest of 577 people. It is estimated that this protest will cost local taxpayers at least $40,000[24]—money that might have been used for social service projects. One conservative group became so irate at this "waste" of taxpayer money that they sued the groups involved for $500,000, charging that, "The public and plaintiffs should not unilaterally be compelled to bear the considerable costs knowingly caused by the planned large-scale illegal actions intended to intimidate the public and attract free media advertising."[25] Whether restitution is legal in this case remains to be determined by the courts. The cost of law enforcement is not usually borne by the criminal, although some might suggest this idea is worthy of study.

Civil disobedience is an affront to public order and, as such, conservatives can be expected to oppose it. The morality of a social movement's cause has little weight against the morality of the legitimate social institutions of a nation.

Moral Development and Social Research

For most students today the decade of the 1960s was not an age of protest and civil disobedience, but one of teething and toilet training. For you the slogan "Make Love, Not War" was not a call to action, but a birthright. The first, and perhaps the most significant, of the protest movements of the 1960s was the free speech movement at the University of California at Berkeley. Students in 1964 conducted an illegal sit-in at the campus administration building, demanding to have a wide variety of speakers on campus. As a consequence of their action, many were arrested.

Norma Haan, a researcher at Berkeley, was curious about the moral reasoning of those involved in this controversy. In order to learn how students justified or condemned the free speech movement, she sent questionnaires to three groups of students: students who were arrested during the protest, students who were members of conservative and/or Republican groups, and a random cross-section of Berkeley students. In this survey, she asked the participants to provide moral justifications to a set of hypothetical situations and specific moral questions about the sit-in (for example, "Do you think it was right or wrong for the students to sit in? Why, or why not?")[26]

The hypothetical and actual moral reasoning responses were then divided by two coders into six moral reasoning categories developed by psychologist Lawrence Kohlberg.[27] Kohlberg believes that individuals progress through six stages of moral reasoning, with the first two, mainly egocentric, primarily characteristic of childhood. Stages three and four, termed "conventional" moral reasoning, focus on the role of authority in determining proper action. Stages five and six, "principled" reasoning, return the responsibility for moral judgment to the individual actor—suggesting either that the rights and duties of individuals be respected (stage five) or that transcendent moral principles be observed (stage six). Kohlberg believes that individuals proceed through these stages sequentially until they reach their highest level of moral reasoning. He suggests that only a small proportion of people will ever base their reasoning on transcendent moral principles. Haan differs from this approach to some degree because she recognizes that the context of reasoning is important. It is her concern for context that makes this study of moral reasoning fall within the interactionist approach. Moral meanings can change depending upon what is going on around you. (We must also be cautious in judging a person's capacity for moral reasoning from their answers to hypothetical issues.)

Haan's methodology might perhaps be called an "experimental survey." She compares the reactions of three different groups of subjects to two types of moral dilemmas (actual and hypothetical). She hypothesizes that there should be systematic differences between a person's reasoning about real situations and about hypothetical ones. Even though this is not the focus of the analysis, she is also able to examine differences among those with different attitudes toward civil disobedience. Haan attempts to incorporate the advantages from survey research and from experimental research. Specifically, she uses a broad sample of subjects who respond to a large set of questions, that allows her to contrast responses of groups of subjects. There is at least one weakness in her research method. Because the questionnaires were mailed to subjects, only half of the potential subjects responded and perhaps those who did were only half-hearted in their responses. And by lumping these subjects into large groups, some of the meanings of their personal situations may have been lost.

Haan's findings support the importance of context in moral reasoning. Focusing on those students who engaged in civil disobedience and were arrested (the group most pertinent to the arguments in this chapter), Haan discovered that 63 percent, a clear majority, showed an *increase* in their level of moral reasoning when discussing their justifications for civil disobedience during the sit-in, as compared to their responses to hypothetical moral questions. Among the broad cross-section of Berkeley students, 54 percent of those who displayed "principled" reasoning sat in, whereas 60 percent of the nonprincipled did not—a finding which is on the borderline of being statistically significant. This finding suggests that students with high moral reasoning ability were the most likely to put their beliefs into action through civil disobedience. Part of the argument for this increase of moral reasoning is that these protestors were developmentally ready to increase their level of moral reasoning, and this dramatic event provided the impetus for positive change. Of course, this developmental readiness is hard to measure in advance and, furthermore, there is no certainty that the moral reasoning of these students will remain high. Even more troubling, is the uncertainty that these stages of moral reasoning are actually hierarchical. Who is to say that "principled" reasoning is better than "conventional" reasoning? Conservatives would not agree that a belief in the power of legitimate authority is undesirable.

Haan's research implicitly supports libertarian theory by

suggesting civil disobedience is characteristic of students who have higher levels of reasoning. Also, by suggesting that the rationales for civil disobedience are "better" than those for other moral problems, this implies that civil disobedience is a profoundly liberating and moral enterprise.

Social Movements and Civil Disobedience

What is the relationship of the individual to the state? Is government based on the consent of the governed, and when must that consent be given? Do people have the right to press for change outside the normal political channels? Widespread civil disobedience seems to give evidence that all is not well, that a sizable number of citizens have rejected the traditional lines of authority. Although these actions may not come from an individual conscience but rather from a political movement, this does not deny their morality. Social movements can educate individual citizens and then provide a channel by which they can express their grievances.

It is important to remember, as I have suggested at several points in this chapter, that the issues on which people might engage in civil disobedience do not neatly fall in any one corner of the political arena. Segregation, abortion, school prayer, and pornographic bookstores can provide as potent a motivation for direct action as nuclear power plants, racism, or military buildups. The theoretical underpinnings of civil disobedience are, rather, tied to how a person perceives the state. To be willing to engage in such acts, a person must concede that there are some cases in which the authority of the government is not supreme. In a democratic system, philosophical conservatives would not agree with this, notwithstanding the support of the supposedly conservative Moral Majority for such action. The social democrat, with an absolute code of morality based on equality and justice, places some organized resistance above a government's right to crush that resistance; libertarians place any resistance over the government's right to intervene. For the libertarian, civil disobedience proves that individuals are still free, as the bonds of consent to the government can be broken at any moment.

We might consider a social movement to be like a collective individual. By bringing individuals with shared values together, a movement is able to express views more forcefully than any single individual could. In time, if the movement proves successful, it comes to speak for all its members even though there are many within the group it claims to speak for who would disagree with what is said. The National Organization for Women (NOW) is often said to speak for "women," but this is obviously a loose use of the word "women." Likewise, the Moral Majority does not represent all fundamentalist Christians. Yet, the existence of such groups allows the social order to function, dealing with these groups as brokers for their constituencies. In a society as large and diverse as ours, it is impossible to deal with citizens as individuals; thus, the ideals of libertarianism function far better in a small state than in a large one, where individualism must be given up in some measure. A social movement as a voluntary collection of like-minded individuals provides a means by which some principles of libertarianism can be incorporated into a nation state. The existence and vitality of social movements, therefore, gives legitimacy to a democratic government and permits this government to maintain the consent of the governed, by providing an avenue for the expression of dissatisfaction.

Questions

1. Is civil disobedience ever justified? If so, under what circumstances?

2. Are people who engage in civil disobedience criminals?

3. Is there any circumstance in which you would refuse to pay your income taxes to protest a government action?

4. Was Thoreau right that the government that governs best, governs not at all?

5. Should people who oppose the nuclear arms race blockade companies doing business with the military?

6. Is America's system of government sufficiently democratic to make inappropriate any form of civil disobedience?

7. Should protestors accept the punishment that they are given or should they use whatever legal techniques they can to avoid being punished?

8. Should social movements organize and direct acts of civil disobedience?

9. Why are religious leaders frequently in the forefront of movements involving civil disobedience?

10. Was civil disobedience justified in the South during the Civil Rights movement of the 1960s?

For Further Study

Bedau, Hugo Adam, ed. *Civil Disobedience: Theory and Practice*. New York: Pegasus, 1969.

Brown, Jr. Stuart M. "Civil Disobedience," *Journal of Philosophy* 58 (1961): 669–681.

Day, Jr., Samuel H. "The New Resistance: Confronting the Nuclear War Machine," *Progressive*, 47 April (1983): 22–30.

Hook, Sidney. "Social Protest and Civil Disobedience," *The Humanist*. 27 (1967): 157–159, 192–193.

Pitkin, Hanna. "Obligation and Consent—I," *American Political Science Review* 59 (1965): 990–999.

Prosch, Harry. "Limits to the Moral Claim in Civil Disobedience," *Ethics*, 75 (1965): 103–111.

Thoreau, Henry David. "Civil Disobedience." This essay can be found in many editions of Thoreau's writings.

Weber, David R. ed. *Civil Disobedience in America*. Ithaca, New York: Cornell University Press, 1978.

Zwiebach, Burton. *Civility and Disobedience*. Cambridge: Cambridge University Press, 1975.

Notes and References

1. William Gamson, *The Strategy of Social Protest* (Homewood, Illinois: Dorsey, 1975).
2. Gustave Le Bon, *The Crowd: A Study of the Popular Mind* (London: T. Fisher Unwin, 1896), pp. 54–56.
3. John D. McCarthy and Mayer N. Zald, "Resource Mobilization and Social Movements: A Partial Theory," *American Journal of Sociology* 82 (1977): 1212–1241.
4. Le Bon, *op. cit.*, pp. xiii–xxi.
5. Ralph Turner and Lewis M. Killian, *Collective Behavior*, 2nd ed. (Englewood Cliffs, New Jersey: Prentice-Hall, 1972), pp. 21–25.
6. Hugo A. Bedau, "On Civil Disobedience," *Journal of Philosophy* 58 (1961): 661.
7. William Sloane Coffin, Jr. and Morris I. Leibman, *Civil Disobedience: Aid or Hindrance to Justice* (Washington, D.C.: American Enterprise Institute for Public Policy Research, 1972), p. 14.
8. Dean Snyder, "Civil Disobedience: What It Means," *Christian Century*, April 27, 1983, p. 403.
9. John Junkerman, "Why Pray for Peace While Paying for War?: Tax Resisters Seek the Path of Conscience," *Progressive*, April 1981, p. 16.
10. "A Blue-Collar Tax Revolt," *Newsweek*, March 9, 1981, p. 33.
11. Henry David Thoreau, *Walden and Civil Disobedience* (Cambridge: Riverside Press, 1960), pp. 235, 252.
12. *Ibid*, p. 256.
13. Frederick C. Foote, "No Nukes—No Consistency," *The Freeman* 33 (1983): 461.
14. For an example of such a person, see Junkerman, *op. cit.*, p. 18.

15. Burton Zwiebach, *Civility and Disobedience* (Cambridge: Cambridge University Press, 1975), p. 150.

16. Hanna Pitkin, "Obligation and Consent—I," *American Political Science Review* 59 (1965): 999.

17. Coffin and Leibman, *op. cit.*, pp. 3–4.

18. Martin Luther King Jr., "Love, Law, and Civil Disobedience," *Civil Disobedience in America*, David R. Weber, ed. (Ithaca, New York: Cornell University Press, 1978), p. 215.

19. David R. Carlin, Jr., "Civil Disobedience, Self-Righteousness, and the Antinuclear Movement," *America*, September 25, 1982, p. 153.

20. Rodney Clapp, "Christian Conviction or Civil Disobedience?" *Christianity Today*, March 4, 1983, p. 31.

21. Charles E. Wyzanski, Jr., "On Civil Disobedience," *The Atlantic*, February 1968, p. 59.

22. Stuart M. Brown, Jr., "Civil Disobedience," *Journal of Philosophy* 58 (1961): 672–673.

23. Sidney Hook, "Social Protest and Civil Disobedience," *Moral Problems in Contemporary Society*, Paul Kurtz, ed. (Englewood Cliffs, New Jersey: Prentice-Hall, 1969), p. 169.

24. Wayne Wangstad, "Protest Runs Up Hefty Bureaucracy Bill," *St. Paul Pioneer Press*, October 25, p. 8A.

25. David Carr, "The Price of Protest," *Twin Cities Reader*, November 9, 1983, p. 6.

26. Norma Haan, "Hypothetical and Actual Moral Reasoning in a Situation of Civil Disobedience," *Journal of Personality and Social Psychology* 32 (1975): 255–270.

27. Lawrence Kohlberg, "A Cognitive-Developmental Approach to Socialization," *Handbook of Socialization*, D. Goslin, ed. (New York: Rand McNally, 1969).

Ten

Deviance and Social Control: Should Drug Use Be Legalized?

SOMETIMES SOCIETY SEEMS like a minuet between the forces of social control and the forces of escape from that control. Whatever is ordered, some resist. Indeed, the enforcement of norms and values may be necessary because the actions that are being controlled are those we "really" would like to do. If we were not unconsciously interested in such things, there would be no need for such control. Freud claimed that the reason for the strength of our taboos against incest was that this form of social behavior represents our fondest, though most socially destructive, wish.

Probably no area of social life has been as closely examined by sociologists as the relationship between deviance and social control. In orderly societies human beings use a variety of institutions to enforce social control. Some social scientists distinguish between the forces of ideological social control and those of direct social control.[1] *Ideological social control* refers to attempts to shape people's perceptions so that they are willing to accept the status quo and the legitimacy of social institutions.

The family, the church, one's peer group, the schools one attends, and the mass media each contribute to the belief that the dominant view of the world is the correct one. Of course, these institutions are not in complete agreement, nor do they work sufficiently well to enforce a total ideology; yet, most people adopt the world view of these institutions. It takes either a person with a very strong (or warped) sense of self or a person in a strong subculture to reject the dominant view of how life should be organized.

With major deviations, society maintains a variety of institutions to force a person into appropriate patterns of behavior or to remove someone from society. Direct social control involves the attempt to punish, change, or isolate those who do not "fit in," including the mentally ill, criminals, and extreme political dissidents. Even institutions that, on their face, have a humanitarian goal, can indirectly serve to enforce social control. For example, some argue that public welfare programs function in times of recession to defuse social unrest.[2] The main elements of direct social control are the police force, the courts, the prison system, and mental hospitals. Although it would be nice to believe that such institutions treat all individuals who come before them equitably and without regard to class or race, many sociological research studies show that, sadly, such is not the case. Blacks and the poor, in particular, are given less leniency than others not similarly damned. Even the bumper sticker on your car may affect the number of traffic citations you will receive.[3] (Stock up on "Support Your Local Police" stickers.) Rich white kids do sometimes get into trouble, but there is a presumption that their "crimes" are just a phase, rather than a career of crime—and this may be right. Still, that is little comfort for those not afforded similar mercy.

These engines of social control are designed to prevent or limit deviant behavior. Simply put, *deviance* is behavior that is thought to be improper by large numbers of people in a society, and that violates their social expectations. For most people, deviance is more than simply behaving in an unusual manner (becoming a surgeon would qualify under that criterion); rather, deviance is negatively valued behavior. Nothing is inherently deviant; what is considered deviant is socially determined, and may differ from one culture to another.

In explaining deviance, some researchers examine the characteristics of those who break the rules. One approach contends that criminals are not like "normal" people. They have, perhaps, a genetic anomaly (an extra male chromosome), special physiques, brain malfunctions, or hereditary factors based on race or ethnicity. Such biological theories have not been shown to be valid. To be taken seriously they will have to be more sophisticated and complex than they are now.

Others examine the psychological characteristics of deviants and suggest they lacked affection in childhood, had psychosexual traumas, or never developed proper attachments to adults or other children. In theory, it should be possible to predict which children will "get in trouble," and then give them appropriate conditioning or training to prevent this. Yet, at current stages of knowledge, such prediction is far from exact and, in any event, raises questions of civil liberties.

Another approach to explaining the behavior of deviants is to look at their environment. Certainly the fact that most deviant behavior occurs in urban areas is of more than passing interest, and some claim that there are psychological and social features of living in cities that contribute to this behavior.[4] A second argument is that the sort of people a person associates with determines their behavior: deviants associate with different individuals than non-deviants. This approach is termed *differential association*.[5] A third view examines the goals and values of potential criminals and argues that they do not follow socially approved means to achieve socially desired ends, mostly because they find these approved means closed to them.[6] Miller's studies focus on the distinctive subculture of the lower class—the so-called culture of poverty—many values of this group run directly counter to the culture of the larger society and are more congruent with deviant behavior.[7] There is, of course, little agreement among social scientists as to which if any of these approaches explains deviant behavior.

Other sociologists do not study the deviants themselves but rather the society they feel makes them so. According to these theorists, society "blames the victim."[8] The leading approach of this type is the *labeling theory*. Almost everyone has been deviant, but not everyone is so labelled. Whether a person gets labelled depends on who he or she is and whether he or she has been fortunate enough to avoid an official stigma. In the case of drugs, since most young adults have tried marijuana, presumably more than half the youthful population could be labelled as drug offenders, yet relatively few have had this misfortune. Once people are labelled, they find themselves being treated differently: their behavior is evaluated differently (and with closer scrutiny), and there is less tolerance for future offenses. Because of these constraints *secondary deviance* occurs, that is, deviance that is the result of the labeling process. How a person is labelled is, from this interactionist perspective, a consequence of the person's relations with others.

As in most things, functionalists and conflict theorists disagree about the nature of deviance. The functionalist believes deviance is illegitimate but has some positive effects. The labeling of some people as deviant brings the non-deviant members of society together and emphasizes their similarities in contrast to the behavior of the deviant. The functionalist sees deviance as ultimately caused by the failure of a social system to socialize its members properly. Conflict theorists, on the other hand, stress the social and political components of deviance. For the conflict theorist deviance, in many cases, is healthy because it sends a message about the injustices of society. To eliminate deviance people must radically restructure their social system, altering the social conditions that cause the deviance and the class system that permits some people the luxury to define others as deviant.

Question:

Should Drug Use Be Legalized?

Two decades ago, Bob Dylan sang, "Everybody must get stoned."[9] With the double meaning of stoned, this lyric has particular relevance to the continuing drug controversy in American society. If we include alcohol and nicotine among drugs, almost everyone has gotten "stoned," yet not everyone has been "stoned" by the legal system.

The National Commission on Marijuana and Drug Abuse defines a drug as any chemical that affects the structure or function of a living organism.[10] Such a definition covers a lot of substances—marijuana, cocaine, heroin, LSD, alcohol, nicotine, and perhaps salt, sugar, and beef fat. Nevertheless, most people agree on what is meant by "chemical abuse," "substance abuse," or "drug abuse." Alcohol, which by all reasonable definitions, is a drug, and a potentially harmful one at that, is legal (with some restrictions), whereas marijuana, which seems to be harmful when used continually, but less clearly so than alcohol, is not legal in the United States.[11] Tobacco, more clearly a health risk than either marijuana or alcohol, is not typically discussed in terms of drug abuse, and so will not be examined here.

Alcohol is the drug of preference for most Americans, due to its easy availability and relatively mild consequences when used in moderation. According to the National Institute on Drug Abuse, over 95 percent of all eighteen to twenty-five year olds have used alcohol, with over 70 percent of those twelve to seventeen having had a drink at least once. Seventy-five percent of young adults now use alcohol, as compared to 37 percent of teenagers. The equivalent figures for marijuana are that 68 percent of young adults and 30 percent of teens have tried it, and 35 percent and 16 percent are regular users. The figures for other drugs are much lower, but still over 25 percent of young adults have tried hallucinogens and cocaine; 3.5 percent of this group have tried heroin.[12] Despite legal constraints, Americans are willing to pay the costs of using a wide variety of mind-altering substances.

Much of the discussion of the legalization of drugs (particularly marijuana, where most of the attention has centered) has dealt with how harmful they are. This is a complicated area about which we are learning more each year, but precise levels of danger are not relevant to this discussion. It is fair to say that drugs are not harmless, but neither are they as harmful as a bullet from a revolver. The specific amount of damage they do is not crucial to the issues I describe here. After all, knowing the evidence about cigarette smoking has not caused our society to outlaw cigarettes, and some high schools even provide rooms in which students can smoke at their leisure.

The first federal law aimed at controlling the use of drugs was the 1914 Harrison Act, which was designed to regulate, license, and tax the distribution of narcotic drugs. Perhaps unexpectedly, the Narcotics Division of the Treasury Department, given the responsibility to enforce the law, criminalized the use of these drugs, turning users into "criminals." The first law regulating marijuana was the 1937 Marijuana Tax Act, which provided severe penalties for the use of the drug—as much as twenty years imprisonment for mere possession. Some state laws were even tougher, providing for life imprisonment. Louisiana and Missouri permitted the death penalty for drug sales to minors.

By the late 1960s and 1970s, sentiment slowly began to change toward control of marijuana, a consequence of the drug's widespread popularity and perhaps the use of the drug by the children of leading politicians. Although no state has legalized marijuana, eleven states from Mississippi to Minnesota, Maine to Oregon, have decriminalized the use of small amounts of it. In 1970 the federal government sharply reduced the penalties for "crimes" involving marijuana. During this period politicians from Barry Goldwater to Jimmy Carter supported its decriminalization. From 1969 to 1977 the percentage of Americans who supported the legalization of marijuana increased from 12 to 28 percent. It seemed by the late 1970s that marijuana would soon be legalized. Since 1978, however, no new states have decriminalized marijuana, and there seems to be greater concern among parents and polticians about the use of all drugs (with support for legalization of marijuana dipping to 25 percent by 1980).[13] New evidence of the health risks of marijuana has perhaps also affected people's attitudes. The use of marijuana has leveled off or even decreased in high schools.[14] It now appears that no public policy changes are likely, and there is no effort to change laws on other types of drugs, other than to tighten drunk driving laws and raise the drinking age.

For good or ill, some four hundred thousand Americans are arrested every year for possession of marijuana. In 1981 the retail value of the marijuana sold in America was $15 to $21 billion; it is the fourth largest cash crop grown in the United States and the largest in the state of California. Marijuana represents a significant portion of the American economy. Other drugs, while not so economically significant, play a role in our unfavorable balance-of-trade picture with other nations.[15]

The Conservative Point of View

Most, though not all conservatives, are opposed to legalizing drugs, and public opinion supports them. Seventy percent of the American population oppose the legalization of marijuana,[16] and almost all Americans oppose the legalization of harder drugs. Drugs, with their mind-altering properties, give people pleasure, and this private pleasure separates them from those social institutions that should be most important; they separate the individual from the community, and they both reflect and cause the rejection of social mores, a major threat to order. This view is reflected in the extreme rhetoric of California's former State Superintendent of Public Instruction, Max Rafferty. "What to do about the dope syndrome, Mom and Pop?" asks Rafferty. "First, recognize it for what it is. Just one more symptom of the nation's unraveling moral fiber. A sign of our times. Then resolve to combat it in your own family mercilessly, with no holds barred. Remember that souls are the things actually at stake in the war you're declaring, and fight accordingly."[17]

First Lady Nancy Reagan has a similar theme as she argues that the "weakening of the family unit" is one factor that contributes to and is a consequence of drug abuse.[18] Some people also contend that drug users display an "amotivational syndrome" that deprives the society of these citizens' work in its behalf. In other words, they remove themselves from the community from which they should be contributing. Consider the remarks of columnist Carl Rowan:

> As surely as if they were nuclear bombs from a dreaded enemy, the tons of heroin from Asia, the mountains of cocaine from Bolivia and Peru, the endless supply of marijuana, Quaaludes and other illicit drugs from Columbia—and from American farms and laboratories—are wrecking this society. . . . Illegal drugs are playing havoc with our business communities, with sales of marijuana, heroin and cocaine commonplace on Wall Street. Drug abuse has become the scourge of professional athletics, the curse of our entertainment world from Hollywood to Broadway, a shame of Congress. It is a tragedy that touches every type of family in this land.[19]

The real threat of drugs for conservatives is the danger they pose to social order. In particular, conservatives are concerned about the effects of drug use on children. If children are not properly socialized, the continuation of an orderly society is hopeless. The fact that the young are likely to indulge in drugs makes them a particular menace for the conservative. Richard Vigilante, an editorial writer for the *Charleston Daily Mail*, recognizes this, commenting, "The special dangers for young users and the prospect of 10 to 15 percent of the adolescent population being too doped up to mature normally or get an education certainly justify, in theory, state intervention."[20]

While conservatives do not like government interference, they do believe that government action is necessary when there is a substantial danger to the fabric or structure of society. Conservatives accept the basic right of government to intervene to protect "core values." Ultimately it is harm to people that justifies action, even though there may be some advantages to letting drugs be widely available. Judianne Densen-Gerber, founder of Odyssey House, an experimental program for young drug abusers, is concerned that

> the major value question brought into focus is whether society values its property more than its people. The legaliza-

tion of all narcotic substances, particularly heroin, would lessen the amount of crime, especially crimes against property. But such legalization would increase the number of the afflicted and the severity of the disease in each individual addict. As an example, during Prohibition, although millions of people violated the law by drinking, the number of alcoholics markedly decreased.[21]

The conservative contends that taking drugs is not a "victimless crime." The drug-user does not live in isolation but is part of a family, a church, a community, and a society. Taking drugs is a sign that a person is refusing to take his or her responsibilities as a citizen. In this way, drugs are a threat to the continuation of social order.

The Libertarian Point of View

As usual, the extreme libertarian is entirely consistent. The 1980 Libertarian platform advocated the repeal of all laws that prohibit the production, sale, possession, or use of drugs. For the libertarian, drug use is a personal matter in which the State has no business. This position was stated eloquently by the radical psychiatrist, Thomas Szasz. Szasz writes, "Every individual is capable of injuring or killing himself. This potentiality is a fundamental expression of human freedom. . . . I believe that just as we regard freedom of speech and religion as fundamental rights, so we should also regard freedom of self-medication as a fundamental right."[22]

Szasz, like most libertarians, believes strongly in individual free-will. The choice of the individual to do well or do ill, to help himself or harm himself is ultimately a personal choice. Szasz even goes so far as to argue that drugs can be likened to ideas. "Although I recognize that some drugs—notably heroin, the amphetamines, and LSD, among those now in vogue—may have undesirable or dangerous consequences, I favor free trade in drugs for the same reason the Founding Fathers favored free trade in ideas. In an open society, it is none of the government's business what idea a man puts into his mind; likewise it should be none of the government's business what drug he puts into his body."[23] This right to control one's body is similar to the argument that pro-choice feminists make about their right to have abortions. Szasz makes an interesting point in generalizing his argument by noting that most medicines are available only with a doctor's prescription. If you wished to give yourself insulin or penicillin, you would need a doctor's signature (and pay him for that signature), rather than just purchasing it for yourself. Szasz sees this control as wrong as restrictive laws on drug use.

For some the issue is the right to privacy, for others it is the right to freedom of choice, and for still others it is the right to pursue happiness. After all, according to Michael Aldrich, a Ph.D. in English and one-time Yippie, drug use is enjoyable. "Marijuana should be legalized because it's fun. Social use of *cannabis* [marijuana] depends primarily on the fact that altering one's perception is pleasurable; if the mental changes produced by smoking, eating, or drinking marijuana are not pleasurable, use will not normally be continued."[24] This assumes that the drug will not control the individual, but the individual will have sufficient powers of thought to decide about his or her own drug use.

Libertarians believe the drug "problem" is created by drug laws, rather than by the drugs themselves. Prohibition turns otherwise honest citizens into criminals. The libertarian disputes the conservative's claim that drug use is not a victimless crime, saying that although some may be indirectly hurt or offended by drug use, and relationships may change, coercion is not involved.

Libertarians perceive a serious problem in that drug laws give the government additional powers. An editorial in *Reason* (a libertarian journal) entitled, "Making War on Americans," articulates this point.

> What the New Right and their allies want is nothing less than an all-out mobilization, enlisting the Army, the Navy,

the Air Force, the IRS, the Justice Department, and the State Department in an all-out war on drug producers and consumers. The price we would pay for all this: the loss of more of our dwindling freedoms. . . . [W]ar is the health of the State . . . the main result of the war on drugs will be to build an ever more powerful and oppressive American State."[25]

Drug laws (particularly those in force in the 1960s) gave the police extensive powers to search homes, cars, and people— powers that libertarians feel are far more deadly than an occasional toke or even an injection of heroin.

The Social Democratic Point of View

Social democrats are of several minds about the government's position toward drug use. They realize that drugs often harm the most vulnerable groups in society—minorities and the young; yet they also recognize that drug enforcement has typically come down hardest on these groups.

The social democrat points out that for most of our history, drugs have not been regulated. Why did this change? The answer: racial and ethnic prejudice. David Richards, in his book *Sex, Drugs, Death and the Law*, writes that, "the use of liquor in the United States was identified with the Catholic immigrants and their subversive (non-Protestant) values; when heroin came under attack, it was identified with Chinese influences from which America, it was said, must be protected; marijuana was associated with undesirable Hispanic influences on American values, and cocaine with black influences."[26] President William Howard Taft, for example, linked cocaine to rape among Southern blacks.[27] More recently, the attack on drugs has been seen by some to be an attack on young people. It is perhaps significant that one of the states with the most liberal drug laws is Utah, which also has a homogeneous population.[28]

Class bias is evident in who gets arrested for drug abuse and who does not. Typically middle-class citizens are not affected by drug laws, whereas the poor, the young, and non-whites receive the brunt of the enforcement. For some on the left, such as Michael Rossman, a San Francisco political activist, this presents a cruel paradox—while the government attacks the young, it ignores other criminal elements. "As for the government, I think it should keep its bloody hands off the young and its sacraments . . . and turn its attention towards cleansing our society of its dreadful ugliness and violence, instead of helping industry turn the sky black for a buck, exploit man as badly as nature, and play at genocide here and there."[29]

Social democrats are not calling for government inaction, but, rather, for it to act in other areas, such as fighting discrimination and pollution. With regard to drug use, social democrats do not call for a free market in drugs, as do libertarians; they want instead a regulated market. This need for regulation is evident in comments made in *Consumer Reports*, about the hazards of marijuana. "The notion that arrest and imprisonment are the proper social responses to possession of a hazardous product or substance appears inconsistent with society's usual approach to products, even to hazardous products. When an electrical appliance constitutes a potentially lethal shock hazard, no one demands the arrest and imprisonment of those who own the offending appliance."[30] Of course, when someone purchases a defective electrical appliance, he or she does not buy it knowing its danger and certainly not because it has that danger, as conservatives suggest is true for someone purchasing drugs. Implicit in the social democrat's view is the extensive government regulation of the quality of drugs. This would require the Food and Drug Administration or the Consumer Product Safety Commission to ensure the purity and quality of the marijuana that is sold and would have the government put a tax on its consumption. Ultimately this approach makes the "problem" of drug "abuse" a medical problem, rather than a legal one because drugs would be treated much like liquor currently is.

There is, however, another side to the social democratic argument—a side that is not as lenient toward legalized drug use. Social democrats who are less tolerant are concerned about the effects of the legalization of drugs on blacks and Hispanics. In 1970 the Board of the American Civil Liberties Union refused to approve a proposal to allow the freedom to use and purchase heroin because of what it might do to minorities.[31] Since social democrats believe in a benevolently paternalistic (or maternalistic) government, such thinking makes sense. Their approach criticizes the "ideology of tolerance." Ronald Bayer, an expert on the history of attitudes toward heroin, sees heroin decriminalization as repressive.

> The ideology of tolerance, present as a critical force in the service of freeing those caught in the web of contemporary social control, actually tends to serve a profoundly repressive function. . . . Instead of assisting in the struggle against human misery those concepts provide the justification for choosing human misery. Because the ideology of tolerance tends to conceal the extent to which certain forms of deviance are reactions to deprivations rooted in the social order—indeed, can be considered as determined by that order—and because it seeks to integrate behavior that should serve as the starting point for a critique of society, it serves to neutralize the possibility of opposition.[32]

This view eliminates some of the drug user's autonomy, but it does so because the proponents believe these individuals do not understand the structural reasons for their drug habit. These users do not recognize that drug use prevents them from asserting their rights and gaining economic and social equality. Such an approach puts decision-making where, some suggest, it rightfully belongs—in the hands of the sociologist.

Marijuana and Social Research

In the 1980s marijuana seems almost as much a part of college life as multiple-choice tests. It was not always so. Prior to the mid-1960s, "blowing smoke" or "sipping tea" was something that "good" people did not do. Marijuana was found in various deviant subcultures—jazz musicians, beat poets, and prostitutes. It was partly for this reason that Howard S. Becker's article "Becoming a Marijuana User" had such a dramatic impact when it was published in the prestigious *American Journal of Sociology* in 1953.[33] Not only did Becker present the thoughts and behaviors of marijuana users in their own words, but he did not even treat them as criminals! He did not ask where these people went wrong.

The problem for Becker, a prominent symbolic interactionist, was: how do people learn to smoke marijuana properly, how do they define the effects of the drug, and how do they decide these effects are pleasurable? In order to answer these questions, Becker (and his colleagues Harold Finestone and Solomon Kobrin) conducted in-depth interviews with fifty marijuana users to learn about their experiences with the drug or how they became socialized to marijuana use.

Unlike the in-depth interview study of transracial adoptive parents discussed in chapter 11, Becker is not particularly concerned with the *people* he interviewed but, rather, with the *process* of becoming a marijuana user or *natural history* of drug use. Becker does not agree with those who suggest that marijuana use is related to some trait in the individual user—a point of view that we can now largely discard since 68 percent of American youth have tried the drug. Instead, Becker's study asks: What must someone *do* to "get high"?

Choosing to rely on in-depth interviews, Becker is, in some sense, at the mercy of the users for his information and, thus, must rely on their perceptions. By treating a deviant as a normal person, this research technique leans toward the libertarian attitude of refusing to condemn this behavior on the basis of societal attitudes. To accept the informants' accounts as accurate implies (although does not insist) someone must see this behavior as an acceptable choice of rational, reasonable people—or why else trust them? While conducting the interviews, Becker moonlighted as a professional jazz musician, so it might reasonably be supposed that he had some familiarity with this subculture. This would have permitted him to check his interview findings with information gained elsewhere.

Have you smoked marijuana? If you have, recall the first time you tried it. Did you try to smoke the reefer as if it were a cigarette? Did you wonder what the fuss was all about? One of Becker's conclusions is that knowing how to smoke dope does not come naturally. Just as we must learn our multiplication tables, so we must learn how to inhale—deeply and long. If you do not draw the marijuana smoke into your lungs, nothing much happens. Without learning the proper technique to get high—often taught by a friend—you are not likely to continue to smoke.

Becker also suggests that you must learn what being "high" feels like. Specifically, you must "feel" the effects caused by marijuana and then must connect them with the use of the drug. At first, you may not be sure how you will react, and so you search for clues. You get high "with a little help from [your] friends." One user explains "I heard little remarks that were made by other people. Somebody said, 'My legs are rubbery,' and I can't remember all the remarks that were made because I was very attentively listening for all these cues for what I was supposed to feel like."[34]

Becker argues that it is crucial to label feelings in such a way that you know you are high. Because the user is focusing so hard on what he or she is feeling, possibly part of being "high" the first time is simply becoming aware of those things that are always present but that are never noticed.

Finally, to continue to use marijuana you must decide that the feelings are pleasant. For some people (usually former users) the experience may be decidedly unpleasant. You could, for example, feel like you are losing your mind. Distortion of spatial relationships and sounds, violent hunger and thirst, and panic are not always fun. Unless you can label your physical reactions as enjoyable, marijuana use will stop. Thus, Becker places great emphasis on the definitions that users have of their experience and on the fact that these experiences are not only chemical but are also social. Your fellow users have a large impact in determining the nature of your experiences, but ultimately it is a personal decision as to whether to continue to smoke:

> It is quite common for experienced users suddenly to have an unpleasant or frightening experience, which they cannot define as pleasurable, either because they have used a larger amount of marijuana than usual or because it turns out to be a higher-quality marijuana than they expected. . . . [He] may make this the occasion for a rethinking of his attitude toward the drug and decide that it no longer can give him pleasure. When this occurs and is not followed by a redefinition of the drug as capable of producing pleasure, use will cease.[35]

Note that Becker discusses drug use as a voluntary decision of the user. People have free will in their marijuana consumption. Since marijuana is not overtly harmful and does not harm others, Becker's conclusions are consistent with the libertarian approach to social order. Why should society prevent rational, reasonable people from doing what they wish? If some poeple do not find marijuana pleasant, they are not forced to smoke it. Like the libertarian, Becker, accepting the word of those he interviewed, appears to advocate personal decision-making, rather than government control of citizens. Marijuana is a "recreational" drug, so this line of reasoning goes, and it would be a highly intrusive government that would limit personal "recreation."

Social Control, Deviance, and Drug Use

What should the role of the state be in dealing with deviance? How tolerant should we be in dealing with behavior that is different from our own? No one wishes to live in a society in which everyone must march in lock-step, but how much diversity is too much? Libertarians have the simplest answer to this problem. If it feels good, do it—just as long as it does not physically coerce others. They see the ability to be deviant as a sign that there is freedom in society. Perhaps the most frightening aspect of George Orwell's *1984* is not the various tortures and murders practiced by the government but the horrifying sameness of the people, the drabness of their lives and world. For the libertarian, then, youthful rebellion is not something to be feared but is simply the attempt of the new generation to demonstrate that they are free. Only to the extent that young people choose to behave like their peers is there danger of deviance actually being subcultural conformity.

The social democrat sees each act of deviance in its own context. Who is doing what to whom, and how does it conform to the ideals of equality and justice. Painting swastikas on Jewish synagogues is deviant, but it is not the sort of deviance that a government should tolerate. On the other hand, dress styles that express ethnic or subcultural values might be seen by the social democrat as an indication of a healthy multicultural state.

A critical issue for the social democrat is the structural conditions of society that gave impetus to the deviant display. Some deviance, crime, for example, is due as much (or more) to the social condition in which the criminal finds him or herself, than it is to any free choice of the criminal. For the social democrat, who generally accepts conflict theory, deviance indicates structural inequalities that need to be corrected by changing the priorities of society. What the powerful do is often considered "normal," but similar behaviors by the powerless are labelled criminal or mentally ill. The powerful have greater access to the means of defining behavior and more control over those who enforce that behavior. Drugs favored by the rich are legal, or not very illegal, whereas the drug preferences of the poor have long prison terms attached to them.

The conservative, of course, sees the issue of deviance in quite a different light. There is within any society an absolute moral order; as a result, there should be little tolerance for behavior that attacks the core values of that order. Drugs, pornography, homosexuality, and abortion fly in the face of what most American conservatives believe is morally proper behavior. These behaviors in one way or another are defined as undermining the family and the work ethic. If we permit behavior that undercuts these fundamental institutions, there is little that will hold us together as a society. Although conservatives do not wish to enforce a rigid uniformity, they are much more willing to draw lines beyond which we must not pass under penalty of law. Because the conservative values order and, thus, a stable functional interrelationship within social systems, the smaller the diversity on important value questions, the stronger will a society be. Thus, drug *use* poses the same bogie for the conservative that drug *laws* pose for the libertarian.

Questions

1. Should marijuana be legalized? If it is legalized, should it be government regulated?

2. Should heroin be legalized? If it is legalized, should it be government regulated?

3. Should marijuana possession be decriminalized?

4. Is the reason that certain drugs are still illegal because of the characteristics of their users?

5. Should there be a free market in drugs?

6. Does drug use undermine the "fabric" of society?

7. Should young people under eighteen be allowed to use drugs if they wish?

8. Does the "ideology of tolerance" actually serve a repressive function in society?

9. Should society welcome deviance or try to outlaw it? Is diversity healthy for society?

For Further Study

Baker, Ronald. "Heroin Decriminalization and the Ideology of Tolerance: A Critical View," *Law and Society* 12 (1978): 301-318.

Becker, Howard. *Outsiders*. New York: Free Press, 1963. (This work includes "Becoming a Marijuana User").

Cloyd, Jerald W. *Drugs and Information Control: The Role of Men and Manipulation in the Control of Drug Trafficking*. Westport, Connecticut: Greenwood Press, 1982.

Duster, Troy. *The Legislation of Morality: Law, Drugs and Moral Judgment*. New York: Free Press, 1970.

Hart, Harold W. ed., *Drugs: For & Against*. New York: Hart, 1970.

Lasagna, Louis, and Lindzey, Gardner. "Marijuana Policy and Drug Mythology," *Society*, 20 (January-February): 1983, pp. 67-78.

Richards, David A. J. *Sex, Drugs, Death, and the Law: An Essay on Human Rights and Overcriminalization*. Totowa, New Jersey: Rowman and Littlefield, 1982.

Szasz, Thomas. *Ceremonial Chemistry: The Ritual Persecution of Drugs, Addicts, and Pushers*. New York: Anchor, 1975.

Notes and References

1. D. Stanley Eitzen, *In Conflict and Order: Understanding Society*, 2nd ed. (Boston: Allyn and Bacon, 1982), pp. 180–199.
2. Frances Fox Piven and Richard Cloward, *Regulating the Poor: The Function of Public Welfare* (New York: Random House, 1971).
3. Frances K. Heussenstamm, "Bumper Stickers and Cops." *Transaction*, February 1971, pp. 32–33.
4. Louis Wirth, "Urbanism as a Way of Life," *American Journal of Sociology* 44, July 1938, pp. 1–24.
5. Edwin H. Sutherland and Donald R. Cressy, *Principles of Criminology*, 7th ed., (Philadelphia: J. B. Lippincott, 1966), pp. 81–82.
6. Robert K. Merton, *Social Theory and Social Structure*, enlarged ed. (New York: Free Press, 1968), pp. 185–214.
7. Walter B. Miller, "Lower Class Culture as a Generating Milieu of Gang Delinquency," *Journal of Social Issues* 14 (1958): p. 5–19.

8. William Ryan, *Blaming the Victim* (New York: Vintage, 1972).

9. Bob Dylan, "Rainy Day Woman #12 and 35," *Blonde on Blonde,* Columbia Records, 1966.

10. National Commission on Marijuana and Drug Abuse, *Drug Use in America: Problem in Perspective* (Washington, D.C.: Goverment Printing Office, 1973), p. 9.

11. Lester Grinspoon, *Marijuana Reconsidered* (Cambridge: Harvard University Press, 1977).

12. National Institute on Drug Abuse, *The National Survey on Drug Abuse: Main Findings, 1979* reported in the U.S. Bureau of the Census, *Statistical Abstract of the United States* (Washington, D.C.: Goverment Printing Office, 1980), p. 129.

13. "Opposition to Legalization of Marijuana Unchanged," *The Gallup Opinion Index,* No.179, July 1980, p. 14.

14. "Marijuana Update," *Editorial Research Reprints*, February 12, 1982, pp. 114–115.

15. *Ibid,* pp. 107–116.

16. *The Gallup Report,* Report No.179, July 1980.

17. Max Rafferty in Harold H. Hart (ed.), *Drugs: For & Against* (New York: Hart, 1970), p. 28.

18. "Nancy Reagan: How Parents Can Help Teenage Drug Users," *U.S. News & World Report,* May 31, 1982, p. 49.

19. Carl T. Rowan, "The Drug Scourge Must Be Stopped," *Readers' Digest,* August 1983, p. 135.

20. Richard Vigilante "Pot-talk: Is Decriminalization Advisable: No," *National Review,* April 29, 1983, p. 489.

21. Judianne Densen-Gerber in Hart, *op. cit.,* p. 113.

22. Thomas S. Szasz, "The Ethics of Addiction," *Harper's,* April 1972, pp. 75, 77.

23. *Ibid,* p. 75.

24. Michael Aldrich, in Hart, *op. cit.,* p. 77.

25. Robert Poole, Jr., "Making War on Americans, *Reason,* October 1981, p. 6.

26. David A. J. Richards, *Sex, Drugs, Death and the Law* (Totowa, New Jersey: Rowman and Littlefield, 1982), p. 179.

27. Michael C. Monson, "The Dirty Little Secret Behind Our Drug Laws," *Reason,* November 1980, p. 49.

28. John F. Galliher and Linda Basilick, "Utah's Liberal Drug Laws: Structural Foundations and Triggering Events," *Social Problems* 26 (1979): 284–297.

29. Michael Rossman, in Hart, *op. cit.*, p. 180.

30. "Marijuana: The Legal Question," *Consumer Reports*, April 1975, p. 265.

31. Ronald Bayer, "Heroin Decriminalization and the Ideology of Tolerance: A Critical View," *Law and Society* 12 (1978): 307.

32. *Ibid*, p. 314.

33. Howard S. Becker, "Becoming a Marijuana User," *American Journal of Sociology* 59 (1953): 235–242.

34. *Ibid*, p. 238.

35. *Ibid*, p. 241.

 **Eleven**

Family: Who Should Be Allowed to Adopt?

WHEN POLITICIANS SCRAMBLE for votes, they often stress their love for family, and may speak of America as being one family. The family is one of the grand rhetorical images in the arsenal of any public speaker. And, of course, the family influences us more than we know in our socialization, culture, education, income, and class position. Most of us have had the experience of growing up in a family, and whatever we might think of that experience there is no denying that we have been much influenced by it. Most of us (96 percent) choose to repeat the pattern at least once in our lifetime.

The family is a central building block of society. But what is a family? Many family structures are possible with widely different roles for the participants. Basically a *family* is a long-term social arrangement in which people who are related through marriage, birth, or adoption reside together as an economic unit, and raise children. Sociologists distinguish between a person's family of origin (the unit he or she was born into) and a person's family of procreation, (the unit in which he or she rears offspring).

Because of its role in propagating and socializing the species, the family is the most basic of all social institutions. Social order would not be possible without *some* institution that performs the tasks we expect of the family. In Israeli agricultural communes (the kibbutz) most child care is organized collectively, but the intense social integration and similarity of goals of the participants makes this unusual form of child rearing possible.

Functionalists see the family as a convincing example of the necessity of social institutions. Families provide the following important social functions in most societies:

1. They regulate and control sexual behavior—determining who will mate with whom. Since intercourse typically involves an intense social and emotional relationship, changing the relations of the two people and their relations with others in society, no society can permit totally free and open sexual behavior. Such free sexuality would produce severe and changing lines of stress because relationships would never be stable.

2. The family provides for the stable replacement of the population. No society can exist for long if the death rate remains higher than the birth rate.

3. Along with the creation of new members, the family provides an efficient means by which these individuals learn the rules and values of a culture. The family is the first, and perhaps most important, means of socialization.

4. The family provides a means by which children are placed into a social structure. Some families are known as wealthy and powerful ("the elite", "the blue bloods", "the Four Hundred"), while other families are stigmatized as poor or uneducated. The children of these families are branded with the position of their parents.

5. The family distributes goods. It is a micro-social welfare agency in providing food, shelter, interaction, and other needs.

The functional services provided by families, however, are only part of the picture. The conflict theorist, while not denying that the family may efficiently provide for certain important societal needs, also sees its darker side. Most societies are patriarchal. That is, men control the major forms of decision-making. Despite the joke made by some chauvinists that "the only way for women to gain equality is for them to come down off their pedestal," most important decisions in a traditional family are usually made by the husband. He decides where the family will live (the right of domicile), how the family budget will be spent, and, in large measure, what the wife shall do (whether she can or must work outside the home). Although this has changed substantially in the last two decades, husbands still have more power than wives in many marriages. This lack of power suggests that the family system may oppress women. Friedrich Engels,[1] Karl Marx's co-author of the *Communist Manifesto*, argued perceptively that the family system represents the first class repression in history and that the relationship between husband and wife is the model on which other types of economic oppression are based. Marx and Engels make the analogy of a wife as a prostitute—both provide sexual favors in return for money and goods.[2] The domination of the male over the family is also seen in the recognition of family violence. While the image of the family in our society is of a loving "team," this team is often wracked by disputes and, sometimes, even bloodshed.

Sociologists distinguish between *nuclear families* and *extended families*. The former refers to the kinship unit that is composed of parents and children, whereas the latter includes other relatives, especially "grown children" and grandparents. Nuclear families are particularly characteristic of our highly mobile society in which each adult generation has sufficient resources to live independently. Some have argued that the Social Security system, with its payments to senior citizens is in part responsible for the decline in extended families. But an increasing number of families fall into neither category— "families" that have a single head of household. These families pose many challenges to the traditional sociological explanations of family life.

Another feature of our mobile society is the extent to which the choice of marriage partners is relatively unconstrained by geographical proximity. Although location is still a good predictor of whom one will marry, it is not as adequate a predictor as it was a few decades ago. A person is more likely today than before to meet his or her mate at school, work, or at a non-neighborhood social event. Despite this, the choice of a marriage partner is still based largely on *homogamy*—that is, the attraction and marriage of partners with similar social backgrounds. Those people who are least likely to marry are also the ones who are most likely to get divorced. The greater the similarity of social experiences, values, beliefs, and expectations, the more likely will we celebrate a marriage, and then raise a family.

Question:

Who Should Be Allowed to Adopt?

"Compared with childbirth, adoption is a civilized business. The preliminaries involve more red tape than passion. The delivery of the child occurs in an office rather than a hospital. It is free of panic, agony, and danger."[3] Yet adoption is not free of emotion. Few images are as sad as a child who is unwanted, who has no home. Every child deserves a family—a happy, loving family. Once the primary purpose of adoption was to fill a family need; today adoption is supposed to be for the child, and adoption procedures are to be in the child's "best interests." But we do not always know what these best interests are; nor do we know for sure what kind of home provides the best environment.

Adoption has had a long history, going back beyond the time when Pharoah's daughter discovered young Moses in the bulrushes. Romulus and Remus, the founders of Rome, were supposedly adopted by a she-wolf and suckled by her. Oedipus was adopted so as to make the murder of his "true" father and marriage to his "true" mother inevitable. The great legal code of Hammurabi contained a detailed treatment of adoption in ancient Babylonia.

The longevity of adoption is but one testimony to its success. Many studies of adoption[4] indicate that children so placed are quite happy and healthy, even compared to children who are raised in their natural family. Since the adopting families often have more social status and wealth than the families of birth this suggests both the power of environment and the flexibility of children in overcoming difficult circumstances.

The present adoption situation demonstrates convincingly the power of rapid social change. Twenty years ago the adoption problem was the reverse of what it is today. At that time there were too many babies and not enough adoptive parents. Today we have a "baby shortage." There is far more demand for certain types of infants than there are infants to meet the need. One estimate is that for every Caucasian infant there are fifteen waiting couples.[5] According to the North American Council on Adoptable Children no more than 100,000 children are likely to be adopted in 1984, compared to 175,000 in 1970.[6]

Why has there been such dramatic change? Several factors are at work. With the change in sexual morality, it is more acceptable for a single mother to keep her child. In the late 1960s, it was estimated 80 percent of single mothers gave up their children for adoption; a decade later 80 percent were keeping their children.[7] Schools have made special provisions so that nursing teenagers will not have to drop out. Second, new methods of birth control and more education about them have decreased the proportion of "accidents." Third, because of the increase in government welfare programs fewer people are below the poverty line and there are more government programs to aid poor, unmarried mothers. Having a child is less of an economic hardship. Finally, the Supreme Court decided in January 1973, in *Roe v. Wade,* to legalize most abortions. Among the unintended consequences of this controversial decision was a decrease in the number of babies available for adoption. Why would any woman wish to deliver a baby she knew she would not keep? Only ethical considerations would lead to that decision, but that has not been enough in many cases. As the supply of babies has dwindled, people have struggled to adopt; now it is virtually impossible to adopt a healthy white infant unless you pass rigorous screening and can prove you are infertile. This has given social workers enormous power in determining who is fit to raise the small number of children available.

Basically three types of non-kin adoptions occur in this country—agency adoptions (the white market), independent adoptions (the grey market), and baby-selling (the black market). The first is the most common form of adoption when relatives are not adopting. The mother signs away her rights to the child to a social welfare agency (either public or private), and the agency's social workers find suitable parents, with the approval of the courts. In independent adoptions, which are legal in all but four states, adoptive parents and mothers who do not wish their children find each other (often through middlemen, such as friends or lawyers) and arrange to have the child transferred. Under this system, money is not supposed to change hands other than for the mother's medical expenses and a reasonable lawyer's fee. Black market adoption is identical to independent adoption except that the money paid is considerably higher, and the transaction amounts to "purchasing" the child. I shall discuss this further in considering the libertarian point of view.

Considering the reality of the baby shortage, it is significant that there are 120,000 to 140,000 children in foster care ("temporary" homes of unadopted children paid for by the state).[8] In New York City in 1975, 25,000 children were wards of the city and state.[9] Obviously these children are not included in the baby shortage, despite their lack of homes. These children are racial minorities, older children, the handicapped, the chronically ill, and the troubled. Our society treats these children as "damaged goods." If those of us who are white consider the matter honestly, we probably long for the healthy blue-eyed, blond cherub and consider the others poor second choices.

The baby shortage has forced potential parents to consider these "hard-to-place" children. Even though they may not be their first choices, these children can still love and be loved. Simultaneously, there has been pressure to broaden the definition of who can adopt a child. In particular, single women (and some men) have argued for their rights to adopt, noting that in 1980 some 12.6 million children under eighteen live with only one of their natural parents. Adoption by single parents through adoption agencies is a fairly recent phenomenon. Even though there is little evidence that having a single parent harms a child, it was not until the mid-1960s that adoption agencies finally agreed to consider single parents.

A second controversial issue is transracial adoptions. The first recorded case in the United States occurred in Minneapolis in 1948 when a white family adopted an unplaceable black child. By 1971 35 percent of all black adopted children were placed in white homes. While this percentage has decreased because of the objections from the black community, there are still transracial adoptions (particularly of foreign children). Estimates are that there are 15,000 American black children in white homes.[10] This can be interpreted as either a hopeful sign for a truly multiracial society or an example of "cultural genocide."

The Libertarian Point of View

What would a system of adoption with minimal state involvement look like? According to some libertarians it would be a "stork market." In a provocative article, two libertarians, Lawrence Alexander and Lyla O'Driscoll, argue that people should be allowed to sell their rights (and duties) as parents. A mother who did not wish to keep her child could just go to an adoption market and sell her interest in the child for whatever she could receive.[11] Note that parents would not sell their children (children are not property, even for the libertarian) but rather would sell their parental rights and duties.

Alexander and O'Driscoll contend that our current system also constitutes a market, but is simply not recognized as such. In independent adoption, for example, prospective parents are permitted to pay for the medical expenses of the mother, and we are not upset by this payment. Surely this is not all that a woman loses by being pregnant. Pregnancy is not a wholly pleasant experience, and a pregnant woman may lose many opportunities. The libertarian believes that it is only reasonable for a mother to be compensated for those lost opportunities. Rather than having cash paid under the table, the system would be open, avoiding the fraud and blackmail that now occur in the current black market. For the libertarian, the major problem with the black market is that it is illegal, and so attracts criminals, leads to criminal behavior, and labels "honest" citizens as criminals.

Critics might ask whether a couple can truly love a child they have purchased. What would their motives be for such a transaction? Although there is no direct evidence on this point, Alexander and O'Driscoll use the analogy of buying a pet:

> In transactions regarding pet animals, people do not . . . seem to believe . . . that those who *buy* pets are likely to have motives or expectations different from—or less suitable than—the motives or expectations of those who pay no cash price. Nor do they seem to think them less likely to love and care for the pet once they have it, or that their having paid cash (as opposed to some other or no medium of exchange) is itself likely to corrupt their attitude toward the pet. Indeed, some who have young animals to distribute prefer to charge at least a nominal cash price rather than to give the animal away; they apparently believe that, other things being equal, the purchaser's willingness to make an explicit sacrifice is a sign that the pet is "really wanted" and will be given good care.[12]

Another example of the relationship between economics and adoption can be found in "companies" of immigrant children sent out to farming communities in the Midwest during the nineteenth century to be adopted:

> The sight of the little company of the children of misfortune always touched the hearts of a population naturally generous. They were soon billeted around among the citizens and the following day a public meeting was called . . . and a committee appointed of leading citizens. The agent then addressed the assembly, stating the benevolent objectives of the society, and something of the history of the children. The sight of their worn faces was a most pathetic enforcement of his arguments. People who were childlesss came forward to adopt children; others who had not intended to

take any into their families were induced to apply for them; and many who really wanted the children's labor pressed forward to obtain it.[13]

While there were complaints at the time about the practice, it does suggest that such a market is not unique. Libertarians assert that under our current system money is involved in all the adoption markets. Adoption agencies regularly consider the financial status and the "cultural atmosphere" of the applicants; the amount of income one has contributes to the likelihood of being able to adopt. Even though being rich does not guarantee that someone will be a good parent, and being poor does not mean that he or she will be a poor parent, most people would probably entrust a child to the family with more wealth, status, and education because care and love are difficult, if not impossible, to measure. If you had to choose an adoptive parent, not knowing their capacity for love, what factors would you look for? Baby-selling, while not without flaws, insures that the purchased child will be wanted and that the family will have the resources to care for it.[14]

The libertarian is also concerned about the state intruding into people's lives. Some resent the "home visits" that adoption agencies make to the homes of prospective clients, suggesting that it would be logically consistent for state welfare officers to pay the same "home visits" to prospective parents before licensing them to have children—an image from George Orwell's *1984*. Libertarians believe, within broad guidelines (for example, preventing extreme child abuse), parents should be allowed to raise children as they wish. Just as the state should not tell natural parents how many children they should have and how to raise them, they should apply this restraint to adoption.

The Conservative Point of View

For the conservative the family is the cornerstone of society. Organized society cannot exist without the family—it is a sacred institution. Conservatives have none of the cold, rational calculation of the libertarians when it comes to buying and selling babies. There is something grossly offensive about such a practice. Perhaps it is the mixing of "filthy" money with "pure" love that is so disturbing. Conservatives look upon adoption as a beautiful and important relationship. By adopting a homeless child, a family can socialize the child properly.

But what is a family to a conservative? For many it is the "Walt Disney model of daddy coming home to mommy in the house with a white picket fence and the boy, the girl and the dog running out to greet [him]."[15] Single parents, handicapped parents, homosexual parents, older parents, and ill parents run families, and they often do so well. But such families are not likely to receive a healthy adopted child. Joyce Ladner in her study of transracial adoption learned that most adoption agencies have a fairly restrictive list of criteria, given the shortage of babies. These requirements include the following.

1. Both parents have to declare a religious faith.

2. Both partners have the same religious faith.

3. They have good physical and mental health.

4. The husband is employed.

5. The wife is a housewife and not otherwise employed.

6. They have a middle-class income and lifestyle, including a separate room for a child.

7. They can not be too old or too young (they must be the age they would have been had the wife given birth).

8. They should not be too intense about their desire for a child, nor too uncaring.

If your parents wished to adopt you, given all these requirements, would they have been allowed to? Mine wouldn't. Ladner suggests that these criteria have the effect of "screening out" parents, rather than "screening them in."[16]

Inevitably the social worker is in the position of God. One can argue for each of these criteria, but taken together they exclude many good parents, and may cause some couples to shade the truth and present themselves in the best light possible. Given the shortage of babies, do these requirements make for the best possible adoptive parents, and serve the best interests of the child?

Ultimately for the conservative, the goal is to place each child in a warm, welcoming, stable family. Joseph Goldstein, Anna Freud, and Albert Solnit, writing from a psychoanalytic perspective, feel the goal of child placement (with the exception of violent juveniles):

> . . . is to assure for each child, membership in a family with at least one partner who wants him. It is to assure for each child and his parents an opportunity to maintain, establish, or reestablish psychological ties to each other free of further interruption by the state. . . . The intact family offers the child a rare and continuing combination of elements to further his growth: reciprocal affection between the child and two, or at least one, caretaking adult; the feeling of being wanted and therefore valued; and the stimulation of inborn capacities.[17]

The conservative, like the libertarian, objects to state intervention except under the greatest provocation. Where the libertarian values the freedom of the individual actor, the conservative points to the necessary stability of a family; even a bad family might be better than a good, temporary foster home.

One of the areas in which the debate over adoption is particularly intense concerns whether a single person can adopt a child. Is a two-parent home always preferable to a single-parent home? Conservatives would say yes, and this appears to be the sentiment of most Americans, despite considerable evidence that a single-parent home is not necessarily a disadvantage to a child.[18] In 1969 *Good Housekeeping* magazine conducted a survey of their readers, asking: Should a single person adopt a child? Of those responding, 73 percent favored the idea, while 23 percent opposed it. But even those who supported the idea did not believe that a single-parent home was as good a setting for bringing up a child as one with two parents present.[19] The sentiment generally suggests that "one parent is better than none," just as it is better to have one eye than to be blind. Howard Stein, the executive director of Family Service of Westchester, however, does not completely agree. He feels "a child really needs both parents—the parent of the same sex to identify with and of the opposite sex as a love object to fix on. A boy brought up only by a woman faces serious psychological hazards; a girl without a father may be limited in her responses. Any child growing up in a one-sided household is deprived of an important life experience and may be poorly prepared for his or her own marriage and parenthood."[20]

While this may be somewhat exaggerated, few people would claim the single-parent home is the best of all possible worlds. Thus, single parents who wish to adopt children must settle for the less desirable children. Such a situation is ironic. These children with special needs are precisely those for whom two parents are particularly desirable, but they are rarely the first choice of first-choice parents. Conservatives believe in the importance of families, but the question of what constitutes a family is something of a puzzle.

The Social Democratic Point of View

The social democrat does not see anything inherently wrong with agencies of the state intervening in family life if the welfare of a child is at stake. The question is what should the government do? What image of the family should it encourage? What is the best upbringing for a child? In this section I will examine one particularly thorny question: Are transracial adoptions morally justified or do they reflect a form of prejudice. This question is particularly difficult for the social democrat because their emphasis on equality may lead to opposite answers.

The first transracial adoption occurred in the late 1940s, but it was not until the late 1960s that many white families began to adopt black children in any numbers. By this time, the shortage of healthy white infants was increasing, and the overt racial discrimination that had characterized American society was decreasing. By the early 1970s, over one-third of all adopted black children were adopted by white parents. In 1972, a federal court struck down a Louisiana law that prohibited such adoptions. Ironically, it was in this same year that the National Association of Black Social Workers went on record as being "in vehement opposition to placing black children in white homes."[21] At the same time the battle had been won against white racists in the South, arguments similar to those being used by segregationists were advanced by black professionals. These arguments pitted the image of a society in which there would be no race consciousness against one in which all racial groups would retain their own identity. Social democrats were caught right in the middle.

Those who argue in favor of transracial adoption contend that society's goal should be a multi-racial society, a melting pot—with race not particularly salient. Race-mixing is healthy and is to be encouraged. The mother of a black child and a Hispanic child expresses this view:

> In our experience the multicultural family has become something positive, something to celebrate. We tell our children that because we are a family, each of us can share in the cultural heritage of all the rest: "Thanks to Mark, we can all celebrate Martin Luther King Day, thanks to Adam we can all have birthday piñatas, thanks to Daddy we can all wear green for St. Patrick's Day, and thanks to Mommy we can all eat garlic bread. Although parenting a multicultural family is a challenge, it suggests practical ways to embody spiritual values in the daily life of the most intimate unit of society.[22]

Some supporters of transracial adoption justifiably point out that the policy now generally adhered to in the aftermath of the objections of black social workers is an instance of reverse discrimination. Although black parents adopt at the same rate as white parents (controlling for their income), there are not enough black parents to meet the demand. There are two major reasons for this: (1) there is a smaller *percentage* of black middle-class parents than whites, and (2) there is a larger number of black children put up for adoption than white children.[23] White people who want to adopt black children feel that if race were not a consideration, they would be able to adopt many of the children who are now placed in black homes or who remain in foster homes. After a Connecticut court decision that ruled that a white family could not adopt a black child which it had raised from birth, black civil rights leader Roy Wilkins commented that this policy

> . . . has the effect of depriving otherwise-adoptable black children of a stable, loving family life. The state which permits such archaic considerations as the race of the prospective parents to bar an adoption bears a heavy responsibility for cruelty to children by sending them instead to institutions or passing them from one foster home to the next. . . . To render a black child "unadoptable" or label his white foster parents "unable" or unfit to adopt him on the grounds of racial incompatability would be the advice of the segregationist.[24]

And so it is. What difference, after all, does race make?

For some, race does make quite a difference. Opponents of transracial adoptions say that the white demand for black babies did not begin until after whites learned they could no longer adopt healthy white babies. Blacks saw that in many (although not all) cases whites who were given black babies did not qualify for white babies.[25] Just as the white parent may see a black baby as a second choice, the black adult may see the white parent as inferior. Blacks are now recommending that adoption agencies make an intense effort to find black parents to adopt black children, even if it means altering their criteria of income and home ownership and subsidizing some of these adoptions.

Opponents of transracial adoption see adoption as a political issue with racial and class implications. Mary Benet notes that opponents of transracial adoption see

> more recent doubts about adoption stem from today's controversies over inequality, imperialism, and the nature of the family itself. . . . Adoption has usually meant the trans-

fer of a child from one social class to another slightly higher one. Today, as always, adopters tend to be richer than the natural parents of the children they adopt. They may also be members of a racial majority, adopting children of a minority; or citizens of a rich country, adopting children from a poor one.[26]

The contention here is that the upper class uses minority or Third World children for their own pleasure, sometimes wiping out the culture of those they adopt. One black man sees the issue in genocidal terms: "Transracial adoption is one of the many conspiracies being waged against Black people. It is one of the white man's latest moves to wipe out the last vestiges of our culture if not us. He made progress in brainwashing us and our young with his churches, his schools, and birth control. And now he wishes to use his latest trick of mental genocide."[27]

This may be an extreme statement, but it captures the sensitivity of blacks toward the preservation of their heritage. While caring white parents can certainly teach black history and literature, they cannot teach a child what it means to be black in white-majority America. Since America is likely to remain color-conscious, some argue that a strong black identity is necessary. This may pose a particular problem once the black child has reached adolescence and must deal with white political institutions and also with his or her own sexuality in a largely white community. While the testimony of many parents and children suggest that transracial adoptions are successful, the difficulties of such adoptions cannot be easily dismissed.

Social democrats want to recognize both of these impulses—the desire to have a color-blind society, and the desire to have a society in which all people are proud of their "roots." For now, most involved in adoption accept that racial matching is desirable, and many black children remain in foster care.

Transracial Adoption and Social Research

Sometimes the best way to find out about someone's behavior is simply to ask them directly. If we wish to understand white parents who have chosen to raise black children—their attitude toward their responsibilities, their philosophy of upbringing, their views on how their neighbors feel, and their fears of the future—we could sit down with them and discuss their concerns. This is precisely what Joyce Ladner, a prominent black sociologist, decided to do in her study, *Mixed Families*. Recounting her experience, she remembers she started her research project with considerable skepticism of whether white parents had the abilities necessary to raise black children. On the other hand, she was also convinced that every child had the right to a happy and stable home life. These two attitudes influenced her research.

An important methodological issue raised in this study is the question of whether a sociological researcher can conduct racially sensitive research with members of another race. Ironically, Ladner had been one of those militant black sociologists who questioned the value of white sociologists examining blacks. Here, some years later, she found herself conducting personal interviews with whites on their racial attitudes.

In in-depth interviews a sociologist must be able to make his or her informants open up and reveal their honest and private thoughts—those that they might only reveal to their closest friends. Good interviews have the ring of truth, and sometimes the sting of pain. Poor interviews consist of subjects merely rattling off what they think the researcher wishes to hear. Interviews, like participant observation, involve understanding the subject; thus, they usually produce sympathetic accounts. It is hard to paint someone you know well, and who has been personally friendly, as a bad person. This is true in Ladner's study of 136 parents in six states and the District of Columbia. Since the focus is on white parents, the study "discovers" that white parents can raise black children.

It would be unfair to characterize this study as suggesting parental race makes no difference in childrearing. Ladner believes deeply that black children should have their own racial identity and that their white parents face particularly difficult challenges in ensuring that this sense of blackness is not lost. While she respects most of the parents in the study and indicates that most appear to be doing a good job in raising their children (recall that she has no objective measures on this), Ladner would clearly prefer for there to be enough black adoptive parents to go around. She summarizes the challenges to white parents of black children as follows:

> Adoptive parents need to be exceptionally strong, well-adjusted, independent-minded, confident individuals who are more prepared for failure in the childrearing than are birth parents. The added dimension of transracial adoption is obvious. It requires courage, commitment, independence, and sensitivity to undertake this awesome responsibility in bringing up a healthy child. . . . The racial attitudes and behavior [of the parents] as well as their attitudes toward adoption itself will, more than anything else, determine these children's outcomes.[28]

Perhaps the most compelling portion of her study, as is often the case in in-depth interviews, is the testimonies of the participants. Although Ladner worried about whether she would receive honest comments, and although not all subjects may have been candid, there are enough "honest-sounding" accounts for us to be able to better understand these people's lives. Consider for example, the ambivalent remarks of one white father: "It is very painful for me to listen to blacks criticize me for what I have done, even if I know that they don't personally know *me.* I used to dismiss their criticisms as trite, irrelevant, and irresponsible. One day I asked myself, 'How would I feel if I were them?' I then realized that I could understand their anger and frustration, even when I also know that many of these children wouldn't have homes if whites had not adopted them."[29]

Ladner's interviews may remind us that ultimately we are talking about people who feel pain, anger, and joy. But aside from this, if we look at each individual as an individual, we do not have certain guidelines for determining the amount of good or harm these parents do. In sociological terms, the in-depth interview does not give us an adequate *operationalization* of the crucial variables of good or harm.

Ladner's position in terms of the points of view present here falls between the two poles of the social democratic argument described in this chapter. On the one hand, she points out that in the real world, race does make a difference and that it should make a difference. Thus, she has a preference for black homes for black children, which is in line with the wishes of black social workers. On the other hand, Ladner does not forget that these children are children, and, while transracial adoption poses special problems, she does not advocate stopping it. Most of these children, she suggests, are being raised lovingly and well.

Adoption and the Family

It is ironic that a healthy, white infant put up for adoption is likely to be placed in the "ideal American family," while babies reared in their families of procreation are often not so fortunate. Such are the whims of biology that many couples, who are unable to have the perfect children they have been told they are supposed to have, must compete with each other for a few children, sometimes paying tens of thousands of dollars to give "someone else's child" the upbringing their natural child would have had. Because of the competition, adoption agencies are able to place children in families that meet the agencies' image of what a family should be. Even many children who are ill or "damaged"—but "perfect" in their love and humanity—are now being placed in permanent homes rather than going to foster homes and institutions.

How we treat children reveals a great deal about what we think about ourselves. First, the existence of a highly bureaucratic and careful adoption procedure suggests that we do not trust individuals to make personal arrangements for their children—perhaps a consequence of a large and complex social system. "Experts" have the power to make the decisions about who should get which children. Second, by placing the "most desirable" children with the "most desirable" parents, society underlines its support for the social elite. Yet, unlike some cultures, we do not let unwanted children die. We do not leave them out on the hillside in the middle of winter to fend for themselves. We do wish to place unwanted children with parents who will make a special effort to raise these children. But we are torn between "the best interests of all children" and the desire to maximize our human capital by giving special treatment to the healthy child.

One question involving how we maximize our human capital is that of whether we should match parents and children racially and culturally. There is a belief that demographic considerations (race, religious background, ethnicity) should not make any difference. Why should a black child not be reared at birth by orthodox Jews and become a member of a Hasidic synagogue? Some people would reply that a person's roots are genetic and that religion, ethnicity, and race should not be lightly discarded. Furthermore, changes in a child's ethnicity or religion have political implications if duplicated often enough; such a pattern of adoption might be enough to do away with a culture, a set of beliefs or traditions of a group—a charge made by Catholics when it was their children who were put up for adoption to Protestant families. Of course, with race, parents and children can never escape public recognition and perhaps sometimes stigma. Americans are of two minds about what to do with matching children to parents. What we consider legitimate for race and, to some extent, for religion would seem ludicrous if we extended it to political beliefs or leisure preferences.

Adoption reminds us that biology is not the only basis on which a family can be built. Just as husbands and wives can love each other, even though they are not biologically related, so, too, can they love someone else's biological child. The social bonds in the family are as strong as any biological bond. Furthermore, the success rate of adoption gives testimony to the fact that, whatever our feelings might be about our own families of origin and procreation, the family remains a viable and much needed institution in our society.

Questions

1. Should the rights to raise unwanted infants be bought and sold openly?

2. Should the government subsidize parents to adopt certain types of "hard-to-place" children?

3. If you were to be adopted, what kind of parents would you wish to have?

4. Should single parents be allowed to adopt children? Should they be allowed to adopt children only after no other suitable parents could be found?

5. Should white parents be allowed to adopt black children? Should they be allowed to adopt black children only after no suitable black parents could be found?

6. Should adoption agencies attempt to match the background of the mother with the background of the adoptive parents?

7. Should adoption agencies attempt to place children with parents of the same religion as the mother?

8. Should homosexual couples be allowed to adopt children?

9. Should private, independent adoptions be outlawed?

10. If you learned that you or your spouse were infertile, would you attempt to adopt a child?

For Further Study

Alexander, Lawrence A. and O'Driscoll, Lyla H. "Stork Markets: An Analysis of 'Baby-Selling,' " *Journal of Libertarian Studies* 4 (1980): 173–196.

Anderson, David C. *Children of Special Value: Interracial Adoption in America*. New York: St. Martin's Press, 1971.

Benet, Mary K. *The Politics of Adoption*. New York: The Free Press, 1976.

Goldstein, Joseph; Freud, Anna; and Solnit, Albert J. *Before the Best Interests of the Child*. New York: Free Press, 1979.

Hartman, Ann. *Finding Families: An Ecological Approach to Family Assessment in Adoption*. Beverly Hills: Sage, 1979.

Kadushin, Alfred. "Single-Parent Adoptions: An Overview and Some Relevant Research," *Social Service Review* 44 (1970): 263–274.

Ladner, Joyce A. *Mixed Families: Adopting Across Racial Boundaries*. Garden City, New York: Anchor, 1977.

Morris, Steven. "The Fight for Black Babies," *Ebony* 28 (September 1973): 32–42.

Trillin, Calvin. "Cultural Differences," *The New Yorker* 51 (January 5, 1976): 63–67.

Notes and References

1. Friedrich Engels, *The Origin of the Family, Private Property, and the State* (New York: International Publishing, 1942, orig. 1884), pp. 59–60.
2. Karl Marx and Friedrich Engles, *The Communist Manifesto* (Arlington Heights, Illinois: AHM Publishing, 1955, orig. 1848), pp. 27–29.
3. David C. Anderson, *Children of Special Value* (New York: St. Martin's Press, 1971), p. 1.
4. Joyce A. Ladner, *Mixed Families* (Garden City, New York: Anchor, 1977), pp. 148–149.
5. Cynthia D. Martin, *Beating the Adoption Game* (La Jolla, California: Oak Tree, 1980), p. 77.

6. Harold Kennedy, "As Adoptions Get More Difficult," *U.S. News & World Report*, June 25, 1984, p. 62.

7. *Ibid*, p. 1.

8. Ann Hartman, *Finding Families* (Beverly Hills: Sage, 1979), p. 14.

9. Ladner, *op. cit.*, p. 216.

10. *Ibid*, p. 248.

11. Lawrence A. Alexander and Lyla H. O'Driscoll, "Stork Markets: An Analysis of 'Baby-Selling,' " *Journal of Libertarian Studies* 4 (1980): 174; see also Elisabeth M. Landes and Richard A. Posner, "The Economics of the Baby Shortage," *Journal of Legal Studies* 7 (1978): 323–348.

12. Alexander and O'Driscoll, *op. cit.*, p. 187.

13. Charles Loring Brace, *The Dangerous Classes of New York* (New York: Wynkoop and Hallenbeck, 1872), pp. 231–232 in Hartman, *op. cit.*, p. 18.

14. Alexander and O'Driscoll (*op. cit.*, p. 196) suggest that there should be a minimum age below which a child could not be "sold." This age should be lower than the age at which the child becomes aware of the market. Otherwise, the child might worry that he or she could be sold to buy a new car—and rightly so.

15. Martin, *op. cit.*, p. 193.

16. Ladner, *op. cit.*, pp. 218–219.

17. Joseph Goldstein, Anna Freud, and Albert J. Solnit, *Before the Best Interests of the Child* (New York: Free Press, 1979), pp. 5, 13.

18. Alfred Kadushin, "Single-Parent Adoptions: An Overview and Some Relevant Research," *Social Service Review* 44 (1970): 263–274.

19. "Should a Single Person Adopt a Child?" *Good Housekeeping*, August 1969, p. 12.

20. *Ibid*, p. 14.

21. Carole Klein, *The Single Parent Experience* (New York: Walker and Company, 1973), p. 96.

22. Jane Zeni Flinn, "Many Cultures, One Family," *America*, October 21, 1981, p. 261.

23. Benet, *op. cit.*, p. 145.

24. Roy Wilkins, "What Color is Love?" *OURS*, March/April 1980, p. 33.

25. Ladner, *op. cit.*, p. 231.

26. Benet, *op. cit.*, p. 12.

27. Ladner, *op. cit.*, p. 88.

28. *Ibid*, p. 257.

29. *Ibid*, p. 212.

 **Twelve**

Human Sexuality: Should Adolescents Engage in Premarital Sexual Intercourse? Should Parents Be Informed If Their Daughters Receive Birth Control Devices?

> When two people are under the influence of the most violent, most insane, most delusive, and most transient of passions, they are required to swear that they will remain in that excited, abnormal, and exhausting condition continuously until death do them part.
> —George Bernard Shaw, Preface to *Getting Married*

Passion is the most prickly of our social relations. By controlling it, we *almost* destroy it. This control is perhaps what makes us distinctively human. Unlike other animals, we *can* redirect or repress our sexual desires in the name of social order. Human beings can sublimate passion.

Even though there are biological components of human sexuality, the form that sexual behavior takes is learned, rather than innate. Men and women are socialized to their places in the sexual order. Cross-culture studies of sexual behavior[1] show a wide variation among what is acceptable. Homosexuality, for example, is treated quite differently among cultures—from being required to being punishable by death. The positions in which men and women practice sexual intercourse reveals the incredible flexibility of the human anatomy. The "missionary position," which our society defines as "normal," is not at all universal, and much sexual satisfaction occurs from other angles.

Research on sexuality has not had a long history, partially as a result of our "Puritan" or "Victorian" belief (until recently) that it is not a fit subject for study. Alfred Kinsey and his colleagues at the Institute for Sex Research at Indiana University undertook the first major studies of human sexuality. Kinsey, a zoologist by training, published lengthy volumes on male and female sexual behavior (in 1948 and 1953 respectively).[2] These volumes, based on large, if biased, samples demonstrated that there was a much greater variety of sexual behavior in America than many people had imagined. For example, Kinsey uncovered that nearly 40 percent of all adult males had engaged in homosexual behavior, nearly 70 percent had visited a prostitute, 60 percent had oral sex, about 25 percent of the married women had committed adultery, and so forth. Based on his figures Kinsey could claim that "a call for a cleanup of sex offenders in the community is, in effect, a proposal that 5 percent of the population should support the other 95 percent in penal institutions."[3] While Kinsey's exact figures cannot be trusted because of the difficulties in obtaining honest responses, his data are reliable enough to demonstrate that there is considerable diversity of sexual behavior in the American population. Kinsey's problem of validity has diminished somewhat in more recent studies.

Although many people speak glibly of the "sexual revolution," what appears to have changed most dramatically in the last quarter century are *attitudes*. Attitudes are becoming increasingly liberalized to conform to more liberal behavior. The *double standard*, which required different sets of behavior for men and women and suggested that women could not enjoy sex, has diminished considerably. Likewise, the moral outrage that many people at one time reserved for homosexuals has been curtailed, although not eliminated entirely. It would have been unthinkable two decades ago for a known homosexual to run for public office, much less to win. It would have been unthinkable for a law to exist that prohibits discrimination against homosexuals. Today there are even marriage manuals for devout, evangelical Christians that suggest that sexual intercourse (inside marriage, of course) can be fun and not simply for procreation. Television movies gain large ratings by dealing with topics such as incest, prostitution, and adultery—words that could not be *mentioned* on the airwaves a few decades ago. American society has become sexualized, and the real losers of the sexual revolution are those people for whom sexuality is not that important. One satirist some years ago wrote an article calling for "asexual liberation" and received hundreds of letters from people asking to join.

Despite the greater openness to discussing sexuality, and the somewhat wider behaviors being practiced, there are still distinctive differences in sexual ideology. Ira Reiss, a noted sex researcher, describes two major ideologies[4] that he claims characterizes American society. The first he defines as the *traditional-romantic* ideology and characterizes it by the following tenets:

1. Gender roles should be distinct and interdependent, with the male gender role as dominant. . . .

2. Body-centered sexuality is to be avoided by females. . . .

3. Sexuality is a very powerful emotion and one that should be particularly feared by females. . . .

4. The major goal of sexuality is heterosexual coitus and that is where the man's focus should be placed. . . .

5. Love redeems sexuality from its guilt, particularly for females.[5]

This perspective sharply contrasts with the *modern-naturalistic* perspective, which currently seems more dominant (at least among many of our opinion leaders). Its tenets consist of the following:

1. Gender roles should be similar for males and females and should promote equalitarian participation in the society.

2. Body-centered sexuality is of less worth than person-centered sexuality, but it still has a positive value for both genders.

3. One's sexual emotions are strong but manageable, by both males and females, in the same way as other basic emotions.

4. The major goals of sexuality are physical pleasure and psychological intimacy in a variety of sexual acts and this is so [for] both genders.

5. A wide range of sexuality should be accepted without guilt by both genders providing it does not involve force or fraud.[6]

Of course, it is altogether possible to accept a stance that merges these two perspectives. An egalitarian view of sexuality might be coupled with certain traditional themes such as the importance of love and marriage. Reiss's two ideologies stress two different functional properties of sexuality: procreation and intimacy. Since the two perspectives are typically held by different groups, the conflict between them is not only ideological, but social as well (for example, religious people versus non-religious people; or less educated Americans versus those with more schooling). Approaches to sexuality are based on attitudes toward human nature (is it good or tainted by selfishness or original sin) and toward social order (should it be open to a wide range of possible behavior or needs to be controlled by social institutions). Nowhere is the dispute over human sexuality more evident than in discussions of teenage sex.

Question:

Should Adolescents Engage in Premarital Sexual Intercourse? Should Parents Be Informed If Their Daughters Receive Birth Control Devices?

An eighth-grader once asked a sex counselor, "Why, if God did not want teenagers to have sex, did He make it possible?" She might also have asked why did He make it so much fun? While figures on the extent of premarital teenage sexuality are not entirely to be trusted, most studies find that approximately half of America's teenagers have engaged in premarital intercourse at least once, with the figures somewhat higher for boys than for girls.[7] By the time that young adults leave college, a substantial majority of them are no longer virgins. Whether or not this is a problem is a matter of opinion. But the number of teenage pregnancies is a social problem. One study estimates that 1,000,000 adolescents become pregnant each year, but only one-third are married.[8] Ira Reiss reports that 240,000 children are born each year to unmarried teenagers.[9] While the precise numbers are not important, these findings do indicate that teenage sexuality is a cause for concern.

This sexual activity occurs within a social context. As mentioned above, attitudes toward sexuality have changed. One study in 1979 found that 83 percent of college students approved of premarital sex if the couple was engaged or in love.[10] A Gallup International Survey in 1973 found that only 23 percent of the American youth, age eighteen to twenty-four, believed that premarital sexual relations were wrong in all circumstances; a figure contrasted to 4 percent in Sweden, 10 percent in France, and 73 percent in India.[11]

As might be expected, adults are less likely to approve of premarital sex than young people, but even here more adults now accept premarital sex than reject it. A 1982 survey found that only 29 percent of adults felt that premarital sex was "always wrong," while 41 percent felt that it was not wrong at all; the rest of the sample fell between these extremes.[12] This increase in permissiveness has been matched by changes in laws regarding sexual behavior. Many states now permit consenting adults to do what they wish in the privacy of their own bedrooms. Likewise, many states have changed their statutory rape laws. Previous laws criminalized a girl's sexual intercourse below a certain age. The fact that a girl was willing and that the boy was her peer was typically not considered. These laws assumed a young girl could never freely choose to have intercourse and that the sexual act was always forced upon her by the male. This is one way in which the double standard worked to the detriment of males. Changes in these rarely-enforced laws have made them sex-blind and lowered the age for consent to make them more socially realistic. Constitutional problems remain nevertheless in terms of government invasion of privacy and age discrimination.[13] Laws are slowly changing, reflecting, and, according to some, *encouraging* the present sexual behavior.

Like any significant portion of the social fabric, a change in something as basic as sex will affect many aspects of social life. Psychologist Dr. Albert Ellis in his book, *The American Sexual Tragedy*, tells how this chain of events could occur.

> Just suppose, for example, that a group of social scientists made an intensive study of the problem of premarital sex relations, and finally recommended that such relations be encouraged and legalized, and that effective birth control and prophylactic measures be taught to all school children. Concomitant with such an acceptance of fornication, the entire meaning of marriage might be radically altered, population statistics might begin to be seriously affected, the vocational plans of millions of young people might have to undergo considerable change, present-day concepts of individualism versus social living might undergo drastic revision, enormous socio-economic changes might be brought about, religious practices and theory might have to alter greatly, and numerous other profound changes in American ways of living might well occur.[14]

The point that Ellis is making it crucial for sociologists. Sex is not simply the pleasant friction produced by two bodies; rather, sexuality has social meaning, and changes in it are not independent of other social changes. For this reason, if for no other, there is a considerable public policy interest in adolescent sexuality.

Ellis was more prescient than he might have imagined in raising the issue of providing birth control information to children. In 1970, in response to the increasing number of teenage births, Congress added "Title X" to the Public Health Service Act. This law provided federal funds to clinics that offered contraceptives to women under eighteen. Now a girl could receive birth control devices, including the "pill," without her parents' approval—free, if she could not afford to pay. The federal government was helping girls to engage in behavior that was illegal under the statutory rape laws. Still, such a provision struck many people as a sensible solution to the growing number of teenage pregnancies. Despite the claims of supporters that this provision would decrease the number of pregnancies and cut down on venereal disease, the incidence of both increased dramatically—although possibly by not as much as they would have if contraceptives had not been made available. One study suggests that 400,000 pregnancies were averted by these family planning clinics.[15] Whatever their effect, by the 1980s these clinics had mushroomed and were heavily used. In 1981 the government spent $162 million on approximately 5,000 family planning clinics that treated 1,300,000 adolescents and gave out half a million prescriptions for birth control pills.[16] Sexual activity had become big business.

In 1981 Congress, perhaps responding to the conservative trend in the country, passed an amendment to the Public Health Service Act that called for encouragement of parental involvement. Following up on this, President Reagan's Department of Health and Human Services instituted a rule in January 1983 that required all federally supported family planning clinics to send notification to a teenager's parents when she received a prescription for birth control devices. As can be imagined, this was not too popular in high school corridors and family planning clinic boardrooms; even the Salvation Army, the American

Medical Association, and the United Church of Christ opposed the rule for fear it would cause an increase in pregnancies. The rule, nicknamed "The Squeal Rule" by opponents (a devastating piece of political labelling), was thrown out by the courts and was never put into effect. The rule, however, produced an interesting debate on how teenage sexuality should be handled—whether it should be subsidized or squashed.

The Conservative Point of View

The conservative has sometimes been pictured as the Scrooge of the Bedroom. It is not so much that conservatives do not enjoy sex, but rather they are more concerned about its effects on society. For the conservative, sexual behavior is potentially dangerous because if left unchecked it could subvert the social order. It needs to be explicitly regulated. David Carlin, Jr. writing in *Commonweal* magazine explains the tie between sex and the social order.

> Though sexual activity might be *performed* in private, it was not really a private act. Others—family, friends, neighbors, potential spouses, and society generally—felt that they had interests which might be jeopardized by one's sexual activity; hence social regulation of that activity was warranted. The traditional rule that sex should be confined within marriage meant that one was not free to act sexually in one's capacity as a mere private or natural individual; instead, one acted in virtue of a kind of public office—husband or wife—that society had artificially created and inducted one into. . . . Since even our genitalia were not available for free private use, society must have powerful claims, indeed, on the use to which we put our hands and brains. Though this lesson was aimed at everyone, its special target was adolescents; if they could be taught to regard so fascinating a business as sex as subject to societal discipline, there was hope they might appreciate the need for social control and social solidarity generally.[17]

The important sociological issue is individual control versus social control. The reason that conservatives want to control sexuality is not because they feel that the physical act is sinful, but because its effects may undermine the stability of the social structure. It is true that some conservatives use religious dicta—particularly in the New Testament—to support the view that this is God's will. This goes only so far since others can point to wonderfully erotic passages in the Song of Solomon and other parts of the Old Testament. Nevertheless the religious rationale serves as a convenient means of enforcing the social order that conservatives feel is vital to a stable society.

At one time a girl under eighteen who lost her virginity was a rebel, today she is a conformist. A teenager must have a strong will to remain chaste in the face of peer pressure. Author Joyce Maynard relates the agony that some teenagers must face if they resist this pressure. "I—the one who slept alone, the one whose only pills were vitamins and aspirin—I was the embarrassed one. How has it happened, what have we come to, that the scarlet letter these days isn't A, but V? . . . Virginity has become not a flower or a jewel, a precious treasure for Prince Charming or a lively, prized and guarded gift, but a dusty relic—an anachronism. Most of all, it's an embarrassment."[18]

Public attitudes toward sexuality have altered. Today most adults, even those who do not like the change in public values, believe there is little they can do about teenage sexuality; so, rather than trying to convince teenagers not to "do it," they try to teach them to use birth control. The attitude seems to be "If you can't be good, at least be careful!"

One way in which conservatives have attempted to control teenage sexuality has been to increase the role of parents, as evidenced by the Reagan administration's unsuccessful attempt to allow parents to know if their daughters have received prescription birth control devices. Even President Reagan did not require parental permission *prior* to prescription but only notice afterward. This angered many conservatives who emphasize that parents are ultimately responsible for their children's health and safety. Since birth control pills may have harmful side effects, parents should be permitted to decide whether their children should take that risk. Conservatives believe that the workers at birth control clinics, however well-intentioned, do not impart morality along with the contraceptives; rather, they merely help the adolescent fulfill her sexual desires. Unlike birth control counselors, parents have the responsibility to help children make moral decisions, but birth control clinics negate this authority. Marjory Mecklenburg, the Reagan appointee who headed the Office of Adolescent Pregnancy Programs, comments, "Without consent, children cannot have their ears pierced or get a shot from the school nurse. Yet somehow, uniquely in the area of contraceptive services, we have closed the parent out."[19] Children even need a note from their parents to take a school trip—unless, presumably, it is to Planned Parenthood!

The conservative believes the availability of birth control devices to adolescents creates an atmosphere that tells the child recreational premarital sex is acceptable, normal, and expected. While others suggest that the choice is between providing birth control or having pregnancies, the Conservative offers a third option: the currently unfashionable one of abstinence. Just as mores have changed to permit open sexuality, they can—should we wish—revert back.

Ultimately the issue is the conservative's belief that the state has the obligation to legislate for morality, rather than legislate against it. Conservative columnist George Will writes,

> Surely the government subverts family relationships when it subsidizes 5,000 clinics that purvey to children medical treatment and counsel on morally important matters, and do so without informing those who have legal, financial and moral responsibilities for children—parents. . . . [W]hen traditional mores are dissolving as fast as ours are, trying to arrest the dissolution with a law is like trying to lasso a locomotive with a thread. However, policy need not passively reflect and accommodate itself to every change, however destructive. . . . Law should express society's core values, such as parental responsibility.[20]

The Social Democratic Point of View

The social democrat tends to take a pragmatic attitude toward sexuality; so long as it does not disrupt the social fabric it should be left alone. To the extent it causes a social problem—such as unwanted pregnancies—it should be dealt with. Since primary social institutions, such as the family and the church, do not have special standing in the eyes of the social democrat, enforcing morality is not that important. Indeed, the support of traditional morality may well direct us away from considering those real social problems that cause inequality and injustice in a society. Writing in 1931, Robert Briffault makes this point in strong terms.

> The grotesque incongruity which, in the current usage of Western culture, assigns the appelation of "morality" to sexual restrictions exclusively, ignoring as appertaining to a lower plane of ethical obligations, justice, intellectual and social honesty, charity, and every moral demand on the conduct of human beings in their social relations, is not only grotesque, but grossly immoral. . . . Western morality is quick at suppressing literature, but slow at suppressing war; zealous in the abolition of obscene postcards, but lukewarm in the abolition of obscene slums; active in putting down white slavery, but apathetic in putting down wage-slavery; alert in preventing vice, but slothful in putting down starvation; shocked at clothing insufficient for purposes of modesty, but indifferent to clothing insufficient for purposes of warmth. It spares no effort to secure a perfectly pure world, but is ready to tolerate a perfectly iniquitous one.[21]

These very same charges might equally well apply to contemporary conservative Republicans. They might object, however, by saying that concern about morality does not exclude concern about social inequality. Yet for social democrats, the questions about sexual behavior take second place to the concerns of economic equality.

When social democrats consider the so-called "Squeal

Rule," their primary concern is with its effects, rather than with its morality. An editorial in the *Detroit Free Press* makes this criticism of the rule: "Moralists may pass what judgments they wish about young people and sex. The public policy choice, however, is between increased education and availability of contraception before a girl becomes pregnant, or increased abortion or unwed motherhood afterward."[22] While we cannot be certain how many teenagers would have gotten pregnant because they did not get contraceptives at a federally-funded clinic, we can be reasonably certain that some young women would have become pregnant. The social democrat assumes that teenagers will remain sexually active, and so the choice is between preventive medicine or cleaning up a mess afterward. Social democrats make a distinction between enforcing an economic morality that decreases group prejudice and interfering with personal morality. Unlike conservatives, social democrats do not place total faith in the family. The image of the family for the conservative is of a moral, loving group. In contrast, the social democrat is more likely to be skeptical of its absolute purity. They note that only about half the teens who visit birth control clinics have voluntarily informed their parents.[23] Why? The reason is some adolescents believe their parents would not respond with cool, clear reason, and they may be correct. Indeed, such a regulation might even harm family relations. Parents may feel hurt that their daughter has not confided in them, or they might punish the girl for her "sin." They might also attack the girl's partner. Although the regulation provided that parents would not be told if violence were possible, this would be hard to know in advance. Families are not necessarily better than professionals at federally-funded clinics in dealing with adolescents' sexual problems and questions.

A final concern among some social democrats is that this rule would affect only young women. Young men, who do not use prescription birth control devices, were not included. *The Nation,* a social democratic magazine, asserts that the rule is just a form of discrimination. "It is actually a reversion to the nineteenth-century double standard, a subclause of which ran: women should bear the onus of disgrace for illicit sex and unwanted pregnancies. . . . In our own day, society has faced up to the increase in teen-age sexuality, and the concomitant rise in premarital pregnancies, by offering birth control assistance to women. . . . The new rule is an invasion of privacy, and since only the woman's parents are notified, it is discriminatory."[24] Social democrats believe the government should provide birth control devices, but has no obligation to foster a single standard of morality. Teenagers are to be treated equally with adults, and women equal to men.

The Libertarian Point of View

Libertarians are likely to be more permissive about sexual activity than either conservatives or social democrats. So long as the act is between two responsible individuals, then the government should not be involved. Unlike the conservative, the libertarian does not see society as having a vested interest in the pleasure two people give to each other. Carlin writes,

> Contemporary sexual morality . . . considers sex to be a strictly private concern. As for pre-marital sex, it regards as absurd the notion that one should be held answerable to others—even, or perhaps especially, to one's ultimate spouse who, according to old-fashioned ideas, was thought to have the right to resent one's early sexual activities with other persons. . . . [A]dolescent sex, at least when practiced with contraception and backstopped by abortion, is essentially unobjectionable.[25]

Libertarians consider sex natural and fun. They believe no one has the right to tell another person what his or her sexual values should be. This goes for teenagers as well as adults. Each teenager should make a personal decision. Birth control counselors, therefore, should help young men and women implement whatever decision they have made, but not help them make it. Libertarians, however, are often vague on when this right of decision-making occurs—for some this includes children as well as adolescents.[26]

The problem of sex is not sex itself, but the laws and repressive values related to it. This attitude of: Do Your Own Thing, Providing It Doesn't Hurt Others is sometimes called the Playboy Philosophy after a series of articles written by *Playboy* editor, Hugh Hefner in 1962–1965. In these articles Hefner proclaims that "sex can be one of the most profound and rewarding elements in the adventure of living; if we recognize it as not necessarily limited to procreation then we should also acknowledge openly that it is not necessarily limited to love either. Sex exists—with and without love—and in both forms it does far more good than harm. The attempts at its suppression, however, are almost universally harmful, both to the individuals involved and to society as a whole."[27] This is not to say libertarians lack values, but rather their values are those that emphasize the desirability of maximizing pleasure. They define sexual freedom as equally important as political freedom. State control is offensive whether it is in the boardroom or in the bedroom, and in this they sharply disagree with social democrats. It is important to remember that libertarians are not necessarily arguing for promiscuity or for "free sex." Instead, they suggest that these are personal issues on which reasonable people can differ.

The debate over the "Squeal Rule" is a curious one for libertarians. They believe the government has no place in subsidizing birth control devices for teenagers nor does it have any business being involved in gossiping to parents. Libertarians are outraged that Planned Parenthood receives one-quarter of a billion dollars each year from the government for their various programs.[28] They see no reason why adolescents should receive free pills from the state. However, the Libertarian offers another choice besides pregnancy, abstinence, or government-subsidized birth control. This choice is to use private birth control clinics—of which there are many. The rules formulated by the Reagan administration only applied to clinics that receive federal aid. At one time, Planned Parenthood suggested that if the rule were enforced they would forego federal funds, a course of action some libertarians felt was economically practical[29]—particularly since a month's worth of birth control pills costs no more than a record album. Yet, such a solution was rarely mentioned in the debate between conservatives and social democrats.

Premarital Sex and Social Research

Sex is one of those topics, like religion, where there is an abundance of opinions, but a minimum of hard facts. Only recently has our society become sufficiently open to allow research on sexual topics to be conducted. Several decades ago a national survey of the sexual behavior of teenage girls would have been impossible. In 1971 and then again in 1976, three sociological demographers, Melvin Zelnik, John F. Kantner, and Kathleen Ford, interviewed several thousand young women between the ages of fifteen and nineteen in their homes to learn about their premarital sexual activity, their use of contraceptives and the frequency with which they became pregnant.[30] The value of this study rests particularly on the fact that it represents a random, representative sample of American young women. To the extent we can trust their responses (which the authors claim we can), these studies provide an accurate cross-section of American female adolescent behavior at two points in time.

By choosing an activity, in this case premarital sex, that is typically considered outside the bounds of "decent society" and treating those involved in an objective and nonjudgmental way, the study is implicitly giving support to the activity under question. Although survey methodology seems congruent with either conflict theory or functionalism, the topic of these two surveys leans more heavily toward a more critical view of conventional morality. This suggestion, however, should not be pressed too far; clearly the researchers do not believe that the pregnancy of unmarried women is desirable and are by no means endorsing that condition.

Zelnik, Kantner, and Ford find that most young women see

sexual intercourse prior to marriage as permissable, particularly if the two parties are planning to marry. In all age and racial groups, the majority of young women believe that premarital sex is acceptable—with over 80 percent of black females over the age of eighteen agreeing.[31] These statistics, however, are not matched by actual behavior. In the 1976 sample, for example, 41 percent of the interviewees were no longer virgins—18 percent of the fifteen-year-olds and 60 percent of the nineteen-year-olds. Interestingly, of those young women who were married at the time of the survey, over 80 percent had had intercourse prior to their nuptials—indicating that the virgin bride is a rarity indeed. Furthermore, the likelihood of premarital intercourse was considerably higher among those women who did not have high educational aspirations. Of those women who intended to graduate from college, more than two-thirds were virgins, whereas those who did not intend to complete high school or who had already dropped out under 30 percent were still virgins.[32] Other factors that are associated with premarital intercourse include religiosity (the less religious, the more likely premarital intercourse occurs, with those who claim to lack religion being the most likely to engage in sexual intercourse), social class (the higher, the less sex), and the age at first menstruation (the younger, the more likely to have had sexual experience).[33] Similar explanations apply to age of first intercourse. Thus, there seem to be both biological and social factors that influence a young woman's decision to have intercourse.

Most American adolescent girls (about 60 percent) have their first sexual experience "unprotected." According to the survey, only about 30 percent of all sexually active adolescent girls regularly use contraception—this includes girls who hope boys will withdraw before ejaculation.[34] Most rely on a wing and a prayer. Apparently part of the problem of using contraception is that the *idea* of contraception is contrary to the meaning of intercourse. If intercourse is a spontaneous dance of passion, then only a premeditating schemer would prepare for it. Many young women apparently find it difficult to reconcile the meaning of sexual intimacy with the meaning of contraception. Only by making sex rational and routine does contraception become possible—a choice that for some people removes the charm of the act. Perhaps not surprisingly, those girls of higher social class, those from more stable families, and those who are older at first intercourse are more likely to use contraception.[35]

Like most scientific surveys, this one is not focused on policy considerations. Instead, its primary goal is to provide factual information for others to use to make a decision. Yet in their conclusions, the authors hew to a social democratic perspective. They suggest premarital sex is inevitable and that government services can help the situation. Specifically, Zelnik, Kantner, and Ford argue

> that some [young women] do become pregnant is hardly sufficient to argue for the elimination of contraceptive service programs. . . . The inability of young people to obtain contraceptive services is unlikely to have a negative effect on the prevalence of pregnancy or of intercourse. . . . It seems likely that to reduce premarital intercourse in the United States would require far more governmental intrusion than now exists, and at a cost of personal rights that many would be unwilling to accept. Thus, teenage sexuality might recede if we could bring ourselves to accept greater censorship of movies, television, books and magazines, including the advertising therein, combined with regulations to discourage the participation of more than one parent in the labor force at any one point in time, combined with greater restrictions on the daily movements of teenagers and on their finances, combined with greater surveillance of their "trysting places"—whether motels or open fields—combined with a drastic reduction in unchaperoned social activities for teenagers and an increase in "family" activities, combined with restrictions to prevent young people from leaving home for either work or school, combined with social sanctions against open displays of affection by young people, combined with the imposition of punishment in some form for those who stray from clearly marked "paths of righteousness". . . . For ourselves, we prefer to cope with the consequences of early sex as an aspect of an emancipated society, rather than pay the social costs its elimination would exact.[36]

A position that combines a belief that government contraceptive programs provide a valuable service with the desire not to take drastic steps to curb premarital sexuality is the hallmark of the social democratic approach to adolescent sexuality.

Human Sexuality, Adolescents, and Society

Human nature is sexual nature. Our conception of human nature, whether is is essentially good or evil, colors our opinion about how people should behave sexually. The libertarian, who believes in the potential of rational behavior, sees little danger in the grand emotion of sexuality. Sexuality is merely pleasurable and has little effect on social intercourse. Sex is a *natural* function that connects human beings with their primate forbears.

Conservatives see sexual passion bubbling beneath human behavior, and while sex is good, unrestrained passion may be too destructive. People are continually struggling against their baser, animal instincts; sex provides an instance in which those instincts win. Conservatives do not wish to eliminate sexuality entirely, but they do believe it needs to be controlled, like a leopard in a cage. Sexuality can undermine the moral order of a fragile social structure. The family, the home of sexuality, is also the police force to suppress its excesses with support from the government. The state should exercise its influence to maintain the family as the bastion of morality and one of the primary institutions of society.

The social democrat feels less strongly about sexuality than either the libertarian or the conservative. Sexuality is not a primary concern of government unless its effects influence the economic order. Thus, teenage pregnancy is a concern, whereas intercourse is not. Discrimination on the basis of age or gender is a proper place for government intervention, whereas family or church concerns should be handled by those institutions alone. Only a philosophy that is concerned with effects could devise the curious system in which the government subsidizes birth control devices and then refuses to inform the caregivers. It is not that social democrats support sexual promiscuity, it is just that they dislike the effects of unwanted pregnancy more.

The broad underlying question in the debate over teenage sexuality is who should be allowed the freedom to experiment sexually? Specifically, should adolescents be given the rights and privileges of adults? If the age of sexual maturity were also the age of marriage, and if prior to marriage, there were no strong desires to experiment sexually, we would have few problems. This biological utopia obviously does not exist. Two trends exacerbate the problem. First, young people are waiting longer to get married, leaving more time to fulfill their sexual desires. Second, and more surprising, the age at which young people become sexually mature is decreasing. On average, menstruation begins at age twelve and a half today as opposed to thirteen and a half in 1940, presumably because of better nutrition and health care. Thus, there is more time in which young people can test the sexual waters, and thus more opportunities for them to conceive children out of wedlock. The "epidemic" of teenage pregnancies may not entirely be due to "moral decay," but to these social and biological changes.[37] Society can suggest to adolescents that they remain sexually abstinent, but many, if not most, of them would find this advice more relevant in theory than in practice. It is a case of young men fighting old men's wars.

The libertarian and the social democrat are united in thinking that the call for teenage chastity is bound to fail. The libertarian believes it should fail, while the social democrat sees failure as inevitable. Although the conservative can point to historical instances in which large numbers of people did remain chaste, this solution cannot be terribly effective when contradictory messages fill the media and peer-group gossip. Sexuality represents a social reward, and the debate over teenage sexuality is one of who should receive the reward. It is not self-evident that all rewards should freely go to all people. Are teenagers full-fledged members of society? If they are not old enough to drink and vote, are they really old enough to make whoopee?

Questions

1. Is sex a purely private act, or does it affect society?
2. Is there any justification for the "double standard"?
3. Should unmarried adolescents engage in sexual intercourse?
4. Are teenagers psychologically prepared for sexual intimacy?
5. Should adolescents be allowed to set their own moral codes?
6. Can laws prevent adolescents from engaging in sexual intercourse?
7. What are the best ways to prevent teenage pregnancies?
8. Should the government subsidize contraceptives for adolescents?
9. Should the government inform parents if their children have received contraceptives?
10. Should the courts have overruled the Reagan administration's implementation of the "Squeal Rule"?

For Further Study

Clayton, Richard R., and Bokemeier, Janet. "Premarital Sex in the Seventies," *Journal of Marriage and the Family* 42 (1980): 759–775.

Davis, Murray S. *Smut: Erotic Reality/Obscene Ideology.* Chicago: University of Chicago Press, 1983.

Eidson, Rita. "The Constitutionality of Statutory Rape Laws," *U.C.L.A. Law Review* 27 (1980): 757–813.

Ellis, Albert. *The American Sexual Tragedy,* 2nd ed. New York: Lyle Stuart, 1962.

Frustenberg, Jr., Frank F., Lincoln, Richard, and Menken, Jane. eds. *Teenage Sexuality, Pregnancy, and Childbearing.* Philadelphia: University of Pennsylvania Press, 1981.

Reiss, Ira L. *The Social Context of Premarital Sexual Permissiveness.* New York: Holt, Rinehart and Winston, 1967.

Reiss, Ira L. "Some Observations on Ideology and Sexuality in America," *Journal of Marriage and the Family* 43 (1981): 271–283.

Zelnik, Melvin, Kantner, John F., and Ford, Kathleen. *Sex and Pregnancy in Adolescence.* Beverly Hills: Sage, 1981.

Notes and References

1. Clellan Ford and Frank Beach, *Patterns of Sexual Behavior* (New York: Harper & Row, 1951).
2. Alfred Kinsey et al., *Sexual Behavior in the Human Male* (Philadelphia: W. B. Saunders, 1948); Alfred Kinsey et al., *Sexual Behavior in the Human Female* (Philadelphia: W. B. Saunders, 1953).
3. Ian Robertson, *Sociology,* 2nd ed. (New York: Worth, 1981), p. 215.
4. Murray Davis divides sexual ideologies into three categories: the Jehovanist (traditional), the Naturalist (the modern Playboy philosophy), and the Gnostic (á la Marquis de Sade). See Murray Davis, *Smut: Erotic Reality/Obscene Ideology* (Chicago: University of Chicago Press, 1983).
5. Ira Reiss, "Some Observations on Ideology and Sexuality in America," *Journal of Marriage and the Family* 43 (1981): 279–280.
6. *Ibid*, p. 280.
7. Richard Clayton and Janet Bokemeier, "Premarital Sex in the Seventies," *Journal of Marriage and the Family* 42 (1980): 762.
8. Beth Brophy, "A Hard Pill to Swallow?" *Forbes*, May 10, 1982, p. 99.

x

9. Ira Reiss, *Family Systems in America*, 3rd ed. (New York: Holt, Rinehart and Winston, 1980), p. 209.
10. Jane Burgess-Kohn, *Straight Talk About Love and Sex for Teenagers* (Boston: Beacon Press, 1979), p. 24.
11. "American Attitudes on Sex, Nudity Have Undergone Dramatic Change," *Gallup Opinion Index*, No.98, August 1973, p. 23.
12. National Opinion Research Center, *General Social Surveys, 1972-1982: Cumulative Codebook* (Chicago: National Opinion Research Center, 1982), p. 162.
13. Rita Eidson, "The Constitutionality of Statutory Rape Laws," *U.C.L.A. Law Review* 27 (1980): 757–813.
14. Albert Ellis, *The American Sexual Tragedy*, 2nd ed. (New York: Lyle Stuart, 1962), pp. 295–296.
15. Editorial, *Denver Post*, January 21, 1982, printed in *Editorials on File*. vol. 13, March 1-15, 1982, p.296.
16. Brophy, *op. cit.*, p. 99.
17. David Carlin, Jr., "The 'Squeal Rule' and 'Lolita Rights,' " *Commonweal*, September 9, 1983, p. 465–466.
18. Joyce Maynard, *Looking Back* (New York: Avon, 1974), pp. 137, 139.
19. Ken Huff and Nancy King, "When Teens Want Contraceptives, Should Their Parents Know? Two Impassioned Advocates Face Off," *People Weekly*, May 24, 1982, p. 44.
20. George Will, "Teenagers and Birth Control," *Newsweek*, February 28, 1983, p. 80.
21. Robert Briffault, *Sin and Sex* (New York: Macaulay, 1931), pp. 192–193.
22. Editorial, *Detroit Free Press*, March 2, 1982, printed in *Editorials on File*, vol. 13, March 1-15, 1982, p. 298.
23. Editorial, *The Saginaw News*, February 13, 1983, printed in *Editorials on File*, vol. 14, February 1-15, 1983, p. 156.
24. "The Sex Police," *The Nation*, February 12, 1983, pp. 164–165.
25. Carlin, *op. cit.*, pp. 465–466.
26. Ellis, *op. cit.*, pp. 299–300.
27. Hugh Hefner, "The Playboy Philosophy," *Playboy*, July 1963, p. 48.
28. Kenneth Kantzer, "Planned Parenthood Attacks A Parent's Need to Know," *Christianity Today*, May 20, 1983, p. 11.

29. L. A. Villadsen, "Cutting the Umbilical Cord: Can Family Planning Clinics Survive Without Government Funding," *Reason*, February 1983, pp. 21–26.

30. Melvin Zelnik, John F. Kantner, and Kathleen Ford, *Sex and Pregnancy in Adolescence* (Beverly Hills: Sage, 1981).

31. *Ibid*, p. 46

32. *Ibid*, p. 65.

33. *Ibid*, p. 70.

34. *Ibid*, p. 95.

35. *Ibid*, pp. 98, 103.

36. *Ibid*, pp. 181–182.

37. Phillips Cutright, "The Teenage Sexual Revolution and the Myth of an Abstinent Past," *Family Planning Perspectives*, January 1972, pp. 24–31.